Everything you need to score high

GRE PSYCHOLOGY

Third Edition

ARCO

Everything you need to score high

GRE
PSYCHOLOGY

Third Edition

Sidney Raphael, Ph.D. and L.H. Halpert, Ph.D.

ARCO
THOMSON LEARNING ™

Australia • Canada • Mexico • Singapore • Spain • United Kingdom • United States

ARCO
THOMSON LEARNING

An ARCO Book

ARCO is a registered trademark of Thomson Learning, Inc., and is used herein under license by Peterson's.

About Peterson's

Founded in 1966, Peterson's, a division of Thomson Learning, is the nation's largest and most respected provider of lifelong learning online resources, software, reference guides, and books. The Education Supersite^SM at petersons.com—the Web's most heavily traveled education resource—has searchable databases and interactive tools for contacting U.S.-accredited institutions and programs. CollegeQuest^SM (CollegeQuest.com) offers a complete solution for every step of the college decision-making process. GradAdvantage^TM (GradAdvantage.org), developed with Educational Testing Service, is the only electronic admissions service capable of sending official graduate test score reports with a candidate's online application. Peterson's serves more than 55 million education consumers annually.

Thomson Learning is among the world's leading providers of lifelong learning, serving the needs of individuals, learning institutions, and corporations with products and services for both traditional classrooms and for online learning. For more information about the products and services offered by Thomson Learning, please visit www.thomsonlearning.com. Headquartered in Stamford, Connecticut, with offices worldwide, Thomson Learning is part of The Thomson Corporation (www.thomson.com), a leading e-information and solutions company in the business, professional, and education marketplaces. The Corporation's common shares are listed on the Toronto and London stock exchanges.

For more information, contact Peterson's, 2000 Lenox Drive, Lawrenceville, NJ 08648; 800-338-3282; or find us on the World Wide Web at: www.petersons.com/about

Third Edition

Library of Congress Number: 97-81113

ISBN: 0-02-862490-4

Printed in the United States of America

10 9 8 7 6 5 4 3 2   02 01 00

Contents

PART IV: *Two Full-Length Practice Examinations*

P A R T   1

About the GRE in Psychology

36. REM sleep is called "paradoxical" because:

    (A) while the sleeper sleeps, the usual restorative functions of sleep are dormant.

    (B) dreaming occurs during REM sleep, but the sleeper is most easily aroused.

    (C) the muscles are at rest while the brain and eyes are active.

    (D) the sleeper's muscles seem to tense and relax in no relation to dream content.

    (E) REM sleep seems unnecessary; REM deprivation has no observable effects.

37. Which of the following choices is *not* characteristic of the id in the Freudian model?

    (A) The id is pleasure seeking.

    (B) The id is without reason.

    (C) The id is structured in terms of time.

    (D) The id includes unconscious processes.

    (E) The id is minimally socialized.

38. Gate control theory provides a plausible explanation of:

    (A) signal-detection theory.

    (B) the operation of health maintenance organizations (HMOs).

    (C) biofeedback.

    (D) acupuncture.

    (E) evoked potentials.

39. Alcohol disrupts memory by:

    (A) acting on the hippocampus.

    (B) confusing the reticular formation.

    (C) overstimulating the corpus callosum.

    (D) inhibiting the formation of ACTH.

    (E) interfering with the neurotransmitter serotonin.

40. According to Loftus, eyewitness recollection of traumatic events:

    (A) can be distorted by the phrasing of questions asked.

    (B) is best for mildly and moderately traumatic events and worst for severely traumatic events.

    (C) is more accurate the more "innocent" the bystander.

    (D) varies according to the witness's cultural biases.

    (E) is surprisingly reliable even under challenge in the courtroom.

41. It does not elicit an operant behavior, yet it serves as a cue that reinforcement is available for operant behaviors. It is a:

    (A) discriminative stimulus.

    (B) higher-order stimulus.

    (C) mental representation.

    (D) secondary stimulus.

    (E) chained stimulus.

42. "The network of individuals and social settings within a culture to which a person must adapt psychologically" is:

    (A) Lewin's field theory.

    (B) Osgood's GRIT.

    (C) Bronfenbrenner's social ecology.

    (D) Marcia's identity status.

    (E) Horney's neoanalytic world.

43. The nonsense syllable is associated with:

    (A) Helmholtz.

    (B) Fechner.

    (C) Jung.

    (D) Titchener.

    (E) Ebbinghaus.

44. In Freudian terms, sublimation is a:

    (A) reaction formation.

    (B) defense mechanism.

    (C) displacement.

    (D) primary process.

    (E) secondary process.

45. The body strives to maintain a particular weight set-point due to the action of the:

    (A) limbic system.

    (B) pons.

    (C) pituitary gland.

    (D) hypothalamus.

    (E) reticular formation.

46. Current American Psychological Association standards include:

    (A) the right of experimental subjects to give prior approval of the behaviors or responses to be elicited from them by the experimenter.

    (B) the right to voluntarily withdraw from a study and be fully compensated.

    (C) the right to be protected from all forms of experimenter deception no matter what the source.

    (D) the right of informed consent during the course of an extended experiment, not solely at the beginning of the study.

    (E) the right of experimental subjects to review research reports before publication.

47. Concerning adult singles:

    (A) a generation ago, 96% of adults married; today only about 75% will marry.

    (B) more women than men are single.

    (C) single women tend to be better educated than married women and single men.

    (D) single women have poorer family relations than single men.

    (E) married adults are more dissatisfied with their lives than are single adults.

48. Köhler's chimp, who learned to get his food by using sticks, was displaying:

    (A) insight learning.

    (B) accommodation.

    (C) the Zeigarnick effect.

    (D) deductive learning.

    (E) a Gestalt.

49. Small, jerky eye movements which occur when a person is fixating on an object are called:

    (A) optic chiasma.

    (B) saccadic movements.

    (C) strabismus.

    (D) phi phenomenon.

    (E) retinal disparity.

50. Ina discovered that her friend forgot to turn in Ina's homework because the friend overslept. The relaxation following Ina's subsequent angry outburst is controlled by the:

    (A) sympathetic nervous system.

    (B) cerebral cortex.

    (C) limbic system.

    (D) brain stem.

    (E) parasympathetic nervous system.

51. Teenage pregnancy:

    (A) decreases in countries with easiest access to abortion.

    (B) has decreased markedly in the US since AIDS.

    (C) is markedly higher in the US than in other industrialized nations.

    (D) correlates significantly with the size of welfare entitlements.

    (E) decreases in countries which provide in-school condom distribution.

52. Breast-fed babies show _____ compared with bottle-fed babies.

    (A) slower cognitive development

    (B) faster cognitive development

    (C) no differences in social or cognitive development

    (D) slower social development

    (E) faster social development

53. Hue depends mainly on:

    (A) wavelength.

    (B) wave amplitude.

    (C) intensity.

    (D) purity.

    (E) saturation.

54. The primary colors of light are:

    (A) red, blue, yellow, green.

    (B) red, blue, green.

    (C) black, white, red, blue, green.

    (D) yellow, blue, red, gray.

    (E) none of the above.

55. The receptor cells for hearing are located:

    (A) in the auditory canal.

    (B) in the basilar membrane.

    (C) on the oval window.

    (D) in the semicircular canals.

    (E) in front of the eardrum.

56. In the classical conditioning paradigm, the learning period is called:

    (A) assimilation.

    (B) accession.

    (C) disinhibition.

    (D) acquisition.

    (E) appropriation.

57. Experimental neurosis has been reported when:

    (A) rewards are abruptly eliminated.

    (B) punishment is introduced.

    (C) schedules of reinforcement are altered.

    (D) stimulus discrimination is too difficult.

    (E) the value of the secondary reinforcer diminishes.

58. The total number of responses emitted before extinction is a measure of:

    (A) shaping.

    (B) learning.

    (C) generalization.

    (D) latent learning.

    (E) spontaneous recovery.

59. In a cumulative learning curve, an asymptote indicates:

    (A) the end of the trial.

    (B) a marked increase in response.

    (C) steady, systematic improvement.

    (D) extinction.

    (E) no response.

60. As compared with fixed schedules of reinforcement, variable schedules:

    (A) produce less learning.

    (B) produce more generalizable learning.

    (C) are best for avoidance learning.

    (D) produce learning which is less extinguishable.

    (E) do none of the above.

61. When a mother feeds her baby she talks to it. Her talking is best described as a:

    (A) primary reinforcer.

    (B) positive reinforcer.

    (C) continuous reinforcer.

    (D) generalized reinforcer.

    (E) secondary reinforcer.

62. In the classical conditioning paradigm, backward conditioning has been found to be:

    (A) ineffective.

    (B) moderately effective.

    (C) more effective than simultaneous conditioning.

    (D) more effective than delayed conditioning.

    (E) effective, although easily extinguished.

63. The model in which the animal's response elicits the reward is called:

    (A) classical conditioning.

    (B) shaping.

    (C) first-order conditioning.

    (D) second-order conditioning.

    (E) operant conditioning.

64. In conditioning, partial or intermittent reinforcement:

    (A) accelerates extinction.

    (B) retards extinction.

    (C) retards conditioning.

    (D) accelerates generalization.

    (E) produces none of the above effects.

65. A rat that learned to climb a stairway, run across a plank, climb a ladder, throw a switch, open a gate, and then press a bar is exhibiting:

    (A) sign learning.

    (B) discrimination learning.

    (C) contiguity learning.

    (D) shaping.

    (E) none of the above.

66. According to Miller and Dollard, the avoidance gradient is:

    (A) less steep than the approach gradient closer to the goal.

    (B) steeper than the approach gradient closer to the goal.

    (C) asymptotic where it crosses the approach gradient.

    (D) generally steeper farther from the goal.

    (E) variable depending on the kind of goal.

67. In the Miller and Dollard learning model, the usual response in an avoidance-avoidance conflict is:

    (A) a very slow approach to the goal.

    (B) initial vacillation, then withdrawal.

    (C) experimental neurosis.

    (D) a period of apparent conflict, followed by approach to the goal.

    (E) a period of apparent conflict, followed by aggression toward the goal.

68. Electrical stimulation of certain areas of the hypothalamus of rats produced fantastically high bar-pressing responses. The researcher associated with this investigation is:

    (A) Hebb.

    (B) Lashley.

    (C) Penfield.

    (D) Olds.

    (E) Sherrington.

69. In the information-processing model of human learning, the term which is synonymous with "long-term memory" is:

    (A) sensory register.

    (B) retrieval pool.

    (C) response generator.

    (D) working memory.

    (E) knowledge base.

70. Which of the following statements about the incidence of male homosexuality is *not* true?

    (A) Homosexuality occurs more frequently among unmarried than among married men.

    (B) Homosexuality occurs more frequently among African Americans than among whites.

    (C) Homosexuality occurs in the same proportion of males as of females.

    (D) Homosexuality occurs more frequently among religiously unaffiliated men than among men affiliated with a religion.

    (E) Homosexuality occurs more frequently among men in low-status occupations than among those in high status occupations.

71. Superstitious behavior can be defined as:

    (A) behavior based on beliefs that are accepted without proof.

    (B) behavior based on secondary reinforcers, not primary reinforcers.

    (C) behavior based on schedules of reinforcement no longer in effect.

    (D) learned behaviors that seem to have no purpose.

    (E) behaviors that have been previously reinforced merely by chance.

72. A light goes on before a noxious stimulus begins. If the animal emits a behavior after the light goes on, there will be no aversive stimulus. This is called:

    (A) escape conditioning.

    (B) avoidance conditioning.

    (C) inhibition conditioning.

    (D) negative conditioning.

    (E) backward conditioning.

73. Bandura found that:

    (A) children learn certain aggressive behaviors by imitating the powerful adult.

    (B) boys more readily imitate male models, while girls more readily imitate female models.

    (C) modeling is more effective if the scene observed is live rather than filmed.

    (D) imitation learning is effective mostly among children and becomes less effective the older the subject.

    (E) children in a group seem more susceptible to imitation than children tested individually.

74. The Seashore test is used to measure:

    (A) spatial abilities.

    (B) motor functioning.

    (C) musical talent.

    (D) handedness.

    (E) compliance.

75. When children were shown various models in the Bobo doll experiment—live adults, filmed humans, cartoons—it was found that:

    (A) cartoon models reinforced for aggression produced more social learning than did non-reinforced adult models.

    (B) live adult models produced the greatest amount of social learning.

    (C) social learning for aggression was greatest for the most heavily reinforced model regardless of the medium.

    (D) filmed adult models are the most difficult to extinguish.

    (E) results from the Bobo doll experiment do not generalize to other situations.

76. The influential autobiography describing mental hospitalization in the early twentieth century, *A Mind That Found Itself*, was written by:

    (A) Plath.

    (B) Rush.

    (C) Menninger.

    (D) Dix.

    (E) Beers.

77. Birth-order studies indicate that last children show:

    (A) higher intelligence test scores the greater the number of siblings.

    (B) poorer intellectual and social adjustment in life than their older siblings.

    (C) poorer social adjustment and greater likelihood of institutionalization.

    (D) greater creativity and original thinking than earlier-born children.

    (E) greater need to achieve than other siblings.

78. If a tester administers a test which includes subtests that measure digit span, picture completion, block design, and similarities, the tester would be administering:

    (A) MMPI.

    (B) CPI.

    (C) SVIB.

    (D) WISC-R.

    (E) Luria-Nebraska.

79. "Hypnosis is a form of voluntary behavior designed to evoke a desired consequence. Such behavior is merely a manifestation of an increase in motivation. Hypnosis is not an altered state of consciousness." This statement comes closest ro representing the position of:

    (A) Mesmer.

    (B) Freud.

    (C) Hilgard.

    (D) Skinner.

    (E) Spanos.

80. In the Hopi culture infants are bound to cradleboards during the first three months of life. The effect of this procedure on their learning to walk is that:

    (A) it retards the onset of walking.

    (B) it facilitates walking.

    (C) it accelerates the beginning of toddling.

    (D) Hopi children spend much more time crawling and begin to walk later than children who were not so bound.

    (E) it has no effect on subsequent walking.

81. The sound "da" uttered by an infant is an example of:

    (A) a filled pause.

    (B) a phoneme.

    (C) a morpheme.

    (D) a semantic equivalent.

    (E) a lexical marker.

82. To investigate whether intelligence can be altered through environmental variables, a researcher would most likely compare:

    (A) fraternal twins reared apart.

    (B) immigrant children reared in their non-native countries with non-immigrant children.

    (C) samples of closely related children with samples of unrelated children.

    (D) children raised by their biological parents with children raised by foster parents.

    (E) identical twins raised in orphanages with identical twins raised in families.

83. Experiments by the Harlows with monkeys reared by wire and cloth mothers showed that when frightened:

    (A) the monkeys clung to the mother that fed them.

    (B) the monkeys clung to each other, avoiding the inanimate mothers.

    (C) the monkeys clung to the cloth mother.

    (D) the monkeys became immobilized and lost a great deal of contact with reality.

    (E) the monkeys exhibited behavior typical of experimental neurosis.

84. Of the following schedules of reinforcement, the highest response rates are maintained through a:

    (A) partial schedule.

    (B) continuous schedule.

    (C) spontaneous schedule.

    (D) noncontingent schedule.

    (E) random schedule.

85. In the Skinner paradigm, operant behavior is controlled through:

    (A) chaining.

    (B) reinforcement.

    (C) punishment.

    (D) shaping.

    (E) stimulus generalization.

86. In the operant conditioning model, reinforcement appears:

    (A) with the onset of the conditioned stimulus.

    (B) after the stimulus but before the response.

    (C) as the animal begins the response.

    (D) after the response is made.

    (E) as the avoidance response is elicited.

87. The operant conditioning model in which the organism's response is followed by the removal of a noxious stimulus is called:

    (A) release conditioning.

    (B) discriminate reinforcement.

    (C) punishment.

    (D) avoidance conditioning.

    (E) escape conditioning.

88. Chimps learning to operate a machine were rewarded with poker chips. The chips were a:

    (A) primary reinforcer.

    (B) positive reinforcer.

    (C) generalized reinforcer.

    (D) secondary reinforcer.

    (E) higher-order reinforcer.

89. Reinforcing closer and closer approximations to the desired behavior is called:

    (A) instruction.

    (B) shaping.

    (C) higher-order conditioning.

    (D) chaining.

    (E) transfer.

90. A researcher reported that through electrical stimulation of pleasure centers in the brain he could condition rats to change autonomic functions such as heart rate and blood pressure. This was an unusual finding because:

    (A) no one had ever located such precise pleasure centers before.

    (B) these functions were not thought to be under voluntary or operant control.

    (C) heart rate and blood pressure were thought to be fixed from birth and unchangeable except under stress.

    (D) for the first time brain centers that control blood pressure were discovered.

    (E) pleasure centers had never previously been found to be associated with heart rate and blood pressure.

91. All of the following are true findings about children raised in institutions where care was minimal *except:*

    (A) they tended to be hyperkinetic.

    (B) they tended to show little vocalization.

    (C) their intelligence scores were below normal.

    (D) they tended toward autistic behaviors.

    (E) they showed little contact with other people.

92. In Piaget's model, the stage at which behavior is most determined by reflexes is:

    (A) preoperational.

    (B) concrete operational.

    (C) prelogical.

    (D) precognitive.

    (E) sensorimotor.

93. A mode of thought characteristic of the stage of formal operations is:

    (A) inductive reasoning.

    (B) punning.

    (C) scolding for transgressions.

    (D) collective monologue.

    (E) pre-scientific experimentation.

94. In DSM-IV, fetishism, bondage, exhibitionism, and sado-masochistic sexual expression are:

    (A) considered disguised homosexuality.

    (B) defended as normal sexual expression in most circumstances.

    (C) classified as antisocial personality disorders.

    (D) considered untreatable if their expression is ego-syntonic.

    (E) classified as paraphilias.

95. In Freudian theory, the superego develops:

    (A) after attaining the genital stage.

    (B) after resolution of the anal stage.

    (C) after resolving the Oedipal conflict.

    (D) during latency.

    (E) throughout life, especially during the phallic stage.

96. In which society is it considered the obligation of the immediate family to assist the dying in abandoning their ties to this world in order to prepare for the next world?

    (A) Muslim.

    (B) African animist.

    (C) Russian Orthodox.

    (D) Hindu.

    (E) Jewish.

97. The brains of schizophrenics show:

    (A) less gray matter in the frontal cortex and displaced cells in the hippocampus.

    (B) less convolution of the cortex and more random electrical activity, as shown on the PET scan.

    (C) dominance of functions of the "old brain" and more brain stem activity.

    (D) marked decrease in endorphin receptor sites and either left or right brain dominance, varying individually.

    (E) no significant differences from the brains of non-schizophrenics.

98. The two-factor theory of intelligence is associated with:

    (A) Thurstone.

    (B) Gardner.

    (C) Cattell.

    (D) Binet.

    (E) Spearman.

99. The primary mental abilities are associated with:

    (A) Thurstone.

    (B) Eysenck.

    (C) Cattell.

    (D) Terman.

    (E) Wechsler.

100. The facility to generate new, creative, and different ideas or hypotheses is called:

    (A) nonconformity.

    (B) convergent thinking.

    (C) insight thinking.

    (D) abstraction.

    (E) divergent thinking.

101. The tasks on the original Binet-Simon intelligence test were:

    (A) scaled according to the average competencies of each age level.

    (B) scaled by an expert panel, including grade school teachers.

    (C) chosen on the basis of results of previously standardized tests.

    (D) purposely made difficult so that scaled scores were always lower than actual intelligence.

    (E) culturally limited.

102. According to the Stanford-Binet intelligence test, an eight-year-old child with an IQ of 125 has a mental age of:

    (A) 12.5

    (B) 10

    (C) 8

    (D) 6

    (E) none of the above.

103. One possible role of an expert psychological witness in a court case is to provide an explanation for the role of situational variables in predisposing people toward certain acts. Most people judge other people on the basis of assumed intrapersonal dynamics, not on the basis of situational determinants. The tendency to interpret other people's behavior on the basis of intrapersonal dynamics rather than situational variables is called:

    (A) the neurotic paradox.

    (B) cognitive dissonance.

    (C) the double bind.

    (D) paradoxical reactions.

    (E) fundamental attribution error.

104. Among the elderly, alcoholism:

    (A) is more common than among younger generations.

    (B) may be less serious because it takes more alcohol to achieve higher blood alcohol levels than among younger drinkers.

    (C) may be less serious because, with age, most people gain greater control over their impulses, including the desire to drink.

    (D) may be more serious because the elderly drinker is more likely to be a binge drinker than is the younger drinker.

    (E) may be more serious because it takes less alcohol to achieve higher blood alcohol levels than among younger drinkers.

105. The concept that asserts that people perform better when they are in competition than when they are alone is called:

    (A) social facilitation.

    (B) social comparison.

    (C) group dynamics.

    (D) Yerkes-Dodson law.

    (E) social reality.

106. Predisposing causes of a disease are referred to as:

    (A) ethology.

    (B) epidemiology.

    (C) ecology.

    (D) etiology.

    (E) environmental factors.

107. The Asch experiment on conformity found that conformity could be reduced by:

    (A) increasing the size of the group.

    (B) varying characteristics of the stimulus.

    (C) contriving responses so they were unanimous.

    (D) contriving responses so they were not unanimous.

    (E) using same-sex experimenters.

108. The Asch and Sherif experiments on conformity behavior indicated that:

    (A) conformity increases as physical reality becomes more uncertain.

    (B) people tend to agree with the judgment of a strong group leader.

    (C) most subjects try to please the experimenter by confirming the hypothesis.

    (D) conformity is highest among first-borns.

    (E) laboratory experiments artificially create a conforming demand characteristic that might not predict non-laboratory behavior.

109. In investigations of the risky-shift phenomenon, it was found that:

    (A) subjects will change their minds if they believe the experimenter wants them to.

    (B) subjects don't generally like to take risks when observers are present.

    (C) subjects are more likely to take risks if the other people nearby have already completed the experiment.

    (D) groups are more conservative than individuals.

    (E) groups are less conservative than the individuals who comprise them.

110. "Whenever a response occurs, that response is immediately and completely associated with all stimuli present at that instant." This statement is most typical of:

    (A) Estes.

    (B) Guthrie.

    (C) Tolman.

    (D) Hull.

    (E) Skinner.

111. In the study by Schacter and Singer, when subjects were given an emotionally arousing drug but weren't told of the effect of the drug, they tended to:

    (A) take on the affect of the experimenter.

    (B) take on the affect of others around them.

    (C) become frightened.

    (D) search out some cognitively consistent explanation.

    (E) want to terminate the experiment.

112. The social distance scale was developed by:

    (A) Katz and Braley.

    (B) Hovland.

    (C) Likert.

    (D) LaPierre.

    (E) Bogardus.

113. The "suppressed rage" hypothesis has been posited to account for which of the following common health disorders?

    (A) Hypertension

    (B) Anorexia nervosa

    (C) Myocardial infarction

    (D) **AIDS**

    (E) **Atherosclerosis**

114. All of the following activities are mediated by the limbic system *except:*

    (A) feeding.

    (B) reasoning.

    (C) mating.

    (D) fighting.

    (E) fleeing.

115. A propensity to think, feel, or act in a certain way toward a certain object is called a(n):

    (A) prejudice.

    (B) habit.

    (C) attitude.

    (D) canalization.

    (E) affect.

116. A measurement technique in which subjects rate statements on a seven-point scale from "agree" to "disagree" is typical of the:

    (A) Guttman scale.

    (B) Q-Sort.

    (C) Likert scale.

    (D) Thurstone scale.

    (E) Marlow-Crowne scale.

117. Attitude change is facilitated if the communicator:

    (A) appeals to the altruistic feelings of the listeners.

    (B) begins by presenting the opposing view.

    (C) appears to the audience to be "one of us."

    (D) puts the communication in moral terms.

    (E) is highly credible.

118. In attitude-change studies, it has been found that presenting both sides of the argument is most effective if the listener:

    (A) doesn't know anything about the subject.

    (B) is initially opposed to the subject.

    (C) is initially in favor of the subject.

    (D) is not well educated.

    (E) hasn't yet committed himself to a position.

119. Of patients with the following diagnoses, which is *least* likely to voluntarily commence psychotherapy?

    (A) The patient with dysthymic reaction

    (B) The patient with anxiety disorder

    (C) The patient with affective disorder

    (D) The patient with personality disorder

    (E) The patient with somatoform disorder

120. The researcher who designed a scale to measure the degree to which a subject's responses are socially desirable is:

    (A) Edwards.

    (B) Thurstone.

    (C) Hovland.

    (D) Rosenthal.

    (E) Osgood.

121. The major biochemical action of most antipsychotic medications is:

    (A) increased production of dopamine.

    (B) sedation of CNS functioning.

    (C) blockage of seratonin and norepinephrine production.

    (D) increased absorption and utilization of vitamins.

    (E) blockage of dopamine receptors.

122. Of the following characteristics of an audience, the one which would have the *least* bearing on attitude change is:

    (A) intelligence.

    (B) self-esteem.

    (C) dependency.

    (D) feeling toward speaker.

    (E) previous knowledge of subject.

123. When people anticipate that they will be taking part in an experiment in which they will be receiving aversive shocks, they generally:

    (A) choose to wait alone.

    (B) choose to wait with others who are also about to take part in the experiment.

    (C) tend not to care if they wait alone or with others.

    (D) choose to wait with subjects who have already completed the experiment.

    (E) prefer to participate in some activity which distracts them.

124. Affiliation needs seem to be strongest in:

    (A) twins.

    (B) females.

    (C) males.

    (D) last-borns.

    (E) firstborns.

125. All of the following are Gestalt principles of perception *except:*

    (A) Pragnanz.

    (B) good continuation.

    (C) closure.

    (D) projection.

    (E) common fate.

126. The phrase, "We learn to love the thing we suffer for," is most characteristic of:

    (A) congruity theory.

    (B) dissonance theory.

    (C) James-Lange theory.

    (D) balance theory.

    (E) Sapir-Whorf theory.

127. According to congruity theory, if a highly valued source makes a positive statement about a negatively valued object, the listener is likely to:

    (A) become confused and search out other opinions.

    (B) disregard the communication.

    (C) alter his opinion about the source only.

    (D) alter his opinion about the source and the object.

    (E) reinterpret the communication to make it more congruent.

128. Stability and change characterize adulthood according to:

    (A) Kübler-Ross.

    (B) Baumrind.

    (C) Levinson.

    (D) Langer.

    (E) Erikson.

129. According to the US Surgeon General, the most preventable cause of illness and premature death is:

    (A) abuse of alcohol.

    (B) abuse of drugs.

    (C) smoking.

    (D) dietary fat.

    (E) lack of exercise.

130. Artificial intelligence (AI):

    (A) refers to neural networks in computers.

    (B) refers to flaws in IQ testing uncovered by modern computer analysis.

    (C) accommodates for differential rates of learning among computer users.

    (D) bases computer algorithms on models of human thought.

    (E) substitutes computers for animals as research subjects.

131. An occasional complication of obesity is upper airway obstruction which can lead to a syndrome characterized by sleep disturbances, irregular nocturnal heartbeat, and snoring. This syndrome is called:

    (A) agnosia.

    (B) narcolepsy.

    (C) amenorrhea.

    (D) arrhythmia.

    (E) apnea.

132. At last year's Thanksgiving dinner you surprised yourself with how much of the delicious meal you were able to put away. The satisfied feeling you experienced is due in large part to the action of the:

    (A) endocrine system.

    (B) hypothalamus.

    (C) basal ganglia.

    (D) limbic system.

    (E) thalamus.

133. Which of the following is *not* a stimulant?

    (A) caffeine

    (B) nicotine

    (C) barbiturates

    (D) cocaine

    (E) amphetamines

134. An art therapist encourages clients to express feelings of frustration in their art work. The clients are engaging in:

    (A) sublimation.

    (B) catharsis.

    (C) displacement.

    (D) projection.

    (E) behavioral identification.

135. Obesity is difficult to overcome because:

    (A) it is associated with well-being in many minority cultures, although not in the majority US culture.

    (B) most commercial weight-loss programs misdirect attention from basic glandular problems.

    (C) metabolic needs decrease as dieting continues, absent other lifestyle changes.

    (D) fat cells require continued caloric maintenance; otherwise they secrete insulin.

    (E) it is now generally accepted that obesity is genetic.

136. According to Bem's theory, gender identity:

    (A) is a product of both nature and nurture.

    (B) is influenced primarily by hormonal balance in utero.

    (C) is more cognitive than biological.

    (D) derives from imitation of the same-sex parent.

    (E) is the product of environmental reinforcement history.

137. As we age, the cognitive ability that declines most is the ability to:

    (A) recall new information.

    (B) remember small details.

    (C) judge the importance of events in daily life.

    (D) learn new information.

    (E) use new information.

138. The adage that best describes the usual trend in cognitive abilities as we age is:

    (A) It only gets worse from here.

    (B) Use it or lose it.

    (C) The older we get, the wiser we get.

    (D) There's no fool like an old fool.

    (E) You can't teach an old dog new tricks.

139. Fisher's contribution to experimental design was:

    (A) inductive analysis.

    (B) correlational analysis.

    (C) validity testing.

    (D) the use of critical ratios.

    (E) hypothesis testing.

140. Hormones that penetrate cell membranes to activate or inhibit structures are:

    (A) steroids.

    (B) peptides.

    (C) neurotransmitters.

    (D) ACTH.

    (E) testosterone.

141. Advocates of "recovered memories" suggest that later in life victims of childhood sexual abuse develop:

    (A) hysterical personality.

    (B) schizophrenia.

    (C) dependent personality.

    (D) sexual paraphrenia.

    (E) multiple personality.

142. The notions of an inferiority complex and compensatory behaviors are associated with:

    (A) Adler.

    (B) Horney.

    (C) Rogers.

    (D) Rank.

    (E) Jung.

143. The effect of touch by caretakers/handlers on neonate humans and many animal species is:

    (A) no obvious systemic changes.

    (B) the retardation of physical growth.

    (C) the stimulation of physical growth.

    (D) the retardation of social attachment.

    (E) social ostracism by cage-mates.

144. We tend to evaluate ourselves by how much we fulfill others' expectations of us. This is an example of:

    (A) Kelley's consensus self.

    (B) Asch's Gestalt.

    (C) Freud's countertransference.

    (D) Cooley's looking-glass self.

    (E) Bem's self-perception theory.

145. The stranger-situation test for infants is associated with:

    (A) Madelaine Horner.

    (B) Anna Freud.

    (C) Jean Piaget.

    (D) Mary Ainsworth.

    (E) Carol Gilligan.

146. Joe Wonderchild perceives himself to be an incredibly important person, a kind of divine gift to humankind. He rarely feels anxiety about himself and is unlikely to volunteer for therapy because he sees himself as nearly perfect. He could be diagnosed as:

    (A) schizotypal disorder.

    (B) sadistic personality.

    (C) borderline personality.

    (D) paranoid personality.

    (E) narcissistic personality.

147. When the ossicles become rigid, _____ ensues.

    (A) tone deafness

    (B) total deafness

    (C) conduction deafness

    (D) tinnitus

    (E) otosclerosis

148. Hormones cause the average woman:

    (A) to have a reduced sex drive during menstruation.

    (B) no major changes in sex drive during menstruation.

    (C) to have an increased sex drive during menstruation.

    (D) to have increased sex drive during ovulation.

    (E) to have decreased sex drive immediately following ovulation.

149. You lose your gym combination lock, then get a new one. Your difficulty learning the new combination is an example of:

    (A) proactive interference.

    (B) retroactive interference.

    (C) primacy.

    (D) recency.

    (E) chunking.

150. The neurotransmitter which seems to be related to both sleep and obsessive-compulsive disorders is:

    (A) dopamine.

    (B) 6-hydroxydopamine.

    (C) GABA.

    (D) acetylcholine.

    (E) serotonin.

151. In psychoanalysis, the patient feels injured by the analyst's remark and throws the tissue box across the room. This is called:

    (A) transference.

    (B) countertransference.

    (C) abreaction.

    (D) resistance.

    (E) displacement.

152. The theorist who postulated neurotic trends moving toward, moving against, and moving away from people was:

    (A) Carl Rogers.

    (B) Rollo May.

    (C) Erich Fromm.

    (D) Harry Stack Sullivan.

    (E) Karen Homey.

153. Parkinson's disease is characterized by the loss of nerve cells in the:

    (A) cingulate cortex.

    (B) substantia nigra.

    (C) reticular formation.

    (D) cerebral cortex.

    (E) caudate nucleus.

154. Cognitive theorists differ from behavior theorists in that cognitive theorists believe:

    (A) behaviorists are too easily misled by the manifest.

    (B) thought precedes behavior.

    (C) biology is destiny.

    (D) inside the black box is a drive-reduction-driven organism.

    (E) behaviorism will inevitably lead to cognitive theory as a next stage.

155. Poisons that enter the bloodstream from the intestines can leave the blood and stimulate vomiting when they leave via the:

    (A) cerebellum.

    (B) endothelial cells.

    (C) area postrema.

    (D) neuroglia.

    (E) corpus callosum.

156. Medical doctors are now taught that it is better "bedside manner" to be:

    (A) realistic, informative, and honest.

    (B) short, direct, and authoritative.

    (C) optimistic, encouraging, and upbeat.

    (D) indirect, cloudy, and nonspecific.

    (E) objective, fact-laden, and scientific.

157. Of the following, the pair that is *incorrectly* matched is:

    (A) Beck—cognitive therapy.

    (B) Ellis—rational-emotive therapy.

    (C) Rogers—client-centered therapy.

    (D) Mahler—behavior therapy.

    (E) Adler—individual therapy.

158. The psychotic state characterized by wild excitement alternating with tearfulness and depression is:

    (A) catatonic schizophrenia.

    (B) paranoid schizophrenia.

    (C) autism.

    (D) simple schizophrenia.

    (E) hebephrenic schizophrenia.

159. The book *On the Integrative Action of the Nervous System* was written by:

    (A) Lashley.

    (B) Sherrington.

    (C) Broca.

    (D) Penfield.

    (E) Pribram.

160. The movement of the striated muscles is controlled by the:

    (A) central nervous system.

    (B) sympathetic nervous system.

    (C) parasympathetic nervous system.

    (D) reticular activating system.

    (E) ductless glands.

161. The test construct which is *least* essential in a test of chronic anxiety is:

    (A) face validity.

    (B) predictive validity.

    (C) scorer reliability.

    (D) test-retest reliability.

    (E) construct validity.

162. The rod-in-frame test is used to measure:

    (A) cognitive functions.

    (B) perception.

    (C) aphasia

    (D) field dependency.

    (E) organic brain disturbances.

163. A chemical substance which acts as a neuromuscular transmitter is:

    (A) epinephrine.

    (B) acetylcholine.

    (C) l-Dopa.

    (D) norepinephrine.

    (E) quinine.

164. Von Bekesy's theory regarding pitch detection is most like the concept of:

    (A) specific nerve energies.

    (B) lateral inhibition.

    (C) volley theory.

    (D) all-or-none effect.

    (E) graded potential.

165. The MMPI was normed by using:

    (A) hospital patients.

    (B) college students.

    (C) psychologists.

    (D) prison inmates.

    (E) a national sample of high school students.

166. The California F-scale is used in assessing:

    (A) response sets.

    (B) ESP.

    (C) fraternal attitudes.

    (D) psychotic disorders.

    (E) fascist tendencies.

167. An approach to personality which does not stress the person's own history is that of:

    (A) Breuer.

    (B) Murray.

    (C) Jung.

    (D) Kretschmer.

    (E) N. Miller.

168. Achievement need is measured by the:

    (A) TAT.

    (B) Rorschach test.

    (C) MMPI.

    (D) Taylor MAS.

    (E) Gough CPI.

169. Cattell arrived at his theory of personality traits using the technique of:

    (A) introspection.

    (B) factor analysis.

    (C) psychoanalysis.

    (D) physiological assessment.

    (E) projective tests.

170. Longitudinal studies of schizophrenia have generally concluded that:

    (A) it tends to be inherited.

    (B) it occurs pretty much randomly.

    (C) girls tend to be schizophrenic to a significantly greater degree than boys.

    (D) it seems to be passed on through the father.

    (E) the incidence among monozygotic twins is quite rare.

171. The WISC-R test is:

    (A) an individual test for adults.

    (B) an individual test for children.

    (C) a group test for children.

    (D) a group test for adults.

    (E) an individual test for infants.

172. A score falling at the modal point of a group of scores is:

    (A) at the exact midpoint.

    (B) equal to the standard deviation in a normal distribution.

    (C) the most common score.

    (D) the square root of the variance.

    (E) equal to the mean.

173. A bimodal distribution indicates that:

    (A) the test was too easy.

    (B) the results are skewed positively.

    (C) the median and the mode fall at the same point.

    (D) there are probably two distinct populations.

    (E) the scores are normally distributed.

174. A correlation between two measures of 0.00 indicates:

    (A) the relationship is absolutely negative.

    (B) there is no relationship.

    (C) the computation was probably in error.

    (D) as one score goes up the other remains the same.

    (E) none of the above.

175. When an experimenter instructed the subjects to administer what seemed to be a very painful shock to another person, most subjects:

    (A) refused.

    (B) complied.

    (C) left the laboratory.

    (D) appeared to enjoy giving the shock.

    (E) realized the other person was a confederate.

176. Drowsiness and sleepiness would result from lesions to the:

    (A) reticular activating system.

    (B) cerebellum.

    (C) thalamus.

    (D) corpus callosum.

    (E) temporal lobe.

177. An implication of the Yerkes-Dodson law is that:

    (A) learning is best if there has been previous experience with the material.

    (B) a person should be totally relaxed when learning new material.

    (C) learning simple tasks requires much concentration.

    (D) slight anxiety will facilitate learning easy tasks.

    (E) maximum learning occurs under minimum stress.

For questions 178 and 179, consider the following color wheel and assume there are no other colors.

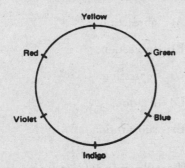

178. Adding red and green in equal proportions produces:

    (A) blue.

    (B) gray.

    (C) yellow.

    (D) white.

    (E) violet.

179. The color that must be added to blue to desaturate it is:

    (A) gray.

    (B) white.

    (C) yellow.

    (D) violet.

    (E) none of the above.

180. A complement to a color is the color which:

    (A) mixes with it to make gray.

    (B) absorbs it.

    (C) is perceived when viewing it against a gray background.

    (D) looks best with it.

    (E) will not desaturate it.

181. Movies exemplify the:

    (A) phi phenomenon.

    (B) autokinetic effect.

    (C) saccadic movement.

    (D) Ponzo illusion.

    (E) Purkinje shift.

182. The number 7 ± 2 described by G. Miller refers to:

    (A) the time taken to retrieve information from short-term memory.

    (B) the number of information chunks which can be held in short-term memory.

    (C) the correlation between visual and auditory short-term memory.

    (D) the number of input channels available for sensory processing.

    (E) the number of phonemes common to all languages.

183. The researcher associated with the concepts of divergent and convergent thinking is:

    (A) Goddard.

    (B) Eysenck.

    (C) Wechsler.

    (D) Guilford.

    (E) Thurstone.

184. The terms *person, shadow,* and *collective unconscious* are associated with:

    (A) Rogers.

    (B) Breuer.

    (C) Jung.

    (D) Bleuler.

    (E) Janet.

185. Mesmer's work was the antecedent of:

    (A) field theory.

    (B) hypnosis.

    (C) sensory deprivation.

    (D) REM sleep research.

    (E) schizophrenia.

186. The sense which is not mediated through the thalamus is:

    (A) sight.

    (B) smell.

    (C) proprioception.

    (D) kinesthesis.

    (E) touch.

187. The therapy technique called *reciprocal inhibition* entails:

    (A) patients communicating in groups about their inhibitions.

    (B) the therapist supporting the patients and revealing his/her own problems.

    (C) the therapist gradually introducing the anxiety-provoking stimulus.

    (D) alternating between strongly positive and strongly negative communications.

    (E) the group cloistering itself at some retreat where alternative communication practices are explored.

188. Reaction formation is to opposite as sublimation is to:

    (A) abreaction.

    (B) projection.

    (C) repression.

    (D) fixation.

    (E) substitution.

189. The volley principle is used to explain the sense of:

    (A) movement.

    (B) hearing.

    (C) sight.

    (D) smell.

    (E) touch.

190. If you hold in your hand two coils with warm water running through one coil and cold water running through the other, you will sense:

    (A) confusion and distraction.

    (B) coldness.

    (C) heat.

    (D) tepidness.

    (E) numbness.

191. Paradoxical sleep is associated with:

    (A) the hypnogogic stage.

    (B) stage four (deep sleep).

    (C) the hypnopompic stage.

    (D) REM sleep.

    (E) NREM sleep.

192. The degree of freedom in a chi-square test depends on:

    (A)   number of observations.

    (B)   number of categories.

    (C)   number of subjects.

    (D)   average variance of the groups.

    (E)   sample means.

193. A forensic technique pioneered by John Douglas of the FBI involves the development of a list of characteristics of possible crime perpetrators by evaluating the crime or crime scene. This controversial technique, which is not to date considered admissible as evidence in court, is called:

    (A)   factor analysis.

    (B)   deductive hypothesis testing.

    (C)   hot pursuit.

    (D)   crystallized intelligence.

    (E)   profiling.

194. Weber's law refers to:

    (A)   imprinting.

    (B)   drive reduction.

    (C)   reinforcement schedules.

    (D)   anxiety thresholds.

    (E)   perceptual differences.

195. Color is associated with the psychological term:

    (A)   brightness.

    (B)   tone.

    (C)   shade.

    (D)   hue.

    (E)   saturation.

196. Studies on influencing attitudes show that a person, after hearing a point of view that he feels is extremely discrepant, tends to:

    (A)   modify his position.

    (B)   accept the discrepant view if the source has high credibility.

    (C)   become more extreme in his adherence to his original view.

    (D)   reinterpret the discrepant message to make it more acceptable.

    (E)   reject the message and reduce his trust in the source.

197. All of the following are tastes *except:*

    (A)   bitter.

    (B)   spicy.

    (C)   sweet.

    (D)   salt.

    (E)   sour.

198. The baby cries. The baby sitter gives him a lollipop to shut him up. He finishes his lollipop and cries again until he gets another one. This kind of reinforcement schedule would be:

    (A)   fixed ratio.

    (B)   variable ratio.

    (C)   fixed interval.

    (D)   variable interval.

    (E)   continuous.

199. In a factory that pays its employees on a piecework system, the schedule of reinforcement can be said to be:

    (A) fixed ratio.

    (B) fixed interval.

    (C) continuous.

    (D) variable interval.

    (E) variable ratio.

200. The Likert scale is used in:

    (A) psychophysics.

    (B) attitude measurement.

    (C) perceptual discrimination.

    (D) intelligence tests.

    (E) statistical inference.

201. The phenomenon of certain colors appearing to change brightness under different levels of illumination is called:

    (A) Emmert's law.

    (B) Young-Helmholz theory.

    (C) Ponzo illusion.

    (D) Yerkes-Dodson law.

    (E) Purkinje shift.

202. The operation of the "one-armed bandit," or slot machine, is an example of:

    (A) continuous reinforcement.

    (B) fixed interval reinforcement.

    (C) variable interval reinforcement.

    (D) fixed ratio reinforcement.

    (E) variable ratio reinforcement.

203. The phenomenon that causes a person to remember unfinished tasks and forget completed ones is called:

    (A) James-Lange theory.

    (B) Emmert's law.

    (C) Weber's law.

    (D) Zeigarnik effect.

    (E) Cannon-Bard theory.

204. Heider is most associated with:

    (A) inoculation theory.

    (B) exchange theory.

    (C) balance theory.

    (D) role theory.

    (E) attribution theory.

205. The theorist who postulated the drive called a *will to power* is:

    (A) Adler.

    (B) May.

    (C) Fromm.

    (D) Binswanger.

    (E) Horney.

206. Experimental neurosis is achieved through:

    (A) similarity of response categories.

    (B) approach-avoidance conflict.

    (C) differential rewarding of indistinguishable stimuli.

    (D) overextinguishing an operant behavior.

    (E) inappropriate response generalizations.

207. The three-color theory of color vision is most associated with:

    (A) Muller.

    (B) Helmholz.

    (C) Hering.

    (D) Von Bekesy.

    (E) Newton.

208. The notion that intellectual faculties can be strengthened through studying subjects like Latin and physics is called the doctrine of:

    (A) convergent thinking.

    (B) primary mental abilities.

    (C) overcompensation.

    (D) formal disciplines.

    (E) reflex arcs.

209. The GSR is a measure of:

    (A) neural activity.

    (B) information-processing functions.

    (C) retinal disparity.

    (D) endocrine hormonal secretions.

    (E) surreptitious behavior.

210. Studies of children raised in institutions where care was minimal indicate that:

    (A) nurses tend to be abusive.

    (B) development depends on genetic factors.

    (C) motor skills develop normally although intelligence is retarded.

    (D) without appropriate stimulation, normal development is retarded.

    (E) there is a higher incidence of schizophrenia as the children mature.

211. A car seen at some distance will still seem about its real size to most drivers. This is explained by the concept of:

    (A) constancy.

    (B) parallax.

    (C) saccadic movement.

    (D) disparity.

    (E) convergence.

212. The frequency of sound waves determines the:

    (A) pitch.

    (B) timbre.

    (C) loudness.

    (D) resonance.

    (E) melody.

213. In a normal distribution, the percentage of cases included within ±3 of the standard deviation from the mean is approximately:

    (A) 50%.

    (B) 68%.

    (C) 32%.

    (D) 95%.

    (E) 98%.

214. The all-or-none principle means that:

    (A) all neurons entering the synapse discharge at the same time.

    (B) the refractory period is complete or there is none at all.

    (C) once the action-potential threshold is reached, the whole neuron fires.

    (D) all fibers in a nerve are activated simultaneously or not at all.

    (E) the perceptual threshold is absolute.

215. It is better to use the median rather than the mean for a distribution when:

    (A) the mean will yield a score too far from the mode.

    (B) the extreme scores would affect the average disproportionately.

    (C) the standard deviation is also needed.

    (D) the mean is not a whole number.

    (E) high reliability is needed.

216. The reliability coefficient is valuable in determining:

    (A) how consistently a person will retain his relative rank in the group if an equivalent test is given.

    (B) how many points a person's score is likely to change if an equivalent test is given.

    (C) whether or not the test is measuring what it is supposed to measure.

    (D) whether or not the test is related to actual performance of the task being assessed.

    (E) if there are fewer factors which can account for the variables measured.

Question 217 is based on the following table giving information on two tests administered to the same group of students.

	Comprehension Test	Word Fluency Test
Number of test items	100	100
Subject A's score	75	45
Group mean	60	35
Standard deviation	10	5

217. From the above scores it can be said that:

    (A) Subject A did better in comprehension than in word fluency.

    (B) Subject A did better in word fluency than in comprehension.

    (C) Subject A did equally well on both tests.

    (D) without the percentile rankings it is impossible to say which test Subject A did better on.

    (E) the comprehension test was difficult for the group.

218. A conditioned stimulus continually presented without reinforcement is likely to produce:

    (A) experimental neurosis.

    (B) retroactive inhibition.

    (C) classical conditioning.

    (D) extinction.

    (E) higher-order conditioning.

219. The mechanical device used to measure the physiological function of hand grip is called the:

    (A) stressor-flexor.

    (B) dynamometer.

    (C) tachistoscope.

    (D) oscilloscope.

    (E) functional glove.

220. The term that does not belong with the others is:

    (A) progression.

    (B) regression.

    (C) sublimation.

    (D) repression.

    (E) fixation.

221. The first experimental laboratory was established in 1879 in:

    (A) Harvard University.

    (B) Clark University.

    (C) Leipzig.

    (D) Vienna.

    (E) Berlin.

222. A student's score falls at the 30th percentile on a 220-item test administered to a group of 100 students. This means that:

    (A) he got 68 items correct.

    (B) he got 30 items correct.

    (C) his score was higher than 70 other students.

    (D) his score was higher than 30 other students.

    (E) his score fell within one standard deviation of the mean.

223. Correlating the GRE scores of entering graduate students with a subsequent measure of success in their graduate studies is an example of assessing:

    (A) construct validity.

    (B) concurrent validity.

    (C) predictive validity.

    (D) equivalent-forms validity.

    (E) none of the above.

224. Each time the baby cries, the baby sitter gives it milk. When the mother comes home, she ignores the baby's crying. From the mother's perspective, the mother's behavior is likely to produce:

    (A) reactivation.

    (B) spontaneous inhibition.

    (C) extinction.

    (D) variable reinforcement.

    (E) adventitious learning.

225. The term "cognitive science" refers to:

    (A) the scientific study of thought processes.

    (B) the scientific study of thought and learning processes (e.g., training) of humans and animals.

    (C) the science of computer programming designed to emulate human thought processes.

    (D) the practice and study of rationally based science.

    (E) the study of human cognition and computer simulations of human cognition.

226. The psychologist associated with non-directed, client-centered therapy is:

    (A) May.

    (B) Maslow.

    (C) Fromm.

    (D) Rogers.

    (E) Perls.

227. Kuder and Strong are associated with:

    (A) balance theory.

    (B) scaling methodology.

    (C) interest inventories.

    (D) special education.

    (E) social learning theory.

228. The defense mechanism in which an undesirable thought is consciously put out of mind is called:

    (A) repression.

    (B) suppression.

    (C) reaction formation.

    (D) abreaction.

    (E) conversion.

229. As compared with one conducted through an unmyelinated fiber, an impulse conducted through a myelinated fiber will:

    (A) go faster.

    (B) go slower.

    (C) be reversed.

    (D) go faster only if the fiber is thicker.

    (E) be inhibited at the synapse.

230. The junction between neurons is called a(n):

    (A) ganglia.

    (B) axon.

    (C) dendrite.

    (D) synapse.

    (E) junction.

231. Brain activity is sometimes studied by using radioactively tagged glucose, which emits positrons as it is consumed by the brain, which in turn emits gamma rays. This technique is called:

    (A) MRI.

    (B) CAT scan.

    (C) PET scan.

    (D) thermograph.

    (E) EEG.

232. A meta-analysis of 81 controlled studies by Andrews and Harvey in 1981 found that neurotics treated with psychotherapy, compared with untreated controls, were:

    (A) improved about 25% of the time.

    (B) deteriorated about 25% of the time.

    (C) improved about 80% of the time.

    (D) deteriorated about 80% of the time.

    (E) neither improved nor deteriorated compared to controls.

233. The term "ideas of reference" refers to:

    (A) self-centered thought patterns in paranoia.

    (B) obsessional ideas about suicide.

    (C) near-conscious thoughts that hover just below awareness.

    (D) ideas that can be confirmed by scholarly research.

    (E) disembodied or dehumanized thoughts, characteristic of the schizoid thought pattern.

234. The experimental design in which neither the experimenter nor the judge knows the hypothesis is called:

    (A) inter-scorer agreement.

    (B) double-blind.

    (C) demand characteristics.

    (D) split-half.

    (E) counterbalance.

235. According to Gilligan, the moral reasoning:

    (A) of men and women shows a surprising convergence with advances in age.

    (B) of men tends to put a higher priority on human needs than does the moral reasoning of women.

    (C) of women tends to put a higher priority on concepts of justice and rights than does the moral reasoning of men.

    (D) of women tends to put a higher priority on human needs than does the moral reasoning of men.

    (E) in both men and women becomes more abstract and less situational with age.

236. A mental shorthand which helps one remember something is called a(n):

    (A) mnemonic device.

    (B) active memory device.

    (C) tip-of-the-tongue phenomenon.

    (D) redintegrative mechanism.

    (E) déjà vu experience.

237. A friend's beliefs are about to be attacked. The effect of your presenting the attacking arguments to her beforehand would likely be that she will:

    (A) accept the arguments when they are presented later.

    (B) feel rejected by you and become defensive.

    (C) alter her feelings about you in a negative direction.

    (D) feel better prepared to refute the attacking argument.

    (E) become less extreme in her position.

238. Congruity theory predicts that if a highly valued communicator supports a negatively valued issue, the listener will tend to:

    (A) not believe what the communicator says.

    (B) feel more positively toward the issue and less positively toward the communicator.

    (C) feel less positively toward the communicator and reject what he has to say.

    (D) feel more positively toward the issue but forget that the communicator originally supported it.

    (E) distrust the communicator in the future.

239. Stimulating the occipital area of the brain produces sensations of:

    (A) vision.

    (B) taste.

    (C) motion.

    (D) memory.

    (E) touch.

240. Prisoner's dilemma is an illustration of:

    (A) role playing.

    (B) non-zero-sum game.

    (C) sensory deprivation.

    (D) reactance theory

    (E) pro-social behavior.

241. According to Maccoby and Jacklin, research on sex differences shows:

    (A) few biologically determined differences.

    (B) many biologically determined differences.

    (C) biology is destiny.

    (D) aggression is the only biological difference shown.

    (E) not enough is known to make a judgment.

242. A method of deriving a person's conception of his ideal self is called the:

    (A) Strong-Campbell Interest Blank.

    (B) Q-Sort.

    (C) Thurstone method.

    (D) REP Test.

    (E) none of the above.

243. The operant reinforcement schedule which produces characteristic scallops in the cumulative response curve is the:

    (A) fixed ratio.

    (B) variable ratio.

    (C) fixed interval.

    (D) variable interval.

    (E) continuous interval.

244. It has been found that an advantage of overlearning is that:

    (A) performance on the task is better.

    (B) relearning the task is quicker.

    (C) speed of recall increases.

    (D) more is retained following sleep.

    (E) fatigue is decreased.

245. A "gateway drug":

    (A) opens the sodium-ion gateway of the action potential.

    (B) increases serotonin absorption, reducing symptoms of schizophrenia.

    (C) increases the likelihood of use and/or abuse of more serious addictive drugs.

    (D) is a drug which can be dispensed by a primary care physician in an HMO without the approval of a medical specialist.

    (E) is a placebo in a drug-use study.

246. Following an extinction trial, if the animal is brought back for another extinction trial, it is likely that:

(A) response rates will show almost complete forgetting.

(B) response rates will be higher than at the end of the previous trial.

(C) response rates will be lower than at the end of the previous trial.

(D) response rates will be lower than at the end of the previous trial only if the interval is longer than the trial time itself.

(E) response rates will be about the same as at the end of the previous trial.

247. Freud contended that dreams:

(A) occur only as neurotic symptoms.

(B) are symptomatic of emotional disorders.

(C) are wish fulfillments.

(D) can at times represent the collective unconscious.

(E) show a latent content derived from the manifest content.

248. If a person stares at a blue square against a neutral background and then looks away, he will generally perceive:

(A) a white square smaller than the original blue square.

(B) a negative afterimage.

(C) a red square which gets larger, then smaller, until it finally fades.

(D) the absence of a perceptual field.

(E) none of the above.

249. In rats, ablation to the ventromedial hypothalamus produces:

(A) excessive overeating.

(B) fatal anorexia.

(C) extreme nausea.

(D) fatal hyperphasia.

(E) loss of appetite.

250. Lewin's field theory is also called:

(A) vector analysis.

(B) typology.

(C) biological homeostasis theory.

(D) topology.

(E) group dynamics.

251. To study the development of a child at different ages, the most appropriate method of investigation is:

(A) longitudinal.

(B) correlational.

(C) naturalistic.

(D) experimental.

(E) cross-sectional.

252. The number of questions in a test is most directly related to:

(A) validity.

(B) reliability.

(C) objectivity.

(D) utility.

(E) homogeneity.

253. If an adult experiences damage to the left hemisphere of his cortex, the likely result is that his:

    (A) vision will be impaired.

    (B) language will be impaired.

    (C) most body functions will be impaired until the right hemisphere can compensate.

    (D) emotions will become extremely disturbed.

    (E) motor functions will be impaired.

254. To extinguish a classically conditioned response, the experimenter should omit the:

    (A) unconditioned stimulus.

    (B) conditioned stimulus.

    (C) unconditioned response.

    (D) discriminative stimulus.

    (E) reinforcement schedule.

255. The prisoner's dilemma game is interesting to psychologists because it:

    (A) compares cooperative and competitive behavior.

    (B) shows how people behave in a confined situation.

    (C) can be used to allow people to act out their aggression.

    (D) shows how involving a role-playing situation can be.

    (E) assesses how much pressure people will inflict on others.

256. The "boomerang" effect in attitude-change research is commonly called:

    (A) scapegoating.

    (B) reactance theory.

    (C) self-perception.

    (D) social disinhibition.

    (E) inoculation theory.

257. The difference between white and gray matter in the brain is evident in the contrast between:

    (A) nuclei and ganglia.

    (B) limbic system and cortex.

    (C) tracts and nerves.

    (D) dorsal roots and ventral roots.

    (E) cell bodies and fibers.

258. Sensory preconditioning is most like:

    (A) superstitious learning.

    (B) habituation.

    (C) shaping.

    (D) pseudoconditioning.

    (E) experimental neurosis.

259. Neural impulses which are conducted from the receptors to the CNS are called:

    (A) reflex arcs.

    (B) somatic responses.

    (C) ganglia.

    (D) efferent impulses.

    (E) afferent impulses.

260. The term "ideation":

    (A) refers to higher-order cognitive functioning.

    (B) describes the disturbed thought patterns of schizophrenics.

    (C) is used by Jungian psychologists instead of the Freudian term "superego."

    (D) refers to the sublimation of sexualized fantasies in Freudian psychology.

    (E) is a commonly used shorthand in clinical psychology for "suicidal ideation."

261. The smallest amount of stimulation needed to produce a perception of that stimulation is called the:

    (A) constant stimulus.

    (B) difference threshold.

    (C) absolute threshold.

    (D) d'.

    (E) point of objective reality.

262. To get a clear image of an object in very dim light, one would fixate the object at the:

    (A) fovea.

    (B) periphery of the retina.

    (C) optic disc.

    (D) cornea.

    (E) point where the cones are most numerous.

263. The cutaneous sensation which has no specific receptor is the sense of:

    (A) coldness.

    (B) heat.

    (C) warmth.

    (D) freezing.

    (E) lightness.

264. Rejecting the null hypothesis when it is true is called:

    (A) the critical ratio.

    (B) the standard error.

    (C) the standard inference.

    (D) Type I error.

    (E) Type II error.

265. The number of chromosomes human cells contain is:

    (A) 24

    (B) 48

    (C) 46

    (D) 23

    (E) none of the above.

266. The results of Harlow's study of monkeys raised with wire and cloth mothers have shown that:

    (A) attachment derives from the mother who does the feeding.

    (B) when frightened, the monkeys fled to the mother they were most used to.

    (C) monkeys raised with wire mothers show more independence than monkeys raised with cloth mothers.

    (D) physical contact seems more important than feeding contact when security needs are aroused.

    (E) once the critical period has passed, the imprinting achieved is irreversible.

267. Terman's study of highly intelligent individuals has shown that:

    (A) they had difficulty maintaining social relationships although their achievements were higher than those of the general population.

    (B) they felt better adjusted, happier, and more successful than the general population.

    (C) they tended to achieve earlier than the general population although their productivity declined sooner than average.

    (D) they were as socially well-adjusted as the general population although they reported more health problems.

    (E) their divorce and suicide rate was higher than that of the general population.

268. The behavior pattern expected of an individual based on his social position is called:

    (A) status.

    (B) role.

    (C) class.

    (D) personal construct.

    (E) inference.

269. The statistical measure of diseases and infirmities of all kinds within a population is called:

    (A) mortality.

    (B) gerontology.

    (C) thanatology.

    (D) morbidity.

    (E) epidemiology.

270. According to the constitutional theory of personality, the person whose muscles are highly developed is classified as:

    (A) endomorphic.

    (B) mesomorphic.

    (C) ectomorphic.

    (D) pyknic.

    (E) asthenic.

271. The highest relationship between two sets of scores is indicated by a coefficient of:

    (A) .51

    (B) .00

    (C) −.78

    (D) .40

    (E) −.40

272. Conflict resolution by means of flight would probably result from:

    (A)   avoidance-avoidance conflict.

    (B)   approach-avoidance conflict.

    (C)   approach-approach conflict.

    (D)   double approach-avoidance conflict.

    (E)   A or B.

273. All the colors of the spectrum can be produced by mixing some combination of:

    (A)   red, green, yellow.

    (B)   blue, green, yellow.

    (C)   red, blue, yellow, green.

    (D)   red, green, blue.

    (E)   red and blue.

274. To prevent material in STM from being forgotten, an individual must:

    (A)   rehearse.

    (B)   overlearn.

    (C)   allow time for consolidation.

    (D)   not engage in any interfering activity.

    (E)   periodically review the material.

275. Which of the following symptoms would least likely be found among patients diagnosed as obsessive-compulsive?

    (A)   Ruminations

    (B)   Amnesia

    (C)   Cognitive rituals

    (D)   Motor rituals

    (E)   Avoidance

276. Hospices:

    (A)   have achieved surprisingly good results restoring previously diagnosed "terminal" patients back to health.

    (B)   are the venues of choice for people desiring proper execution of their living wills.

    (C)   have conducted research indicating the validity of the stages of bereavement, as described by Kübler-Ross.

    (D)   provide an alternative to usual hospital care for the terminally ill.

    (E)   have been found to passively encourage assisted suicide.

277. The group that is *least* advanced in language development is:

    (A)   same-sex monozygotic twins.

    (B)   dizygotic twins.

    (C)   firstborns.

    (D)   girls in general.

    (E)   boys in general.

278. According to Loftus, one of the most common sources of contamination of eyewitnesses' memories of crime scenes is:

    (A)   conflicting traumatic childhood events.

    (B)   the unreliable nature of the long-term memory process, especially with age.

    (C)   the tendency of most people to avoid controversy.

    (D)   the deleterious effects of sex- and race-bias.

    (E)   questions asked after-the-fact by investigators suggesting elements not originally present.

279. Regarding hypnosis, Hilgard says that:

   (A) the lower the IQ, the more susceptible the subject.

   (B) it is a hoax perpetrated by charlatans.

   (C) it is like REM sleep without dreaming.

   (D) it is an exaggeration of normal processes.

   (E) it is preferable to medical anesthesia.

280. Tourette syndrome is associated with
dysfunction of the:

   (A) cingulate cortex.

   (B) limbic striatum.

   (C) neostriatum.

   (D) brain stem.

   (E) substantia nigra.

281. The modern version of the EEG is (are):

   (A) microelectrodes.

   (B) PET.

   (C) CT (or CAT).

   (D) histofluorescence.

   (E) MRI.

282. Follicle-stimulating hormones:

   (A) increase female secondary sex traits.

   (B) play a role in maturation of the ova.

   (C) cause the follicles to release the ovum.

   (D) help the ovum to be received by the
   uterus.

   (E) are associated with sex-drive.

283. Latané is known for his work on:

   (A) bystander intervention.

   (B) experimenter expectancies.

   (C) perception and cognition.

   (D) field theory.

   (E) group dynamics.

284. As opposed to an experimental study, a
correlational research design:

   (A) does not operationally define the
   variables.

   (B) controls for concomitant variables.

   (C) is the only viable technique for longitudinal studies.

   (D) does not manipulate the independent
   variables.

   (E) uses parametric statistical analysis and
   levels of confidence.

285. If a cumulative response curve shows a
decline after 20 minutes, it would indicate
that:

   (A) there was spontaneous recovery.

   (B) the number of errors exceeded the
   number of correct responses.

   (C) the trial period was ending.

   (D) the US should be reintroduced.

   (E) there was an error in drawing the
   curve.

286. Schacter found that, compared with normal-weight subjects, overweight subjects tend to:

(A) show less affect.

(B) respond more to external eating cues.

(C) be more defensive in responding to questions.

(D) ignore external cues and respond only to internal physical eating cues.

(E) forget more quickly what they had eaten.

287. Most patients hospitalized for mental disorders suffer from:

(A) neurosis.

(B) dissociation.

(C) depression.

(D) hysteria.

(E) schizophrenia.

288. For most learning tasks, the optimal use of practice time would be to engage in:

(A) spontaneous practice.

(B) massed practice.

(C) distributed practice.

(D) contingent practice.

(E) noncontingent practice.

289. The Young-Helmholz theory proposes that:

(A) there are three types of cones in the retina that are responsive to the colors red, blue, and green.

(B) in response to auditory stimuli, the receptors fire in groups or volleys.

(C) changes in illumination produce changes in the perception of color.

(D) perceptions of most physical shapes, once learned, exist as cell assemblies in the brain and are strengthened with increased use.

(E) taste is not a unitary perception but depends also on the senses of touch and smell.

290. Korsakov's syndrome is most often associated with:

(A) aphasia.

(B) insomnia.

(C) anorexia.

(D) alcoholism.

(E) epilepsy.

291. The TAT and House-Tree-Person are:

(A) tests of special abilities.

(B) tests for organic brain damage.

(C) tests of infant development.

(D) projective tests.

(E) interest inventories.

292. The originator(s) of the notion of the "myth of mental illness" is (are):

    (A) HMOs.

    (B) May.

    (C) Szasz.

    (D) Laing.

    (E) Masters and Johnson.

293. Infertility rates among married couples are:

    (A) increasing because of increasing environmental taeratogens.

    (B) about 15%.

    (C) usually due to problems in the man.

    (D) usually due to problems in the woman.

    (E) decreasing because of greater education in sexual behavior.

294. The hormone ACTH is secreted primarily in periods of:

    (A) increased pressure.

    (B) REM sleep.

    (C) NREM sleep.

    (D) euphoria.

    (E) sexual arousal.

295. Lesions to Broca's area of the frontal lobe are likely to result in:

    (A) insomnia.

    (B) decrease of visual acuity.

    (C) some loss of memory.

    (D) inability to maintain balance.

    (E) expressive aphasia.

296. The effect of severing the corpus callosum is that:

    (A) the organism will not be able to maintain arousal.

    (B) efferent impulses will not reach the appropriate muscles.

    (C) coordination between the two hemispheres is eliminated.

    (D) rage responses will more readily be elicited.

    (E) sequential activities will be impaired.

297. The part of the retina where the optic nerve exits is known as the:

    (A) blind spot.

    (B) fovea.

    (C) bipolar synapse.

    (D) ganglia cell.

    (E) lateral geniculate nucleus.

298. Of the following list of symptoms, which one is most likely to be applicable to an autistic child?

    (A) Dyslexia

    (B) Echolalia

    (C) Metacognition

    (D) Identity diffusion

    (E) ADHD

299. A major difference between the Freudians and the neo-Freudians is that the neo-Freudians:

   (A) place more emphasis on pre-Oedipal stages.

   (B) do not accept the concept of psychic determinism.

   (C) believe the ego is more independent of the id.

   (D) do not accept a stage-sequence of development.

   (E) try to explain neurotic behavior more in terms of the person's socialization history.

300. The drug l-Dopa is used in the treatment of:

   (A) schizophrenia.

   (B) anxiety.

   (C) epilepsy.

   (D) Parkinson's disease.

   (E) depression.

301. The drug that is most effective in treating epilepsy is:

   (A) lithium carbonate.

   (B) Dilantin.

   (C) Thorazine.

   (D) l-Dopa.

   (E) ACTH.

302. Physiological zero is:

   (A) the range of skin temperature at which neither warmth nor cold is sensed.

   (B) the point at which the subject just detects the stimulus.

   (C) equivalent to slow-wave sleep.

   (D) the state that results from severing the RAS.

   (E) the point at which the EEG recording shows the least desynchronization.

303. The drug that is most effective in treating manic-depressives is:

   (A) Dilantin.

   (B) l-Dopa.

   (C) Librium.

   (D) Thorazine.

   (E) lithium carbonate.

304. The operant reinforcement schedule which will produce the highest response rate during extinction is:

   (A) fixed ratio.

   (B) variable ratio.

   (C) variable interval.

   (D) continuous.

   (E) fixed interval.

305. The operant reinforcement schedule which will produce the highest response rate during initial acquisition is:

    (A) fixed ratio.

    (B) variable ratio.

    (C) variable interval.

    (D) continuous.

    (E) fixed interval.

306. The duplicity theory in vision refers to:

    (A) crossing of the optic tract at the optic chiasma.

    (B) joining of the visual cortexes at the corpus callosum.

    (C) retinal disparity.

    (D) the opponent process theory of color vision.

    (E) the structure of the photoreceptors in the retina.

307. A young animal's impaired behavior resulting from brain damage is later corrected when the animal regains the behavior. The term Lashley would use to explain this is:

    (A) regeneration.

    (B) refinement.

    (C) final common path.

    (D) reverberation.

    (E) none of the above.

308. The degree to which one variable may be said to cause another variable can be predicted by:

    (A) analyzing the regression line.

    (B) squaring the correlation coefficient.

    (C) using a rank-order correlation.

    (D) using a t-test.

    (E) using a chi-square test.

309. Which of the following terms describes a mental disorder of short duration?

    (A) Acute

    (B) Episodic

    (C) Chronic

    (D) Factitious

    (E) Secondary

310. Many clinicians object to the inclusion of Axis IV of the DSM-IV on insurance reimbursement forms. Axis IV evaluates:

    (A) clinical syndromes.

    (B) personality or developmental disorders.

    (C) physical disorders.

    (D) severity of psychosocial stressors.

    (E) highest level of adaptive functioning in the past year.

311. Szasz proposed that the concept of mental illness:

    (A) should be redefined.

    (B) is not valid.

    (C) has come to mean physical illness.

    (D) is too tied to biological constructs to remain meaningful.

    (E) cannot be operationally defined.

312. The therapeutic technique of reciprocal inhibition is primarily based on the paradigm of:

    (A) operant conditioning.

    (B) classical conditioning.

    (C) latent learning.

    (D) drive reduction learning.

    (E) insight learning.

313. Primal scream and implosion therapy models are based on the Freudian principle of:

    (A) introjection.

    (B) sublimation.

    (C) identification.

    (D) projection.

    (E) catharsis.

314. A distribution with a negative standard deviation is one which:

    (A) is negatively skewed.

    (B) is bimodal.

    (C) has been incorrectly computed.

    (D) has too small an n to be statistically significant.

    (E) cannot be factor-analyzed.

315. If you remember nothing else from your studies of remembering, remember SQ3R, which stands for:

    (A) survey, question, read, recite, review.

    (B) search, question, read, redo, retrieve.

    (C) store, quiet, read, rehearse, relearn.

    (D) search, question, read, recite, retain.

    (E) sample, question, read, review, recite.

316. Gilligan's additions to the research on moral development by Kohlberg include:

    (A) the criticism that Kohlberg found women's scores lagging men's scores primarily because of testers' gender bias.

    (B) the claim that women tend to be more concerned with the welfare of others than with moral abstractions.

    (C) a reduction in the number of moral stages from six to three, in keeping with Freudian psychology.

    (D) a clear demonstration that women's moral behavior is more consistent than men's moral behavior.

    (E) a demonstration that the "morality of nonviolence" cannot be successfully implemented in men.

317. Roger Shepard is most associated with work in:

    (A) psychophysical scaling.

    (B) vision.

    (C) sleep.

    (D) hemispheric localization.

    (E) cortical deactivation.

318. Alzheimer patients:

    (A) show deterioration of the hippocampus and cerebral cortex.

    (B) have an extra chromosome.

    (C) produce excess ACTH.

    (D) show diminished blood flow in the frontal lobes.

    (E) release excess amounts of dopamine.

319. Bowlby's ethological theory of infant-mother attachment claims:

    (A) mother-infant attachment is controlled by nature, not nurture.

    (B) the mother leads the child's learning by modeling.

    (C) multiple mothering figures have little effect on infants until late in development.

    (D) feeding alone does not necessarily lead to attachment.

    (E) the mother's primary role is reduction of raging drives.

320. Gale's cognitive therapist trains Gale to interrupt his undesirable thoughts by shouting "Stop!" to himself whenever the thoughts appear. Gale is being taught:

    (A) thought stoppage.

    (B) stress inoculation.

    (C) implosion therapy.

    (D) desensitization.

    (E) aversion therapy.

321. Julie gains sexual excitement and arousal from rubbing her body against unsuspecting standees in elevators, buses, and other public places. Julie could be diagnosed as:

    (A) a narcissistic personality.

    (B) having a paraphilia.

    (C) a paraphrenic.

    (D) having a fetish.

    (E) a pedophiliac.

322. The term "animal magnetism" is associated with:

    (A) Tinbergen.

    (B) Lorenz.

    (C) the MRI.

    (D) Mesmer.

    (E) the PET scan.

323. A cumulative response curve is:

    (A) a dependent variable.

    (B) an independent variable.

    (C) an operational variable.

    (D) a transitional variable.

    (E) none of the above.

324. Some ranchers wish to protect their sheep from wolves and coyotes. They place pieces of meat injected with lithium carbonate (a substance distasteful, though harmless, to predators) in fields, hoping it is eaten by the predators. In this example, the bait (the injected meat) is a:

    (A) CS.

    (B) CR.

    (C) UCS.

    (D) UCR.

    (E) vicarious reinforcement.

325. Phenomenology is closest to:

    (A) information-processing.

    (B) behavioral therapy.

    (C) psychoanalysis.

    (D) stress-reduction therapy.

    (E) Gestalt psychology.

326. A person with a high score on a personality test measuring aggression is actually aggressive. This shows:

    (A) test reliability.

    (B) predictive validity.

    (C) concurrent validity.

    (D) content validity.

    (E) face validity.

327. Drugs prescribed for Alzheimer's disease block transmission of:

    (A) acetylcholine.

    (B) motor neurons.

    (C) epinephrine.

    (D) norepinephrine.

    (E) endorphins.

328. Laymen frequently use the term "psycho-somatic" to describe physical symptoms that have a dubious physical cause. The closest modern DSM equivalent term is:

    (A) hypochondria.

    (B) psychogenic disorders.

    (C) conversion hysteria.

    (D) malingering.

    (E) somatoform disorders.

329. Memory formation is disrupted most by:

    (A) stimulants.

    (B) steroids.

    (C) depressants.

    (D) sleep.

    (E) nicotine.

330. A major brain structure that determines the timing and force of movements and muscle contractions is the:

    (A) cerebral cortex.

    (B) thalamus.

    (C) medulla oblongata.

    (D) hypothalamus.

    (E) cerebellum.

331. Two measures of different variables with a correlation of 1.0 would have regression lines that:

    (A) are orthogonal.

    (B) cross.

    (C) coincide.

    (D) have negative slopes and are parallel.

    (E) have positive slopes and are parallel.

332. Chomsky's theory of language development:

    (A) stresses the role of explicit instruction.

    (B) stresses hypothesis testing and self-correction.

    (C) is the basis for computer AI programming.

    (D) assumes humans have a biological predisposition to develop language.

    (E) assumes language development is generally one stage behind cognitive development.

333. The brain wave showing 8 to 12 cps with large variations is called:

    (A) alpha.

    (B) beta.

    (C) theta.

    (D) delta.

    (E) omega.

334. The differences between rods and cones show up on:

    (A) color constancy.

    (B) experiments of visual deprivation.

    (C) tests of binocular vision.

    (D) dark adaptation.

    (E) afterimages.

335. Fractional estimation and magnitude estimation are methods for arriving at:

    (A) sensory thresholds.

    (B) Weber functions.

    (C) signal detection.

    (D) difference thresholds.

    (E) subliminal thresholds.

336. The statement, "I'm afraid because I run," would be supported by the theory of:

    (A) Cannon-Bard.

    (B) James-Lange.

    (C) Muller-Lyre.

    (D) Miller-Dollard.

    (E) Schacter-Singer.

337. Synchronized EEG recordings are caused by:

    (A) lesions to the RAS.

    (B) suppressed neural activity.

    (C) neurons firing in unison.

    (D) conscious alertness.

    (E) thalamic inactivity.

338. Signal detection is most likely to be used in tasks measuring:

    (A) eidetic imagery.

    (B) vigilance.

    (C) daydreaming.

    (D) iconic memory.

    (E) echoic elaboration.

339. Existential psychology most closely approximates the approach of:

    (A) psychoanalysis.

    (B) empiricism.

    (C) functionalism.

    (D) associationism.

    (E) phenomenology.

340. The stage of sleep showing sleep spindles and/or K-complexes is:

    (A) stage one.

    (B) stage two.

    (C) stage three.

    (D) stage four.

    (E) REM sleep.

341. A large 1985 study of Vietnam veterans found that the most severe psychopathology developed in those who had:

    (A) participated in abusive combat violence.

    (B) been injured in combat.

    (C) been recruited, as opposed to volunteering.

    (D) come from dysfunctional families.

    (E) come from the lowest socioeconomic levels.

342. Of the following, the pair that is incorrectly matched is:

    (A) Bowlby—stranger anxiety.

    (B) Spitz—anaclitic depression.

    (C) Mahler—symbiotic psychosis.

    (D) Kanner—autism.

    (E) Hartmann—ego autonomy.

343. The "cathartic method":

    (A) is associated with the use of ECT (electro-convulsive therapy).

    (B) was developed by Freud as a result of his treatment of Anna O, a woman diagnosed as a "hysteric."

    (C) is a form of therapy, predominantly for the treatment of phobias, in which a patient is encouraged to vigorously confront objects or people he or she had previously feared.

    (D) is encouraged by neo-Freudian therapists to overcome inhibitions.

    (E) is synonymous with "ablation," the removal of brain sections.

344. Of the following, the pair that is incorrectly matched is:

    (A) Rotter—Internal-External Scale.

    (B) Witkin—Blacky Test.

    (C) Kelly—REP Test.

    (D) Rokeach—Dogmatism Scale.

    (E) Rogers—Q-Sort.

345. A researcher beginning the study of a problem would most likely be using:

    (A) Buros's MMY.

    (B) NIMH Index.

    (C) APA Publications Manual.

    (D) Psychological Abstracts.

    (E) Psychological Bulletin.

346. A controversial issue in forensic matters is whether a body of knowledge, say handwriting analysis, is sufficiently scientific to be admissible as evidence in court or whether the body of knowledge is a "pseudoscience." The court case most often cited to determine the scientific status of a body of testimony is:

    (A) M'Naghten.

    (B) Tarasoff.

    (C) Durham.

    (D) Daubert.

    (E) Brown v. Board of Education.

347. An idiot savant would most likely *not* show extraordinary abilities in the area of:

    (A) linguistics.

    (B) memory.

    (C) numbers.

    (D) music.

    (E) speed of calculations.

348. Behaviors that cause satisfaction tend to be repeated while behaviors that cause annoyance tend not to be repeated. This is known as the:

    (A) law of reinforcement.

    (B) law of contiguity.

    (C) law of exercise.

    (D) law of effect.

    (E) law of action.

349. The theorist most associated with the concept of drive reduction is:

    (A) Hebb.

    (B) Skinner.

    (C) Olds.

    (D) Hull.

    (E) Spence.

350. A person applying for disability benefits claims to have numerous obscure symptoms. The interviewing psychologist, suspicious of the applicant's truthfulness, suggests some additional, fanciful symptoms and inquires whether the interviewee has these symptoms also. The psychologist is likely testing for:

    (A) memory impairment.

    (B) malingering.

    (C) brain injury.

    (D) hypochondria.

    (E) neurolepsia.

351. The serial position effect in learning a list of words predicts that:

    (A) words occurring at the beginning of the list are remembered better than words occurring at the end of the list.

    (B) there is a monotonic decreasing effect of word position on memory.

    (C) words in the middle of the list are not remembered as well as words occurring at the beginning of the list.

    (D) the last words heard will most likely be the first words reported.

    (E) there is a monotonic increasing effect of word position on memory.

352. An infant's attention to a novel stimulus decreases over time. The best explanation for this is:

    (A) habituation.

    (B) maturation.

    (C) inhibition.

    (D) reminiscence.

    (E) delayed response.

353. The perception of cutaneous pressure often decreases over time even when the pressure remains constant. The best explanation for this is:

    (A) inhibition.

    (B) interaction effects.

    (C) all-or-none effect.

    (D) adaptation.

    (E) interference.

354. Based on information obtained from crisis hotlines, walk-in clinics, and suicide prevention centers, studies have found that:

    (A) suicide rates are highest for unemployed individuals who have had a history of hospitalization.

    (B) the greatest danger of suicide occurs at the point of deepest depression.

    (C) more females than males attempt suicide while more males than females actually commit suicide.

    (D) threatening suicide is not typically an indication that someone will actually commit suicide.

    (E) suicide among minority groups is higher than suicide among non-minority groups.

355. For a behavior to be considered instinctual, it must be shown that:

    (A) it occurs in all normal individuals of the species.

    (B) it cannot be altered by environmental input.

    (C) it is achieved by everyone at the same time.

    (D) it is apparent at birth.

    (E) it is not related to learning.

356. According to accepted practice, a job selection test should have high:

    (A) predictive validity.

    (B) face validity.

    (C) congruent validity.

    (D) content validity.

    (E) construct validity.

357. A phobia could be considered the behavioral manifestation of the defense mechanism of:

    (A) reaction formation.

    (B) isolation.

    (C) displacement.

    (D) denial.

    (E) introjection.

358. According to anthropologists like Malinowski and Benedict, what is considered "abnormal" in one society may be considered "normal" in another. This finding has led some psychologists to the belief in:

    (A) racial diversity.

    (B) genetic markers.

    (C) eclecticism.

    (D) cultural relativism.

    (E) field theory.

359. The point-biserial correlation is used to relate:

    (A) a continuous variable with a dichotomous variable.

    (B) two continuous variables.

    (C) two dichotomous variables.

    (D) three dichotomous variables.

    (E) one continuous and two dichotomous variables.

360. The scale used for numbering uniforms of football players is:

    (A) ratio.

    (B) nominal.

    (C) categorical.

    (D) interval.

    (E) ordinal.

361. After REM deprivation, the phenomenon most likely to occur would be:

    (A) lack of REM during subsequent sleep periods.

    (B) nightmares during subsequent sleep periods.

    (C) REM rebound during subsequent sleep periods.

    (D) decreased hypnogogic imagery during subsequent sleep periods.

    (E) increased hypnopompic imagery during subsequent sleep periods.

362. The behavioral view of reactive depression involves:

    (A) increased negative reinforcers.

    (B) lack of positive reinforcers.

    (C) lowered self-esteem.

    (D) social learning effect.

    (E) perceived negative consequences.

363. An example of a Piagetian task testing the child's notion of conservation would be:

    (A) seriating sticks of various lengths.

    (B) categorizing geometric figures by shape and color.

    (C) having the child take the view of someone else.

    (D) asking the child to explain how rules are made.

    (E) having the child pour all the water from a tall glass into a shorter glass of the same volume and asking the child if the two glasses are the same size.

364. Explanations for most forms of mental disorders due to genes, such as Klinefelter's syndrome and Huntington's chorea, place emphasis on:

(A) polygenic inheritance.

(B) a dominant gene.

(C) a recessive gene.

(D) a sex-linked gene.

(E) genetic anomalies.

365. If a patient shows signs of short-term memory loss and the problem is assumed to be neurological, the most likely place of damage would be the:

(A) hippocampus.

(B) amygdala.

(C) frontal lobe.

(D) septal area.

(E) hypothalamus.

366. The theorist who is least likely to be associated with the concept of drive reduction as a motivator is:

(A) Freud.

(B) Hull.

(C) Dollard.

(D) Skinner.

(E) Miller.

367. One of the bodies of research literature most frequently cited during Congressional hearings on the topic of violence on television was conducted by:

(A) Bandura.

(B) Gilligan.

(C) Tavros.

(D) Hinkley.

(E) Zimbardo.

368. Rogers' client-centered therapy stresses the therapist's:

(A) intelligence.

(B) training.

(C) genuineness.

(D) eclecticism.

(E) theoretical orientation.

369. The t-test is used to test the significance of the:

(A) difference in the means of two groups.

(B) difference in the standard deviations of two groups.

(C) difference in the variances of two groups.

(D) difference in the means of three groups.

(E) correlation in the scores of two groups.

370. A child who has been identified as being high in achievement orientation would probably choose a task that is:

    (A) easy.

    (B) highly structured.

    (C) very difficult.

    (D) moderately difficult.

    (E) very ambiguous.

371. A piano student practices a new piece for a while and then stops. The next day she comes back to the piano and finds she can play the piece better than at the end of the previous day's practice period. This is an example of:

    (A) reminiscence.

    (B) spontaneous recovery.

    (C) proactive recovery.

    (D) forward masking.

    (E) canalization.

372. When a risky venture is being considered, the decision reached by group consensus, as compared with an average of the individual decisions reached by group members, will tend to be:

    (A) more conservative.

    (B) riskier.

    (C) unpredictable.

    (D) the same.

    (E) dependent on gender makeup of groups.

373. Some drugs act on dopamine receptors, blocking them and preventing dopamine activity. These drugs are members of the class of:

    (A) antagonists.

    (B) agonists.

    (C) binders.

    (D) antigens.

    (E) antibodies.

374. Severe malnutrition during the third trimester of pregnancy:

    (A) produces fewer permanent aftereffects than first trimester malnutrition.

    (B) is frequently associated with impaired mother-infant bonding.

    (C) is frequently associated with autism.

    (D) is frequently associated with schizophrenia.

    (E) is frequently associated with stillbirth and premature birth.

375. The chemical action of many drugs which alleviate schizophrenic symptoms is to:

    (A) block the action of serotonin.

    (B) increase levels of acetylcholine.

    (C) stimulate the action of norepinephrine.

    (D) block receptors for dopamine.

    (E) inhibit levels of epinephrine.

376. The thalamus receives signals from all the following sensory systems *except:*

    (A) proprioception.

    (B) vision.

    (C) olfaction.

    (D) audition.

    (E) gustation.

377. Belle indifference would most typically be found among patients diagnosed:

    (A) as hysterical.

    (B) with psychogenic pain disorder.

    (C) with somatoform disorder.

    (D) as obsessive-compulsive.

    (E) with paranoid character.

378. As afferent impulses move higher up the nervous system, the number of nerve cells mediating these impulses:

    (A) multiplies arithmetically.

    (B) multiplies exponentially.

    (C) remains the same.

    (D) decreases exponentially.

    (E) decreases in absolute numbers.

379. A patient complains of chronic pain. The brain structure most associated with the conscious experience of pain is the:

    (A) hippocampus.

    (B) hypothalamus.

    (C) cortex.

    (D) thalamus.

    (E) none of the above, since pain is a psychological sensation.

380. Depression is treated with:

    (A) MAO inhibitors.

    (B) chlorpromazine.

    (C) lithium carbonate.

    (D) phenothiazine.

    (E) haldoperidol.

381. Apu doesn't like fighting and arguments. He tends to deny unpleasantness by saying, "Tomorrow is another day." Of the following, he would most likely suffer from:

    (A) ulcers.

    (B) high blood pressure.

    (C) diseases of the immune system.

    (D) eczema.

    (E) cancer.

382. Experiments on split-brain patients show:

    (A) the left hemisphere specializes in verbal information and the right hemisphere specializes in spatial information.

    (B) the right hemisphere specializes in verbal information and the left hemisphere specializes in spatial information.

    (C) severing the corpus callosum results in generally degraded mental performance.

    (D) the left hemisphere specializes in athletic performance and the right hemisphere specializes in cognition.

    (E) the right hemisphere specializes in athletic performance and the left hemisphere specializes in cognition.

383. Parkinson's disease is associated with deterioration of neurons terminating in the:

    (A) limbic system.

    (B) parasympathetic nervous system.

    (C) hypothalamus.

    (D) basal ganglia.

    (E) thalamus.

384. The primary target of adolescent rebellion, according to Erikson and numerous independent studies, is:

    (A) clash with school values and authorities.

    (B) conflict with peers and social pressures.

    (C) identity confusion.

    (D) clash with perceived parental constraints.

    (E) clash with perceived social injustices.

385. Rodin's studies of response to food cues found:

    (A) overweight people had the highest insulin responses.

    (B) externals had a higher insulin response than internals.

    (C) insulin response was dependent on level of food deprivation.

    (D) internals had insulin responses equal to externals, but had better control.

    (E) when food is denied for over 18 hours, insulin responses of externals and internals are similar.

386. A person's knowledge and control of his or her own rational processes is called:

    (A) observing ego.

    (B) internalization.

    (C) metacognition.

    (D) epistemology.

    (E) ego syntonicity.

387. The brain structure that plays an important role in food intake and also affects sexual behavior, especially in females, is the:

    (A) cerebellum.

    (B) hypothalamus.

    (C) medulla.

    (D) midbrain.

    (E) thalamus.

388. Of these common childhood fears, the one that diminishes last and least is fear:

    (A) of stranger-caused injury.

    (B) of imaginary creatures.

    (C) for personal safety.

    (D) of animals.

    (E) of stranger intrusion into household.

389. The expression of this emotion tends to develop last among infants. The emotion is:

    (A) fear.

    (B) startle.

    (C) distress.

    (D) disgust.

    (E) happiness.

ANSWERS TO QUESTIONS

1. **D**	31. **A**	61. **E**	91. **A**	121. **E**
2. **C**	32. **B**	62. **A**	92. **E**	122. **A**
3. **A**	33. **E**	63. **E**	93. **A**	123. **B**
4. **A**	34. **D**	64. **B**	94. **E**	124. **E**
5. **B**	35. **D**	65. **E**	95. **C**	125. **D**
6. **D**	36. **C**	66. **B**	96. **D**	126. **B**
7. **C**	37. **C**	67. **B**	97. **A**	127. **D**
8. **C**	38. **C**	68. **D**	98. **E**	128. **C**
9. **C**	39. **E**	69. **E**	99. **A**	129. **C**
10. **C**	40. **A**	70. **C**	100. **E**	130. **D**
11. **C**	41. **A**	71. **E**	101. **A**	131. **E**
12. **D**	42. **C**	72. **B**	102. **B**	132. **D**
13. **B**	43. **E**	73. **A**	103. **E**	133. **C**
14. **C**	44. **B**	74. **C**	104. **E**	134. **B**
15. **B**	45. **D**	75. **B**	105. **A**	135. **C**
16. **D**	46. **B**	76. **E**	106. **D**	136. **C**
17. **B**	47. **C**	77. **D**	107. **D**	137. **A**
18. **A**	48. **A**	78. **D**	108. **A**	138. **B**
19. **A**	49. **B**	79. **E**	109. **E**	139. **E**
20. **C**	50. **E**	80. **E**	110. **B**	140. **A**
21. **D**	51. **A**	81. **B**	111. **B**	141. **E**
22. **C**	52. **C**	82. **A**	112. **E**	142. **A**
23. **A**	53. **A**	83. **C**	113. **A**	143. **C**
24. **E**	54. **B**	84. **A**	114. **B**	144. **D**
25. **E**	55. **B**	85. **B**	115. **C**	145. **D**
26. **A**	56. **D**	86. **D**	116. **C**	146. **E**
27. **E**	57. **D**	87. **E**	117. **E**	147. **C**
28. **C**	58. **B**	88. **D**	118. **B**	148. **B**
29. **D**	59. **E**	89. **B**	119. **D**	149. **A**
30. **D**	60. **D**	90. **B**	120. **A**	150. **E**

151. C	182. B	213. E	244. B	275. B
152. E	183. D	214. C	245. C	276. D
153. B	184. C	215. B	246. B	277. E
154. A	185. B	216. A	247. C	278. E
155. C	186. B	217. B	248. B	279. D
156. A	187. C	218. D	249. A	280. A
157. D	188. E	219. B	250. D	281. B
158. E	189. B	220. A	251. A	282. B
159. B	190. C	221. C	252. B	283. A
160. A	191. D	222. D	253. B	284. D
161. A	192. B	223. C	254. A	285. E
162. D	193. E	224. C	255. A	286. B
163. B	194. E	225. E	256. B	287. E
164. A	195. D	226. D	257. E	288. C
165. A	196. E	227. C	258. D	289. A
166. E	197. B	228. B	259. E	290. D
167. D	198. E	229. A	260. E	291. D
168. A	199. A	230. D	261. C	292. C
169. B	200. B	231. C	262. B	293. B
170. A	201. E	232. C	263. B	294. A
171. B	202. E	233. A	264. D	295. E
172. C	203. D	234. B	265. C	296. C
173. D	204. C	235. D	266. D	297. A
174. B	205. A	236. A	267. B	298. B
175. B	206. C	237. D	268. B	299. C
176. A	207. B	238. B	269. D	300. D
177. D	208. D	239. A	270. B	301. B
178. C	209. A	240. B	271. C	302. A
179. E	210. D	241. A	272. A	303. E
180. A	211. A	242. B	273. D	304. B
181. A	212. A	243. C	274. A	305. D

306. **E**	323. **A**	340. **B**	357. **C**	374. **E**
307. **E**	324. **C**	341. **A**	358. **D**	375. **D**
308. **B**	325. **E**	342. **A**	359. **A**	376. **C**
309. **A**	326. **C**	343. **B**	360. **B**	377. **C**
310. **D**	327. **A**	344. **B**	361. **C**	378. **E**
311. **B**	328. **E**	345. **D**	362. **B**	379. **D**
312. **B**	329. **C**	346. **D**	363. **E**	380. **A**
313. **E**	330. **E**	347. **A**	364. **A**	381. **C**
314. **C**	331. **C**	348. **D**	365. **A**	382. **A**
315. **A**	332. **D**	349. **D**	366. **D**	383. **D**
316. **B**	333. **A**	350. **B**	367. **A**	384. **D**
317. **A**	334. **D**	351. **C**	368. **C**	385. **B**
318. **A**	335. **A**	352. **A**	369. **A**	386. **C**
319. **D**	336. **B**	353. **D**	370. **D**	387. **B**
320. **A**	337. **C**	354. **C**	371. **A**	388. **E**
321. **B**	338. **B**	355. **A**	372. **B**	389. **A**
322. **D**	339. **E**	356. **A**	373. **A**	

PART III

Instructional Review

Response Sets

Some subjects have particular response sets. They might always answer yes-no questions with a "yes," or they might always choose the middle response on a 1-to-7-point scale, or they might give *socially desirable* answers that don't really reflect their own feelings. Another response set is *acquiescence,* the tendency to agree with statements irrespective of their content. The authors of some of the most popular personality tests, such as the MMPI, go to great effort to create methods to detect response biases that some people use to mask their answers.

Experimenter Effects

Experimenter effects can confound the experiment in subtle ways. The researcher can make unconscious errors in the direction of his hypothesis when obtaining, scoring, or reporting results. The experimenter—despite his or her best efforts—might communicate expectations to the subjects. The sex or demeanor of the experimenter can affect a subject's behavior. The classic study of **Rosenthal and Jacobson,** *Pygmalion in the Classroom* (1968), demonstrated how a teacher's preconceived notions of a student's ability resulted in the student's grades and even IQ scores moving in the expected direction. Exactly how and to what degree biases of this kind occur is a matter of great controversy. The original Rosenthal and Jacobson study was eventually shown to be confounded and its findings not so clear-cut. Nevertheless, the possibility that experimenter effects might creep into experimental results cannot be ignored.

Experimenter effects can be reduced through various means, such as automating the equipment, using unbiased third parties to administer the experiment to subjects, or by doing *blind studies.* An experiment is said to be blind when one or more of the participants do not know which condition or experimental group they are participating in. If a pill taker does not know if he or she is being administered the experimental pill or a placebo, the subject is said to be blind. If, in addition to the pill taker's being blind, the person giving the pill does not know whether the pill is the experimental drug or a placebo, the study is said to be *double-blind.*

Demand Characteristics

The *demand characteristics* of experiments have been investigated by **Orne.** Demand characteristics are the total of all the clues that interact with the subject's nature to confound the dependent variable behavior. In other words, subjects feel there is a demand to behave in a certain way no matter what the manipulation is. Good subjects try to find out the hypothesis and confirm it; faithful subjects try to follow instructions; apprehensive subjects try to present themselves favorably rather than follow directions; negativistic subjects try to disprove the hypothesis. An experimenter can overcome the demand characteristics through deception, role-playing, and embedding the real experiment in another situation.

A classic example of demand characteristics is the *Hawthorne effect.* Workers at the Hawthorne Works of the Western Electric Company who took part in a productivity experiment increased their output whether the conditions were improved or made worse. They seemed to respond more to being in an experiment than to the conditions of the experiment.

STATISTICS

Frequencies and Distributions

A basic curve in statistics is the *frequency polygon*. It is useful in representing the occurrence of an observation. Values or scores (the independent variables) are represented along the horizontal axis called the *abscissa*. Frequencies (the dependent variables) are represented along the vertical axis called the *ordinate*.

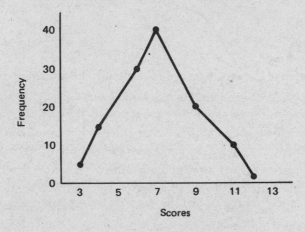

A *histogram* is another way of displaying frequencies. In this graphic distribution, scores are grouped into *class intervals,* and the height of each column represents the frequency for that class interval.

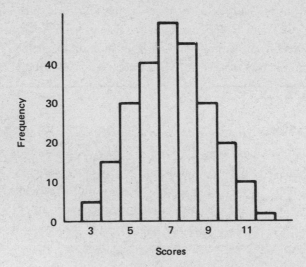

The statistically ideal frequency polygon is called a *normal distribution* or *bell curve*. Considering any single variable, if enough data were collected—in other words, if the sample population were infinitely large—the observations would fall into a symmetrical or normal distribution. Most cases would fall near the mean with fewer and fewer cases occurring as the values get farther from the mean.

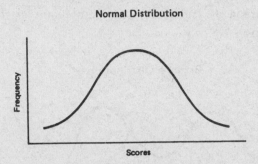

Normal Distribution

Sometimes the frequencies do not fall in the normal distribution pictured above. They could be *skewed* toward one end. If a distribution is skewed to the left it is *negatively skewed,* with most of the scores falling at the high end. We say negatively skewed because the *tail,* that line leading off to the side, is on the negative, or low-score, side of the continuum. This would happen if an exam were easy for most people.

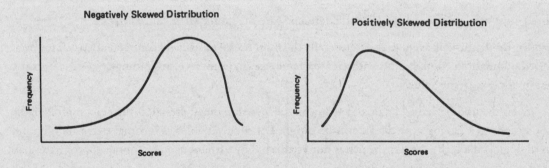

Negatively Skewed Distribution   **Positively Skewed Distribution**

If the distribution is skewed to the right, or *positively skewed,* most scores fall at the low end. This occurs, for example, if a test is too difficult and only a few individuals achieve high scores. Another example of positive skewness is income. If a survey is made of the incomes of every resident of a country, it would be found that most people are in the low or middle ranges, but some individuals, like Bill Gates and Donald Trump, are at the very, very high end. Exceptional individuals represent an *outlying* group. If a plot is made of the income distribution, one would get a picture similar to the one on the right, above. The tail trails off to the high, or positive, end of the scale, representing these very high-income people.

Sometimes a distribution has two humps. If scores tend to cluster around two different points, or *modes,* the distribution is *bimodal.* An example of bimodal distribution is ratings. If a group of people gives a rating of something or someone, a bimodal distribution is often obtained. Imagine the case in which some people very much like the thing or person being studied while other people very much dislike the thing or person. Consider ratings of a controversial political figure. Some people love the figure; others think he or she is awful. Very few people are in the middle. Bimodal distributions are clues that we are probably dealing with two different groups.

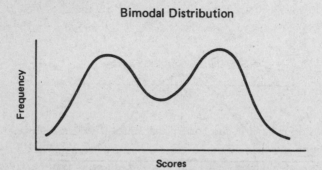

Bimodal Distribution

Measures of Central Tendency

The three most common measures of central tendency are the *mean, mode,* and *median.*

The *mean* is the arithmetic average and is generally the most useful measure of central tendency. However, for skewed populations (populations with a few extreme cases), the mean is misleading because it is greatly affected by these extreme values.

The *median* is the middle value of data ordered from the lowest to the highest. It is the exact middle in the sense of a highway's having a median down its center. For such variables as income, size of family, and certain biological data, the median, which is not as affected by extreme scores, is more appropriate than the mean as a measure of central tendency.

The *mode* is the most frequent value obtained. It is the point of maximum concentration. Sometimes, as in a bimodal distribution, there are two modes.

In a normal population, the mean, median, and mode are at or near the same point, and the distribution falls in a normal curve. When the distribution is skewed, the three measures of central tendency fall at different points.

Measures of Variation

The variability of a population refers to how individuals vary among themselves. Variation is an inherent property of a population or of a sample. Three measures of variation are the *range,* the *variance,* and the *standard deviation.*

The *range* is the extent of the difference between the highest and the lowest values. A disadvantage of using the range as a descriptive statistic is that it is affected by sample size. It tends to be larger when the sample is larger, since then more extreme observations are likely to be selected.

The *variance* shows the variability of the scores by computing the average of the squared differences of each observation from the mean.

The *standard deviation* (SD) is the square root of the variance. The SD is particularly useful if the population is normally distributed. In such cases, characteristic proportions of the population are located within specified standard deviations around the mean. The mean ±1 SD includes 68% of the population. The mean ±2 SD includes 95% of the population. The mean ±3 SD includes 99.7% of the population.

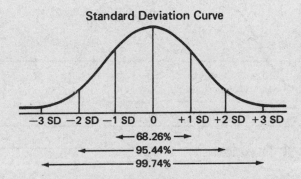

While the curve above shows the percentages falling between the standard deviations, the curve below shows the *cumulative percentages* at each standard deviation.

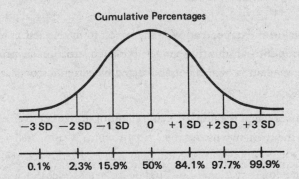

Other ways of analyzing the normal distribution are to divide it into *Z-scores*, *T-scores* and *stanine scores*. Z-scores are the same as standard deviations. For example, Z = 1.5 means $1\frac{1}{2}$ SDs above the mean.

T-scores are based on 10-point intervals with T = 50 being the distribution's mean and every 10 points above or below that being a standard deviation away from the mean. Stanine scores divide the distribution into nine equal intervals with stanine 1 being the lowest ninth and stanine 9 being the highest ninth of the distribution. The following chart shows these standard scores.

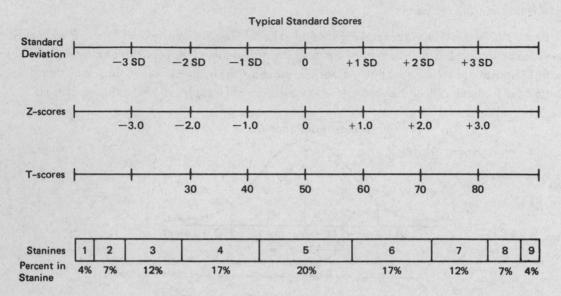

Typical Standard Scores

Test of Significance

If a researcher could test every member of a population, he or she wouldn't need very sophisticated statistics. All the data would be right there. In most cases, however, the entire population isn't available, so the investigator assesses *samples* from the population. The samples are selected in various ways, the most technically correct being a random sample that shows no bias in selection. In practice, however, sample populations turn out to be whoever is available, frequently college sophomores in beginning psychology classes.

Once the sample population is given the task, or manipulation, or has been tested according to the particular requirements of the experiment, that sample's performance is compared with another measure of performance. The other measure could be a standard, as in standardized IQ scores, or it could be the same group's average score on a previous occasion, or it could be the average score of a control group. Whatever the comparison, the statistical operation is to compare two or more sets of scores. The question asked in the comparison is: "Is the difference I find among the scores or sets of scores a *significant* difference, or did I get this difference merely by chance?"

The statistical procedure is to assume a *null hypothesis.* This statistical hypothesis states that there really is no difference between the groups, and any differences obtained are strictly due to error or chance. In order for the experimenter to believe that the obtained differences are real—in other words, in order to *reject the null hypothesis*—the experimenter must be quite sure that the results did not occur by chance. For example, if the differences between two samples could happen just by chance 10% of the time, the researcher wouldn't believe the differences were caused by manipulation. But, if the probability (p) is only 5% that the differences would occur by chance, then the differences might be accepted as real and the null hypothesis rejected. In this case, the experimenter is saying that the differences really exist and are not an accident, and that the same results would be obtained 95 times out of 100. Sometimes even a probability of 5% is too great, and the researcher will put confidence only in a result that would occur by chance 1% of the time. In this case the null hypothesis would not be rejected unless the probability were less than .01. Normally, experimental results are assumed to be significant when p<.05, that is, when the probability of getting this result by chance is less than 5%. The other common significance values are p<.01 and p<.001.

But since there always remains a chance that the results really were just chance happenings, the researcher is accepting the results with some risk of error. A *type I error* is just that: rejecting the null hypothesis when it is applicable.

A *type II error* is just the opposite: not rejecting the null hypothesis when it is not applicable. In this case, differences really exist between the two populations, but just by chance the differences did not show up as significant.

The following table shows the conditions of type I and type II errors.

Risk of Making an Error in Use of Null Hypothesis

		DECISION	
		Accept Null Hypothesis	Reject Null Hypothesis
ACTUAL SITUATION	Null Hypothesis is True	No Error	TYPE I ERROR
	Null Hypothesis is False	TYPE II ERROR	No Error

Results of measures of significance also depend on the size of the sample. A slight difference is not significant if the samples are small. But if the samples are very large, a small difference could be significant. As the sample size increases, the probability of results occurring by chance decreases because differences occurring by chance tend to cancel each other out. A difference obtained with a large sample is more likely to be real than a similar-size difference obtained with a small sample.

Statistics Used in Significance Testing

Analysis of Variance

When comparing results from only two sample groups, the *t-test,* a simple kind of analysis of variance, is used to test the null hypothesis. If there are more than two groups to be compared (say running speed of rats under three different conditions of food deprivation on four different days), an *analysis of variance* (ANOVA) is used. Basically, the analysis of variance determines if the results of the different manipulations are significant. This is done by comparing two estimates of variance—the variance between the groups with the variance within the groups. If only chance is operating and the null hypothesis is true, the two estimates of variance should be about the same. However, if the independent variable has an effect, the two variances should differ. If the *between-group variance* (the degree to which the groups as a whole differ from each other) is significantly larger than the *within-group variance* (the estimate of how much variation there is normally in the groups without any manipulation), the null hypothesis can be rejected. The results of an analysis of variance are expressed as an *F-statistic* or *f-test,* named after **R.A. Fisher.**

The number of independent variables determines how many ways the analysis will be performed. Thus, if the researcher is testing the effect of different levels of alcohol on performance, there is really only one independent variable (alcohol) even though there might be different levels of alcohol given. As an example, if three groups are given three different amounts of alcohol and one group is given a placebo (an inert substance), there are four levels of a single independent variable, and the statistic used is a one-way analysis of variance, or one-way ANOVA. If a second independent variable is used, for instance gender, then the design would be "gender by alcohol level," and the statistic used would be a two-way ANOVA.

Main Effects and Interaction Effects

Sometimes, when there are two or more independent variables, the effect of one depends on the level of the other. This is called an *interaction effect.* The *main effect,* as the name implies, shows if the independent variable had an effect over all conditions. These two effects can be shown using an example from attitude change research. The study investigated the effect of one-sided versus two-sided communication. The subjects were in two groups, very intelligent and of low intelligence. A hypothetical set of results for the experiment might be presented as follows:

**Mean Attitude Change for Subjects
of Different Intelligence Levels
Under Two Different Communication
Conditions**

Kind of Communication	Very Intelligent Subjects	Low Intelligence Subjects	
One-sided	0.30	0.45	0.375 → Marginal Means
Two-sided	0.55	0.20	0.375
	0.425	0.325	0.375 ← Grand Mean
	↑ Marginal Means		

The main effect can be quickly seen by examining the difference between the marginal means and the grand mean. In this case, the marginal means for communication are the same as the grand mean. This shows no main effect for type of communication. However, there is a main effect for intelligence. For intelligence levels, the marginal means differ from the grand mean.

In this study it was found that even though there was no main effect for type of communication, there was an interaction effect. The type of communication interacted with the level of intelligence. A quick way to see if there is an interaction effect is to plot the scores in each cell. If the two lines cross, there is an interaction; if they are parallel, there is no interaction. For the example, the graph would look like this:

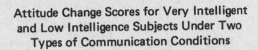

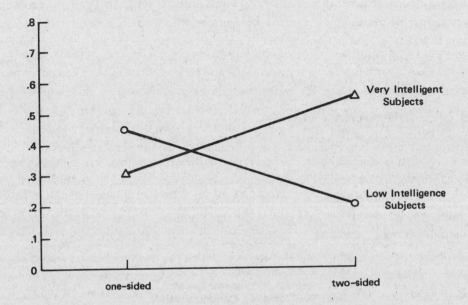

The interaction effect is shown by the crossing lines.

Chi-Square Test

When the dependent variable is measured by frequency or counting, the chi-square is the statistical test used. This test assesses whether the obtained frequencies in a set of categories differ significantly from the expected frequencies. A simple example would be that in a random sample population, the assumed expected frequency of preference for Coke versus Pepsi versus RC Cola would be about equal. Each category should get about one-third of the votes. If the obtained frequencies are found by the chi-square test to differ significantly from these expected frequencies, the experimenter would conclude that there is a preference for one beverage over the others and would reject the null hypothesis.

Degrees of Freedom

The significance values for statistical tests are tabled based on *degrees of freedom* (df). The degrees of freedom are essentially the number of category frequencies that are "free to vary" given that the total number of subjects is known. For instance, in the previous example, there are three categories (Coke, Pepsi, RC Cola). The *df* is 2; since the total number of subjects is known, only two categories are free to include an unknown number of observations. Once the observations in those two categories are known, the observations in the third category are known by subtracting the sum of the first two from the total. In a chi-square test the degrees of freedom depend on the number of categories. In ANOVA the *df* depends on the number of observations and the number of factors in the design.

Correlation Coefficient

If the relationship between two variables exists, the nature of the relationship can be expressed by the *correlation coefficient,* or *r.* For instance, shoe size and height are related. This relationship can be expressed as a correlation coefficient.

The coefficient gives two measures—*direction* and *magnitude. Direction* indicates whether high scores on one variable are associated with high scores or with low scores on a second variable. Direction is shown by positive or negative coefficients. A positive coefficient indicates that the two variables move in the same direction. Those individuals who get high scores on variable X tend to get high scores on variable Y, and those who get low scores on X tend to get low scores on Y. For example, a positive correlation is found between IQ scores and grades in school—students with high IQs tend to get high grades.

A negative correlation indicates that as one variable goes up, the other goes down. Those who get high scores on variable X tend to get low scores on variable Y, and vice versa. For example, a negative correlation has been found to exist between test anxiety and grades in school—students high in test anxiety tend to get low grades. Prejudice and tolerance for ambiguity have also been found to be negatively related.

The *magnitude* of the relationship indicates the degree to which the two variables are related. A perfect, positive correlation is indicated by the coefficient 1.00; a perfect negative correlation is –1.00. No correlation can exceed 1.00 or –1.00. The measured degree of relationship between two variables thus falls between –1.00 and 1.00. When there is absolutely no relationship between two variables, the correlation is 0.00.

The closer the coefficient is to 1.00 or –1.00 the more certain the relationship. The closer the coefficient is to zero the less certain the relationship.

Scattergrams of different degrees of relationships are pictured below. The scattergram shows the plots of each variable pair. The resulting picture is an indication of the direction and magnitude of the relationship.

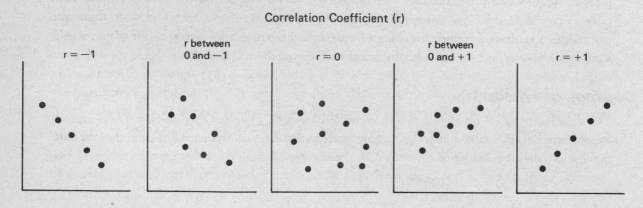

Correlation Coefficient (r)

Correlations do not necessarily imply causation. However, sometimes valid causation inferences are drawn, as in the high relationship between smoking and lung cancer or between years spent working in coal mines and lung disease.

Squaring the correlation coefficient will show how much of the variance of one factor can be accounted for by another factor. For instance, if the correlation between IQ and grade point average is calculated to be .80, one could infer that approximately 64% of a person's school grades can be accounted for by his or her IQ.

TEST CONSTRUCTION

Reliability and Validity

The most important characteristics of psychological tests that can be evaluated statistically are *validity* and *reliability*. Validity is an assessment of how well the test measures what it is supposed to measure. Reliability is an assessment of how consistent the results are. Validity is more critical than reliability since a test showing high validity must also be reliable. If a test measures the intended trait or quality, it should produce approximately the same results on each administration.

The measures of validity and reliability are given as correlation coefficients and range from 0.00 to plus or minus 1.00 (see STATISTICS).

Reliability

If the results of a measuring instrument are to be trustworthy, they must be reliable. They must be dependable and reproducible—they must consistently yield the same results. Reliability is measured by one of three methods. The *test-retest* procedure requires administering the test to the same subjects on two different occasions. The *equivalent-form* procedure entails using two different but equivalent forms of the same test. The *split-half* procedure compares halves of the same test separately as if they were two different tests. For example, answers given to odd-numbered items are compared with responses to even-numbered items.

The reliability coefficient describes how much *error variance* (unwanted "noise") there is in the test. The perfectly reliable test yields a reliability coefficient of 1.00, which indicates that the score obtained is the subject's true score—there is no error in the score. Such a perfect result is unlikely when measuring psychological variables, but might be obtained when measuring physical dimensions, say when correlating height measured in inches with height measured in centimeters. A good psychological test will have a reliability coefficient approaching .90. A score of .90 indicates that 90% of the subject's obtained score on the test represents the true score of the attribute measured, while 10% of the subject's obtained score represents error. Personality tests generally have reliability coefficients of about 0.70 and above.

Reliability is directly related to test length. Shorter tests tend to have lower reliability since they are more influenced by chance variability.

Validity

The most important property of a test is its validity. Validity answers the question, "Does this test really measure what I want to measure?" Validity coefficients are obtained by correlating the test scores with some appropriate standard, called a *criterion*. The result of an analysis of validity is a statement of what the test measures and how well it does so.

Validity can be described in three ways—*content validity, criterion validity,* and *construct validity.*

Content validity refers to the adequacy with which the test samples the thing to be measured. Content validity answers the question: "Do the questions or items in the test measure the property or quality that the test is supposed to measure?" When the questions asked of the subject are clearly and directly aimed at the property the test is designed to measure, the test is said to have high *face validity.* For example, in a test of psychological mood states, a test item might read: "Do you frequently feel anxious?" Face validity is very deceptive. Many test items may appear to measure a particular quality, when in fact they do not. For this reason, test designers rarely rely on face validity or intuitive impressions alone when designing tests.

To determine *criterion validity,* test scores are correlated or compared with an outside criterion. The criterion is usually an independent index of those behavioral characteristics that the test is designed to measure. *Concurrent* validity correlates scores on a test with actual present performance at the task or behavior being assessed. *Predictive* validity predicts some future behavior with which the intended attribute can presumably be correlated. GRE scores have fairly high predictive validity for graduate school success.

Construct validity covers a wide variety of validation procedures. It generally assesses the degree to which a test measures the intended attribute. IQ tests have construct validity because, over the years, it has been found that people who score high on these standardized tests display other attributes consistent with the concept of intelligence—e.g., high achievement in school and life.

One of the statistical measures most frequently used to investigate construct validity is *factor analysis.* This procedure indicates if there is one factor or several factors underlying a given test. In simpler terms, this technique reduces a large number of test data to a smaller number of basic factors. The result is a determination of the test's basic *factorial construction.* Among the leading authors of personality tests, **Cattell** reduced personality to sixteen factors; **Eysenck** reduced it to two factors. **Thurstone** reduced intelligence to about a dozen primary mental factors. Factor analysis has demonstrated that often relatively few factors are being measured by a large group of tests.

FOR FURTHER READING

Cronbach, L.J. *Essentials of psychological testing.* 4th ed. New York: Harper and Row, 1984.

Psychophysics

INTRODUCTION

Psychophysics is a method of assessing the relationship between the psychological variable of perception and the physical variable of a stimulus. It was developed by the early experimental psychologists **Weber** and **Fechner.**

DETERMINING THRESHOLDS

One of the most important concepts in psychophysics is the *threshold,* also called a *limen.* There are two properties of thresholds—*absolute* and *difference.*

Absolute Threshold

An *absolute threshold* is the minimal intensity necessary for a stimulus to be detected. For example, light must be of a certain brightness before it can be seen. Intensities below the threshold of perception are called *subliminal.* Absolute thresholds differ from person to person, but thresholds for the general population are approximately as follows:

- Vision—A candle flame can be seen at 30 miles on a dark, clear night.

- Hearing—The tick of a watch can be heard under quiet conditions at 20 feet.

- Taste—One teaspoon of sugar can be tasted in two gallons of water.

- Smell—One drop of perfume can be smelled when diffused into the entire volume of a six-room apartment.

- Touch—The wing of a fly can be felt falling on a cheek from a distance of one centimeter.

Difference Threshold

The *difference threshold* refers to the smallest difference that can be perceived between two stimuli. For example, how much of a weight difference must exist before a subject can feel that two pieces of metal are of different weights? When the difference becomes just barely perceptible, the *just noticeable difference* (j.n.d.) is said to be reached.

Laws Governing Thresholds

Thresholds are described by two mathematical laws—*Weber's law* and *Stevens' power function.*

According to *Weber's law,* the increase in intensity needed to reach the difference threshold is a constant. In each sense modality (hearing, vision, taste, etc.), there is a reliable ratio, expressed as a constant, that predicts difference thresholds. To illustrate: while a subject is holding a 200-gram weight, she adds 1 gram to it. The subject doesn't perceive that the weight has increased. The subject then adds a second gram to the 201-gram weight. She reports that the weight is now heavier. In this illustration, the difference threshold is 2 grams for the 200-gram weight. If the standard weight is doubled to 400 grams, the added weight must also be doubled to 4 grams to achieve a noticeable difference. Thus the ratio is 2/200 or 4/400, or 0.01. The difference threshold for weight in this example is 0.01, or 1%. No matter what the weight, one must add more than 1% to it or take more than 1% away from it before one can perceive the second weight as different.

Weber's ratios work in the middle ranges of stimulus intensities, but not at extreme levels.

According to *Stevens' power function,* not all sense receptors increase in the linear way Weber's law indicates. Stevens contended that perception of an increase in stimulation increases as an exponential power of the stimulus standard. Some stimuli, such as electric shocks, seem much stronger as they increase in intensity. Others, such as increased brightness, do not seem to increase as dramatically.

METHODS OF CLASSICAL PSYCHOPHYSICS

There are three classical methods of psychophysics—*the method of limits, the method of constant stimuli,* and *the method of adjustments.*

Method of Limits

To use the *method of limits,* the experimenter starts with a value of the variable far enough above the threshold that it will certainly be perceived. For instance, if the experimenter is testing the subject's visual ability, a light source within the subject's range of vision will be shown. Gradually the experimenter decreases the variable until the subject reports he or she no longer perceives it. That is, the light is turned down until it can no longer be detected. The experimenter then starts a sequence of exposures with values far enough below the threshold that the stimulus certainly cannot be perceived, and the experimenter increases the stimulus until the subject reports detection. Many of these alternating ascending and descending trials are run and the average reported threshold is calculated.

Method of Constant Stimuli

The *method of constant stimuli* is similar to the method of limits except that the values presented to the subject are varied randomly—they are not presented in an ascending or descending order. The response categories are usually simply "Yes" and "No." Also, *catch trials* are used in this method. Catch trials occur when the stimulus is not presented at all. Responses to these catch trials can be used to evaluate the subject's response set and reliability.

Method of Adjustments

In the *method of adjustments,* the subject makes adjustments to the measuring apparatus until the adjusted value is perceived as equivalent to some standard. The subject does this many times, again starting the adjustment at values above, then below, the standard. The average value perceived to be the same as the standard is the *point of subjective equality.* Usually the point of subjective equality is not the same as the *point of objective equality.* In other words, the physical stimulus and the sensory perception are not equivalent. The difference between what the standard is in reality (the point of objective equality) and the subject's perception of it (the point of subjective equality) is called the *constant error.*

METHODS OF MODERN PSYCHOPHYSICS

Magnitude Estimation

The method of magnitude estimation was developed by **S.S. Stevens.** The observer is asked to assign values he or she feels are appropriate to his or her perceptions, without regard to any method imposed by the experimenter, such as the methods discussed above. For example, the subject is exposed to an odor that he is to consider as a standard with a number, say, 10. Other odors are then presented in an irregular order, each with the same smell but varying in intensity. The subject judges the intensity of the smell and assigns a number. If he feels an odor is half as strong as the standard, he would assign it a 5, twice as strong would get a 20, and so on. The results of such direct scaling tend to support a power-function psychophysical relationship.

Signal Detection

Signal detection was developed originally to deal with the problems of attention and vigilance associated with radar tracking. This method determines a value called *D-prime (d'),* which is a measure of a person's sensitivity free from personal variables (called *noise*) such as motivation, response sets, or strategy. The process teases out the detection of a stimulus from the noise background. Signal detection emphasizes the observer's judgment and the conditions under which it changes rather than the actual intensity of the stimulus.

For instance, in testing a sense like hearing, the tone can be "on" or "off," and the subject can perceive it as being "on" or "off." The categories of responses form a 2×2 matrix.

Subject's Perception

Signal	On	Off
On	Hit	Miss
Off	False Alarm	Correct Rejection

If the signal is "off" but the subject perceives it as "on," the detection is a false alarm. If the signal is "on" and the subject perceives it as "on," there is a hit. An "off" signal perceived as "off" is a correct rejection, while an "on" signal perceived as "off" is a miss. The perceptual sensitivity (d') is the difference between hits and false alarms.

The subject's criterion for perceiving the stimulus will change depending upon his expectancy. In the above example, if he expects that the tone will be presented more often than not, the probability of his getting both hits and false alarms will be great.

The consequences of the observer's judgments, called the *payoff matrix,* will also alter his criterion for detecting the stimulus. If, for example, the task is to detect enemy planes on a radar screen, it is imperative to maximize the number of hits and minimize the number of misses, while false alarms and correct rejections are not so important. The observer will consequently lower his criterion for detecting the stimulus and raise his criterion for rejecting it. Changing the payoff will thus cause the observer to change his probability of detection.

Physiology

NEUROPHYSIOLOGY

The Nerve Cell

The nervous system is made up of some 10 billion cells, called *neurons*. The nerve cell, or neuron, is the basic functional subunit in the nervous system. Each neuron is a living cell and contains three main parts: *cell body, dendrites,* and *axon.* The *cell body* contains the nucleus of the neuron. The *dendrites* are short fibers projecting from the cell body. The *axon* is a fiber, sometimes quite long, emerging from one side of the cell body.

The many kinds of neurons vary in the length of their dendrites and axons but all have these three parts. The dendrites respond to stimulation and carry a nerve impulse toward the cell body. The axon carries the impulse away from the cell body. The following drawing shows major components of a neuron and the direction of the neural impulse.

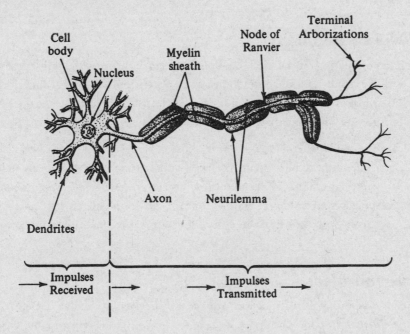

Nerve cells are distinguished by their axons. Some axons are covered by an insulating fatty sheath called *myelin.* Myelination increases the speed of conduction of the nerve impulse. Axons also differ in diameter. Conduction speed increases as the diameter of the axon increases. The myelinated axons are white *(white matter)* and the cell bodies are gray *(gray matter).*

The Nerve Impulse

Transmission of Nerve Impulses

The nerve impulse generally moves from the dendrites or cell body of the receiving neuron out through the axons, making contact with other cells or with effector muscles. Recent research indicates that communication between nerve cells can also occur through dendrite-dendrite synapses.

Connections between neurons are almost always synaptic. A *synapse* is a very small space separating two nerve cells or a nerve cell and an effector system such as a muscle. A bioelectrical impulse is transmitted across the synapse through neurotransmitters released from the *bouton,* an enlargement at the end of the axon. The bouton contains catalytic proteins called *enzymes.* Some of these enzymes are capable of destroying the neurotransmitter, thus inhibiting the nerve transmission. Other enzymes are capable of manufacturing the neurotransmitters. Different neurons release different transmitters. The major transmitters so far identified are *acetylcholine* (the transmitter at the neuromuscular junction), *norepinephrine, dopamine,* and *serotonin.* The neurotransmitters *depolarize* or *hyperpolarize* (i.e., excite or inhibit) the receiving neuron. The effects are determined by the nature of the receptors. For example, acetylcholine excites motor-voluntary muscles but inhibits the heart muscle.

The neurotransmitters in the brain seem to be related to certain affective disorders. It is believed that a deficit of the *monoamines* (this group includes the catecholamines dopamine and norepinephrine and the indolamine serotonin) is associated with endogenous depression while an excess of the monamines is associated with schizophrenia.

Conduction of Nerve Impulses

Neurons are capable of conducting bioelectrical impulses over long distances without loss of signal strength. The impulse moves fairly rapidly, although not as fast as an electric current. Nerve impulses move from 20 feet per second to as fast as 300 feet per second, whereas electric current moves at the speed of light. Impulses move faster through myelinated axons and thick axon fibers.

For animals higher on the phylogenetic scale—that is, those more recently evolved—the nerve impulse typically moves in one direction. The human intestines and stomach are exceptions, revealing their primitive history. An intestinal cramp is hard to localize because the whole intestinal nerve network is affected. The entire nervous systems of lower animals, like the flatworm and jellyfish, are like the human intestine. In these organisms impulses travel in either direction, so response to stimulation affects the whole organism.

Nature of Nerve Impulses

The nerve impulse itself is initiated by the dendrite or the *cell body* being stimulated. Before stimulation, the neuron is in a *resting potential* in which potassium (K+) ions inside the cell are more or less balanced *(polarized)* with sodium (Na+) ions outside the cell, the inside being negatively charged with respect to the outside. When the neurotransmitters make contact with a part of the cell membrane, they change the permeability of the membrane and cause an interchange *(depolarization)* of the ions. As a result, the potassium ions begin to flow outward and the sodium ions flow inward. The interchange starts a kind of chain reaction, and the impulse moves along the cell and out through the axon. This initial voltage change is called the *generator potential* or *generator current.*

If the initial stimulation is not quite strong enough for complete depolarization, a slight impulse called a *graded potential* occurs. The graded potential is a local change that is not sufficient to travel the full length of the neuron. Once the intensity passes the threshold of the *action potential,* however, the impulse travels the full length. The neuron will fire to its fullest extent whether the stimulation is sufficient or more than sufficient. The firing is thus said to be *all-or-none.* The graded response is in the dendrite and cell body. The initial segment of the axon, called the *axon hillock,* is the critical site at which the action potential is initiated.

After the firing, the nerve fiber takes time to re-establish its *resting potential* and regain its polarization. The first stage of this period is the *absolute refractory* period, during which the cell will not fire no matter how strong the stimulation. After this brief period, there is a *relative refractory* period during which only more intense stimuli will cause it to fire. Therefore, to increase the frequency of nerve firings, the intensity of stimulation must be increased. Since nerve fibers form bundles called nerves, increasing the stimulation also activates more fibers.

If the chemicals in the neurotransmitters facilitate depolarization, they excite the nerve cell and produce *excitatory postsynaptic potential* (EPSP). If the chemicals in the neurotransmitters inhibit depolarization, they reduce the action potential and produce *inhibitory postsynaptic potential* (IPSP).

Neurons adapt to stimulation; that is, there is decreased receptor activity in response to steady and continuous stimulation.

Nerve impulses are *transmitted* across a synapse and *conducted* through a neuron.

The Nervous System

Pioneer research in neurophysiology was done by **Sir Charles Sherrington.** His book, *The Integrative Action of the Nervous System* (1906), is a classic. It was Sherrington who investigated the extraordinary importance of the synapses for facilitating and inhibiting neural processes.

Central Nervous System

The *central nervous system* (CNS) consists of the spinal cord and the brain. (The brain is described in another section.) Sensory information received by the brain and spinal cord originates through the response of specialized receptors to physical stimuli. These receptors include rods and cones in the retina of the eye, hair cells of the ears, taste buds of the tongue, dendrites of the olfactory neurons, cutaneous receptors in the skin, and kinesthetic receptors in the inner ear.

The nerve impulses generated by these receptors travel along the *afferent* fibers to the spinal cord and the brain. They enter the spinal cord at the *dorsal,* or back, section. Afferent impulses bring information to the CNS.

All consequences of CNS activity must ultimately be expressed through *efferent* fibers. Efferent fibers go from the CNS out to the muscles and glands. They exit the spinal cord at the *ventral,* or front, side.

Some afferent-efferent circuits had been thought to be entirely outside the brain, unmediated by any higher mental processes. The knee jerk response is an example of this. The afferent impulse goes to a point in the gray matter of the spinal cord. There the impulse is transmitted to an *effector axon* that proceeds to the appropriate leg muscles. This action is called a *reflex arc,* or simply a reflex. Criticism of this reflex arc notion, however, dates from the end of the last century. In a classic article, **John Dewey** (1896) posited that motor discharge is not just a response to disjointed sensory stimulation. Rather, the reflex results from complex interconnections and relationships throughout the central nervous system. Looking only at the stimulus and the response, he felt, ignores the real psychical event.

The efferent nerves can be classified into two groups: the *somatic* and the *autonomic* divisions.

Somatic Division

The somatic division controls voluntary movement of the *striated* muscles such as those that move arms and legs. When a number of efferent nerves converge on a motor neuron, the term used is *final common path.*

Autonomic Nervous System

The autonomic system controls nerves running to the smooth muscles and glands. These regulate the automatic activities such as digestion, circulation, respiration, and heartbeat. There are two divisions in the autonomic system—*sympathetic* and *parasympathetic.*

The *sympathetic system* controls the mobilization of body resources for emergencies. For example, when the organism gets excited, the heart rate increases, pupils dilate, and glands secrete. Everything tends to act as a unit with the effect of preparing the organism for *"fight or flight."* The sympathetic system regulates all this. This system is made up of masses of cell bodies and nerve fibers called *ganglia,* lying on either side of the spinal column. Fibers leave the spinal cord and synapse at these ganglia. From there other fibers project to the various organs. It is believed that *acetylcholine* is the neurotransmitter released at the first synapse and *norepinephrine* at the second.

The *parasympathetic system* is complementary to the sympathetic system. It quiets down an organ that the sympathetic system has activated. The fibers of the parasympathetic system leave the spinal cord and synapse at ganglia lying near the target organs. It is believed that acetylcholine is the neurotransmitter released at both synapses. It has been suggested that the parasympathetic system is implicated in psychosomatic illnesses in that it is this system that attempts to control rage reactions mediated through the sympathetic system.

Measures of autonomic nervous system activity include the EKG *(electrocardiogram)* measuring changes in electrical potential of the heartbeat and the GSR *(galvanic skin response)* measuring changes in electrical conductance of the skin.

Blood System: Endocrine Glands

Body functions are organized through the chemical actions of the blood system as well as through the fibers of the nervous systems. The blood carries *hormones,* which are discharged by the *ductless glands.* These are called the *endocrine* glands and are important in regulating body processes. The endocrine glands are regulated through the *hypothalamus.* Their functions are described below.

The *pituitary* gland is at the base of the brain. It is called the *master gland* because it influences secretions of other endocrine glands. It secretes *somatotropic hormones* (STH), which stimulate normal growth. Oversecretion of STH in childhood results in a *pituitary giant;* undersecretion in childhood results in a *pituitary dwarf. Gonadotropic hormones* (GTH) produced by the pituitary affect the output of the gonads.

The *adrenocorticotropic hormone* (ACTH) secreted by the pituitary stimulates and regulates secretions of the adrenal glands. ACTH output is increased under stress and in turn it stimulates the adrenal cortex to secrete hormones that increase the excitability of the nervous system. ACTH also stimulates the adrenal-regulated functions of sexual vigor and the development of secondary sex characteristics.

The *thyroid* gland controls metabolism, the rate at which the body burns calories. Thyroid deficiency results in physical maldevelopment and intellectual impairment, a condition called *cretinism*.

The *parathyroid* controls calcium metabolism and the maintenance of the body's normal level of arousal. If calcium concentration is reduced, severe muscle weakness may appear.

The *thymus* controls the development of immune reactions in the body through the stimulation of *antibodies*. The thymus increases in size as the child grows but becomes nonfunctional and atrophies after about age ten.

The *pancreas* secretes *insulin,* which controls sugar metabolism. Undersecretion of insulin leads to *diabetes* (oversupply of blood sugar). Oversecretion of insulin results in *hypoglycemia* (low blood-sugar level).

The *adrenal* gland is composed of two distinct systems, the *cortex* and the *medulla,* or core. The adrenal cortex secretes male sex-related hormones and is made of the same type of tissues as the gonads. Secretions of the adrenal cortex are stimulated by the pituitary hormone ACTH. These hormones maintain the excitability of cells. Undersecretion of corticoids results in a syndrome called *Addison's disease,* whose symptoms include depression, weakness, anorexia, and irritability. Oversecretion of these hormones is rare and results in sexual precocity in children and masculine characteristics in women.

The medulla of the adrenal gland is innervated by the autonomic nervous system. The medulla secretes the hormones *epinephrine* (also called *adrenaline*) and *norepinephrine* (also called *noradrenaline*) when the body is aroused and in an emotionally stressed state. Once epinephrine is released, it has the effect of stimulating the pituitary gland to produce ACTH, which in turn stimulates the adrenal cortex to release the corticoid hormones that increase excitability.

The *gonads* control secondary sex characteristics and reproductive apparatus. The male gonads are the testes, which secrete steroids called *androgens*. The female gonads are the ovaries, which secrete *estrogens*.

The *pineal* gland is a small pea-shaped structure found in the brain. In primitive organisms it is a rudimentary visual receptor. In man it responds to the daily light-dark cycle. It produces the hormone *melatonin,* which acts to suppress or inhibit the activity of the gonads. Light suppresses the secretion of melatonin, which has the effect of increasing gonad (sexual) activity, hence the increased sunlight of spring and summer results in increased sexual drive in many species.

BRAIN PHYSIOLOGY

Anatomy

The human brain is composed of (1) a *primitive core* built around the top end of the spinal cord and regulating basic somatic activities; (2) an *"old brain"* (the *limbic system*) built around the primitive core and mediating basic drives such as hunger and thirst and emotions such as rage, fear, and pleasure; and (3) a *"new brain"* (the *cerebrum*), a wrinkled, convoluted, gray mass of nerve cells built around the old brain and responsible for the higher mental functions such as abstract reasoning and sequential thought.

Central Core

The more primitive structures can be thought of as the central core of the brain. The activities regulated at this level are functions affecting basic life-maintaining processes such as temperature control, metabolism, respiration, equilibrium, and deep sleep. The central core includes the *lower brainstem, medulla oblongata, pons,* parts of the *thalamus* and *hypothalamus,* and the *cerebellum.*

The *brainstem* is the top of the spinal cord, the stalk upon which the later-evolved structures are attached. The human brainstem is about three inches long.

Central Core of Brain

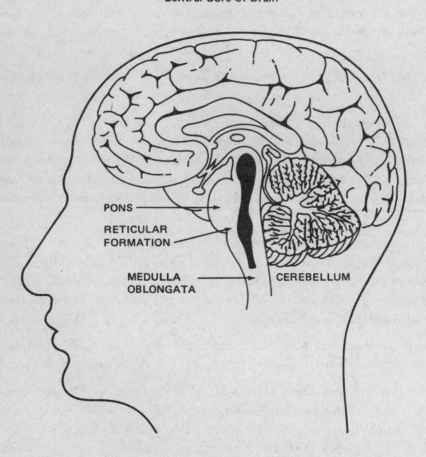

One specialized area of the brainstem, the *medulla oblongata,* is composed of fiber tracts that conduct impulses from higher to lower centers and vice versa. It also contains vital centers that regulate important bodily functions such as breathing, swallowing, digestion, and heartbeat.

The *pons* lies immediately above the medulla. The pons contains regulatory centers especially for the control of slow-wave deep sleep.

The *thalamus* lies on top of the brainstem and acts as a central switching station for affector signals going to the brain from the sense organs and for effector signals leaving the cortex and running to the muscles and glands.

The *hypothalamus* lies under the thalamus and regulates endocrine activity and life-maintaining processes such as metabolism, temperature control, appetite, thirst, and certain emotions such as rage and pleasure.

Behind the medulla is the "little brain," or *cerebellum,* the major mechanism for coordinating movements of different parts of the body and for maintaining posture. Afferent impulses are fed into the cerebellum from receptors in the muscles, tendons, and joints.

Reticular Activating System (RAS)

The RAS consists of undifferentiated neurons that extend from the top of the spinal cord through the brainstem on up into the thalamus. This complex network of fibers and nuclei influences the activity level of the cortex. The RAS is responsible for arousing the organism. Centers within the RAS are considered to be the primary mechanisms for the control of alertness and sleep.

Limbic System

Around the primitive core, the "old brain" structures, now called the *limbic system,* evolved. These structures developed as a consequence of the evolving organism's need for survival mechanisms. Hence the limbic system regulates the emotions and sequential activities necessary to adapt and survive: feeding, fighting, fleeing, and mating (sometimes known as the four "f's").

The limbic system was first identified by **Broca** and later investigated by others, including **MacLean** and **Pribram.** It includes parts of the *thalamus* and *hypothalamus* as well as the *amygdala, hippocampus, septum,* and *cingulate gyrus.*

It has been shown that certain centers in the hypothalamus mediate the expression of emotional behavior, sexual behavior, and appetite. **James Olds** (1956) discovered that a slight electric current delivered through electrodes implanted in the hypothalamus of rats would be felt as a pleasurable experience. The rats seemed to enjoy the sensations and soon learned to self-stimulate by pressing a lever. With suitably located electrodes, animals would stimulate themselves several thousand times an hour, stopping only when physically exhausted.

Other areas of the hypothalamus that have been stimulated have produced manifestations of rage, fright, or pain. **Walter Hess,** experimenting during the 1930s, found areas of the hypothalamus that produced hissing and clawing in otherwise friendly cats.

The two hypothalamic areas associated with food intake are the *ventromedial hypothalamus* (VMH) and the *lateral hypothalamus* (LH). Direct stimulation of the VMH produces cessation of eating, while ablation produces extreme overeating, stopping only when a grossly overweight level is reached. The LH functions in an opposite way. Stimulation of the LH produces eating behaviors, while ablation or anesthetization results in a cessation of eating. Animals with an ablated LH will starve to death unless force-fed.

The *amygdala* has been implicated in aggressive behaviors. Stimulating or lesioning the proper divisions of the amygdala elicits responses that either facilitate or inhibit aggressive behavior. The *Kluver-Bucy syndrome* results from removal of the temporal lobes, including underlying limbic structures, particularly the amygdala. Normally vicious monkeys become placid after this procedure.

The *hippocampus* appears to be related to memory. Hippocampal damage, either through vitamin deficiencies as found in *Korsakov's syndrome* or through direct surgery, such as bilateral surgery for epilepsy, typically leads to *anterograde amnesia*—that is, the inability to remember things occurring after the onset of the brain damage. Patients with less severe damage to this area display less severe memory deficits. It has thus been suggested that the hippocampus serves some function in converting short-term memory into long-term memory.

Cerebrum and Cerebral Cortex

Overlying the lower brain regions is the deeply wrinkled *cerebrum*. The outer surface of the cerebrum is the *cerebral cortex*, which means "brain bark." The cortex is made up largely of masses of grayish cell bodies. This *gray matter* does the brain's work. Beneath the gray matter, the rest of the cerebrum consists mainly of long white axons. These tracts of white tissue are the fibers that conduct nerve impulses between the various parts of the brain.

The cortex is the seat of consciousness, conscious sensation, and voluntary control of behavior. In phylogenetic development, the cortex becomes larger and its surface becomes more convoluted, thus allowing for more surface area.

The cortex is divided into two symmetrical hemispheres. The *right hemisphere* controls functions on the left side of the body. The *left hemisphere* controls functions on the right side of the body. **Broca,** while working with brain-injured patients, discovered that left hemispheric lesions led to poorer performance on verbal tests while right hemispheric lesions were associated with decreased performance on nonverbal tests. This suggests that verbal mental activities are mediated by the left hemisphere.

Mapping Brain Functions

Each hemisphere is divided into four lobes: *frontal, parietal, occipital,* and *temporal.* The lobe areas are divided by *fissures.* The picture on page 111 shows the lobes and fissures for the left hemisphere. The picture on page 112 shows the localized brain functions.

The *frontal lobe* regulates judgment and abstract thought, certain personality characteristics, the ability to focus attention, and motor activities. It is the area most clearly associated with the *limbic system* and probably acts to suppress limbic-regulated behaviors, such as rage reactions.

Human brain damage in the frontal lobes (as in *prefrontal lobotomy*) results in reduced affect, impulsiveness, indifference to pain, and inability to focus attention. Expressive speech disturbances *(motor aphasia)* may result from lesions to an area of the frontal lobe called *Broca's area.*

The *parietal lobe* mediates somatic sensory stimuli. This lobe mediates orientation in space. Lesions in the parietal lobe result in disorders of body image. Lesions in certain areas of the parietal lobe may be associated with *dyslexia.*

The *occipital lobe* is devoted to the visual system. Lesions may produce disturbances of spatial orientation and discrimination, illusions and hallucinations, and the inability to recognize visual stimuli.

The *temporal lobe* is related to the auditory system and the limbic system. Stimulation of the temporal lobe may evoke past memories. *Wernicke's area,* located at the top of the temporal lobe, has been identified as the locus of speech reception. Lesions to this area will usually result in receptive or sensory aphasia. Lesions to parts of the temporal lobe cause loss of recent memory. Lesions can also produce partial deafness and disturbance of auditory localization. The temporal lobe also makes connections to the limbic system and controls some sexual activities and emotions.

Bilateral removal of the temporal lobes produces a characteristic syndrome called the *Kluver-Bucy syndrome.* In humans, the symptoms include loss of recognition of people, loss of fear and rage reactions, increased sexual activity, insatiable hunger, memory deficits, and the inability to ignore stimuli regardless of their novelty.

The Split Brain

The right and left hemispheres are connected via axon fibers that cross at the *corpus callosum*. **Sperry** experimented in the 1950s with severing this connection in laboratory animals so that sensory input was confined to one hemisphere. He showed that the two hemispheres could operate independently of each other. The split-brain animals could learn discrimination tasks independently in the two hemispheres, and the learning thus produced in one hemisphere would not facilitate learning the task in the other hemisphere.

The split-brain research was continued with human subjects who suffered from severe epilepsy. Here it was found that language activities are specialized by hemisphere. Verbal functions are controlled by the *dominant* (usually left) hemisphere, while spatial activities are controlled by the *nondominant* (usually right) hemisphere.

In surgical operations on these epileptic subjects, the corpus callosum was cut so that epileptic seizures could not spread from one hemisphere to the other. When tested later, the patients were not able to give correct names to pictures of objects or words flashed exclusively to the right hemisphere. Other studies demonstrated that the right hand (mediated through the left hemisphere) could copy words but not draw pictures or complete spatial problems. With the left hand (mediated by the right hemisphere) the patients could draw adequately but had difficulty copying words.

Human Cortex Showing Lobes and Fissures

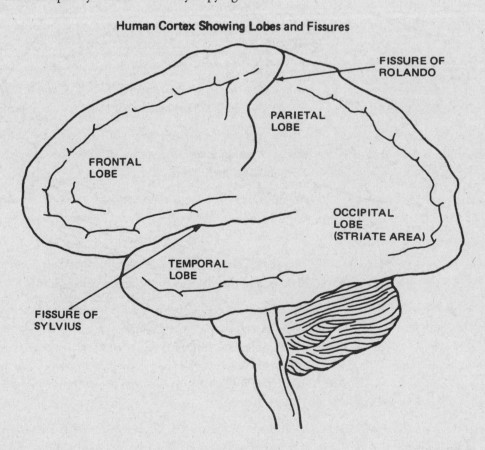

FISSURE OF ROLANDO

PARIETAL LOBE

FRONTAL LOBE

OCCIPITAL LOBE (STRIATE AREA)

TEMPORAL LOBE

FISSURE OF SYLVIUS

A more recent study of hemispheric lateralization by **Bakan** (1971) demonstrated that subjects tend to gaze to the right while solving verbal problems, while they tend to look to the left while solving spatial problems. **Ornstein** (1972) found increased brain wave synchronization *(alpha activity)* in the right hemisphere during verbal tasks and increased synchronization in the left hemisphere during spatial tasks. Since synchronization is indicative of decreased activity, these results tend to support the conclusion that the left hemisphere is organized for linear thought and verbal logic while the right hemisphere is oriented toward intuitive and conceptual processes.

Localized Areas

Visual Area

At the very back of each cerebral hemisphere in the occipital lobe is the area that mediates vision. This is also known as the *striate area.*

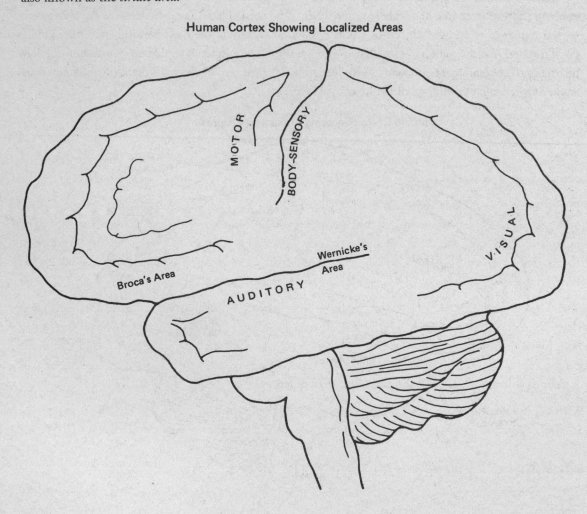

Human Cortex Showing Localized Areas

Auditory Area

In the temporal lobe is the area mediating audition. There is no specialized hemispheric laterality; both ears are mediated on both sides. Thus the loss of one temporal lobe has little effect on hearing.

Speech Area

In the normal brain, the left hemisphere controls speech. There are two separate regions in the left hemisphere that mediate speech—*Wernicke's area* in the temporal lobe and *Broca's area* in the frontal lobe. Damage to Wernicke's area typically results in receptive aphasia, while damage to Broca's area typically results in expressive aphasia.

Association Area

The frontal lobe regulates delayed response, abstract thought, and motor regulation. It is here that the strictly human attributes of thinking are mediated. The association area has shown the greatest increase in size during phylogenetic development.

Function

Memory Storage

Karl Lashley spent many years at Harvard researching the location of specific memories. He taught laboratory rats to perform maze tasks, then *ablated* (removed) portions of their frontal lobes. He found that no matter what part of the lobe was removed, the rats were still able to remember and perform the tasks. Even with large portions removed, the rats remembered some part of what they had learned. These findings suggested that the function of memory is carried out over large areas of the cortex.

Lashley concluded that for higher mental functions like intelligence the brain operates on a principle of *mass action* or *equipotentiality*, which means that complex functions are equally represented at various parts of the cortex.

During the 1950s, **Wilder Penfield** found that when he stimulated points in the temporal lobe of the patient's exposed cortex while performing preliminary brain surgery, the patient recalled a specific vivid memory. In each case, the electric probe brought back incredibly accurate and real memories. However, if the memory site was removed through an operation, the memory itself was not lost. As Lashley had found, the memory experience is apparently laid down throughout the brain.

The *planarian* (flatworm) has been used to investigate memory. Worms are the simplest life forms that have a brain. Worms were taught a simple task, then cut in two (**McConnell,** 1962). When so severed, each piece grew into a complete, new worm. The regenerated worms remembered almost as well as the original ones. These researchers also cut up some trained worms and fed them to untrained worms. The untrained worms later learned the task faster than unfed, untrained control worms.

Memory has been associated with increased production of *ribonucleic acid,* or RNA. Training or experience increases the amount of RNA in cells, and different kinds of experiences produce different kinds of RNA.

Brain Waves: Electroencephalography

The EEG is a recording of brain waves. It measures the spontaneous voltage changes in the cerebrum. The recordings are a kind of picture of the "state of mind." Typically, electrodes attached to or just under the scalp of a human subject will pick up electrical activity from a circular area of the underlying cortex. The EEG is a kind of recording of the summed dendrite potentials (excitatory and inhibitory) of cortical neurons.

Wave Frequencies

The most familiar aspect of the EEG is the frequency. Wave patterns are commonly identified by Greek letters.

A *delta* wave occurs when the impulse is less than 4 cycles per second (cps). This is a high-voltage slow wave that predominates during deep sleep.

A *theta* wave is 4 to 8 cps. A theta wave occurs frequently during emotional states. It is associated with uncertainty, daydreaming, and restful alertness.

An *alpha* wave is 8 to 12 cps. Alpha activity is the "idling" condition of a waking but nonactivated cortex. It is associated with pleasurable feelings of well-being, relaxation, and increased awareness.

A *beta* wave occurs when the impulse is more than 12 cps. Betas are fast waves with low voltage. Beta activity is indicative of an alert, activated cortex.

One type of EEG measurement is the cortical *evoked response* (ER), or *evoked potential*. An ER is a spike of electrical activation occurring in response to a specific sensory input, such as a tone. A tone will elicit an ER in the auditory cortex but not in the visual cortex, whereas for a flash of light, the result is the reverse. The amplitudes of evoked responses are related to the intensity of the stimuli. Evoked potentials normally *habituate* (gradually decrease) when a non-reinforced sensory stimulus of low intensity is repeatedly presented.

Biofeedback

An interesting development in brain research is the application of *biofeedback* techniques to conditioning of the human EEG. Techniques for learning a degree of conscious regulation over alpha activity have become popularized. With the proper equipment, the subject can be presented with a visual or auditory signal that gives feedback about alpha waves. Whatever is done to maintain alpha can be learned and can be repeated at will. Since alpha waves are the dominant rhythm of a relaxed but wakeful mind, increasing alpha results in pleasurable feelings and relief of tension. Biofeedback shows that the central nervous system has some control over the autonomic nervous system, something that was once derided as impossible.

More recent research has found that the efficacy of biofeedback is disappointing. It has been observed that people can put themselves into an alpha state, yet still be tense. The clinical applications of biofeedback have been shown to be overstated. Further, the same results could be obtained merely by having the subject or patient concentrate on some image or word. As many health insurers have found out, one does not need expensive biofeedback equipment to get equivalent results.

Sleep and Dreams

Sleep was once considered a passive phenomenon. It was thought that without stimulation to maintain wakefulness, the brain would cease to remain active. We now know this is not true. The *sleep-wake cycle* is a process actively and carefully regulated by the brain. Psychologists have devoted a great deal of effort ro researching sleeping and dreaming, beginning with the pioneering work of **Aserinsky and Kleitman** (1953), followed by the more thorough work of **Dement** (1960, 1973).

Spontaneous Recovery

When the organism no longer responds to the conditioned stimulus, it might appear that the effects of the conditioning have been wiped out. However, after a period of rest, the response is very likely to reappear, although in a weak form. The reappearance of the response is referred to as *spontaneous recovery*. This phenomenon suggests that a lack of response is not necessarily caused by forgetting, but by some sort of inhibition or suppression.

Stimulus Generalization

A conditioned stimulus will elicit a conditioned response; in our example the bell elicits the salivation. If a slightly different sound is presented, it will also elicit the response. The learning can *generalize* to similar stimuli. If a child is frightened by a white rat, she might generalize this fright to any furry white animal. Pavlov called this *irradiation*.

Stimulus Discrimination

The converse of stimulus generalization is *stimulus discrimination*. An animal or person can be conditioned to discriminate between different stimuli. If one is reinforced and the other not, the reinforced stimulus will evoke the conditioned response. For instance, if a bell is reinforced with food while other sounds, such as a buzzer or chime, are presented without being reinforced with food, a dog will learn to salivate only to the bell.

Sensory Preconditioning

In *sensory preconditioning*, two CSs, say a light and a tone, are paired during preconditioning sessions. The tone is then paired with a US, say food, and the orienting response originally exhibited at the sight of food is now given at the presentation of the tone. If the light is then presented, the animal might exhibit the same response to this stimulus due to its previous pairing with the tone. It is typically found, though, that the power of the second CS to elicit the conditioned response is weak.

Experimental Neurosis

If the discrimination task is too difficult for the subject and the stimuli cannot be differentiated readily enough, the evoked response is confusion. Pavlov called this *experimental neurosis*. In a well-known example, Pavlov conditioned a dog to respond to a circle. The dog was also conditioned *not to respond* to an ellipse. The conditioned response to the circle was salivation; there was no conditioned response to the ellipse. Once the sequence of responses had been well established, the figures were gradually changed over a period of trials—a process that in modern computer terms is called *morphed*—until they were almost identical. As the figures became more and more alike, it became impossible for the dog to differentiate them. At a point of maximal confusion, the dog began exhibiting signs of emotional disturbance resembling symptoms of human emotional disturbances. The previously quiet dog began to bark and snap, and she tore at her harness straps with her teeth.

Higher-Order Conditioning

Once conditioning is well established, the conditioned stimulus can in turn become an unconditioned stimulus for another stimulus. For example, once a dog is well conditioned to salivate to a bell, a light can be associated with the bell. After several pairings of the light with the bell, the light alone is likely to elicit the response. Pavlov called this model *higher-order conditioning*. Pavlov himself failed to achieve higher than second-order conditioning in dogs. The difficulty Pavlov found is that extinction of the original conditioned stimulus occurs unless it is intermittently reinforced.

Pseudoconditioning

Sometimes the experimental conditions themselves become, in effect, the CS. This is especially true for conditioning of fear responses. If, for example, a bell is paired with a shock, an animal will become conditioned to the bell. But the bell might not elicit the fear response outside the experimental room. Thus it is the contextual stimuli—the apparatus, the room, the experimenter, etc.—that are the CS. In the experimental room any loud noise, not just the bell, would elicit the fear response. This is known as *pseudoconditioning,* since the change in behavior is not conditioned to the bell, but rather the response is an artifact of the experimental method.

OPERANT CONDITIONING

The paradigm for operant conditioning was developed by **B.F. Skinner.** He differentiated responses that are elicited as a consequence of a known stimulus *(respondents)* from responses with no apparent stimulus *(operants).*

Respondents are behaviors such as a dog's salivating to food or the constriction of the pupil after an intense light goes on. The respondent behavior fits the classical conditioning model. Stimuli that can elicit salivation in dogs are quite well known.

Operants, however, cannot be traced to any particular stimulus; they simply occur—a dog walks; a bird flies; a baby babbles. Operant responses do not fit the classical conditioning model because there are no known unconditioned stimuli for them. The initial cause of operant behavior is within the organism itself. According to Skinner, most of human behavior is operant in nature.

Skinner felt he could control operant behavior by *reinforcing* it. The desired response could be strengthened by following it with a reward. The undesired operant behavior could be weakened by failing to follow it with a reward or, in limited cases, following it with a punishment.

In the operant conditioning model, reinforcement appears only after the response is *emitted.* This is different from classical conditioning, in which reinforcement precedes and *elicits* the behavior.

A rat being taught to press a lever gets rewarded after actually pressing the bar. Each time the bar is pressed the rat gets rewarded. Since the response is being reinforced, it will tend to be repeated. The rat is taught to "operate" on his environment in order to get food; hence this is called *operant behavior.*

Positive and Negative Reinforcers

The reinforcer may add something to the environment or take something away from it. In the former case, it is a *positive reinforcer,* one which, when added following an operant, strengthens the probability of that behavior's occurring in the future. A *negative reinforcer* is one which, when taken away following a response, results in an increased probability that the response will recur. A negative reinforcer could be a noxious stimulus like a loud noise or electric shock. If the organism's response is followed by the removal of the noxious stimulus, the response will tend to be repeated.

The choice of reinforcer is especially important when using operant techniques in a human therapeutic situation. Sometimes patients participating in a behavior modification program are given tokens for performing targeted behaviors, and the tokens are later traded in for rewards. Rewards that the individual likes or likes to do are offered by the administrator of the behavior modification. This is known as the *Premack principle*. Thus, if a patient likes to watch TV, she would be allowed to trade in her tokens for a chance to watch the tube. In a more informal way, if a father allows a child to go out to play (her own choice of reinforcer) only after she has finished her homework, the father is also employing the Premack principle.

Operant Strength

The effectiveness of conditioning is called *operant strength*. Operant strength can be measured in two ways: (1) by the rate of response during the acquisition, or (2) by the total number of responses before extinction. In a given time interval, the higher the response rate the stronger the operant conditioning. Also, the more resistant the response is to extinction, the stronger is the operant conditioning.

The measure of response rate is usually represented as a *cumulative learning curve*. The practice period, or *elapsed time*, is represented along the *abscissa;* the measure of performance is represented along the *ordinate*. When response curves reach a plateau or *asymptote,* there is a uniform level of response.

Cumulative Learning Curve

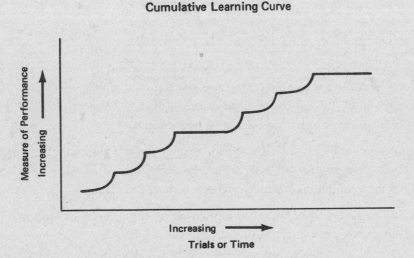

Schedules of Reinforcement

The operant strength varies with the subject and with the *schedule of reinforcement*. In rare instances, the response may be reinforced every time it is emitted. But in most situations, responses are only partially reinforced according to an *intermittent* reinforcement schedule. Various forms of intermittent reinforcement schedules result in characteristic and predictable patterns of acquisition and extinction. Under some schedules, resistance to extinction becomes extremely high.

Simple schedules of reinforcement can be classified into two types—*ratio* and *interval*. In *ratio* schedules, a certain number of responses must be emitted before one response is reinforced. In *interval* schedules, a given interval of time elapses before a response can be reinforced. The most common schedules are *fixed ratio, fixed interval, variable ratio,* and *variable interval*.

In *fixed ratio* (FR) schedules, reinforcement occurs after a fixed number of responses. For example, in a 10 to 1 ratio, the animal has to emit ten bar presses to get a single pellet of food. This typically generates a rapid burst of activity to accomplish the required ratio.

In *fixed interval* (FI) schedules, reinforcement occurs following the first response after a fixed time period. Until the fixed time interval elapses, no response is reinforced. This typically generates a *scallop;* responses decrease, then rapidly increase just before the next reinforcement period approaches.

In a *variable ratio* (VR) schedule, reinforcement occurs after a fixed number of responses but the ratio of responses to reinforcement varies around an average ratio. For example, a variable ratio of 6 to 1 might reinforce the sixth response, then the tenth, then the second. This schedule generates a fairly high and constant rate of response, and the responses are highly resistant to extinction.

In a *variable interval* (VI) schedule, reinforcement occurs following the first response after different time periods. The schedule varies around an average time interval. The unpredictability of reinforcement tends to generate a fairly constant response rate.

The following graph shows the cumulative acquisition and extinction curves for four schedules:

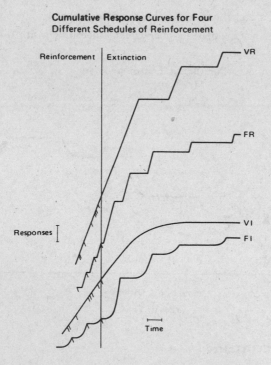

In *fixed ratio* (FR) schedules.

Secondary Reinforcement

The immediate reinforcer, such as food for a hungry animal, is the *primary reinforcer.* A stimulus that accompanies a primary reinforcer can acquire reinforcing capabilities of its own—it becomes a *secondary reinforcer.* For example, a rat is conditioned to press a bar by being reinforced with food pellets. Every time the pellet drops in his cup a light goes on. Soon the light gets associated with the food, and it too begins to serve to reinforce the bar pressing. The sound of a mother's voice while she is feeding a baby can be thought of as a secondary reinforcer for the baby's satisfaction.

Secondary reinforcers can generalize to other responses. This is because some secondary reinforcers tend to accompany a variety of primary reinforcers and acquire their own rewarding value. Money is a generalized reinforcer because it provides food, shelter, entertainment, etc.

Chimps learning to operate a machine were reinforced with a grape and an associated poker chip (**Cowles, 1937**). The chip became a secondary reinforcer, and after a while the chimps worked for the poker chips alone. These are called *token rewards*. This model of giving token rewards has been tried in schools, especially with children who are difficult to teach. The results have been disappointing.

Secondary reinforcers are themselves subject to extinction. Unless the primary reinforcer is occasionally re-presented, the secondary reinforcers gradually lose their effectiveness.

Shaping

Novel behaviors can be elicited by reinforcing responses that gradually approach the behavior that is desired. This is called *shaping*. It requires reinforcing closer and closer approximations to the desired behavior, much as a sculptor shapes clay. For example, the goal might be to teach a child to write the letter *A*. The teacher will shape the behavior by first reinforcing marks on the page, then only reinforcing straight lines, then only reinforcing lines that are connected, and then only reinforcing lines that look like the letter *A*.

Escape Conditioning

Escape conditioning, also called *negative reinforcement*, occurs when the subject is allowed to escape from an adverse situation. For example, a pigeon's cage floor is equipped with a grid that delivers electric shocks. The pigeon can terminate the shock by pressing the lever. It can escape the noxious stimulus by responding with a bar press.

Avoidance Conditioning

Avoidance conditioning is similar to escape conditioning except that the subject can avoid the pain even before it begins by emitting the appropriate response. If a light goes on before the shock begins, the animal can avoid the shock by pressing the lever as soon as the light appears. Avoidance conditioning is very resistant to extinction: if you get poison ivy from walking though the woods, you avoid exposure to that area for a long time afterward.

Punishment

Punishment is the presentation of an aversive stimulus dependent upon the occurrence of a behavior. Punishment works best if it is extreme and continual. Intense punishment, for instance, will suppress behavior more than moderate punishment. Moderate punishment will suppress behavior more than mild punishment, etc. Once punishment is removed, behavior will tend to return to baseline. In fact, at first, it will reach a higher level than baseline. What this tells us is that punishment will suppress or deter behavior, but it won't completely extinguish or abolish it. Hence the preferred method of intervention is to reinforce desired responses at the same time as punishing undesired behaviors.

Chaining

A response can be a reinforcer for another response, which in turn can be a reinforcer for a third response. In the operant conditioning paradigm, this is called *chaining*. Chaining is learning a series of related behaviors and is used in the acquisition of complex behaviors. Each response serves as a stimulus for the next response.

A rat was first trained to eat from a food dispenser. Then the rat learned to press a lever to obtain food. Once the pressing response was established, it was possible to shape a number of responses chained in a complex fashion. The rat learned to climb a spiral stairway, run across a drawbridge, climb a ladder, enter a cable car, pull itself across a gap a few feet above the floor of its experimental box, climb another stairway, and play a toy piano that activated a switch that opened a crossing gate that it had to go through to get to an elevator to get to the bar that it pressed to get its food.

Superstitious Learning (Adventitious Reinforcement)

There are times when responses are reinforced adventitiously (accidentally) by the coincidental pairing of response and reinforcement. This produces *superstitious behavior*. For example, primitive rain dances can be seen as superstitious behavior; they occasionally have been followed by rain, although the behavior is completely independent of the reinforcement. Ritualistic behavior is superstitious behavior that has been reinforced merely by chance and therefore becomes habitual.

Extinction

The nonreinforcement of a previously reinforced response sooner or later results in a gradual reduction of the frequency of response. A common example of *extinction* is that of a mother not picking up a crying baby. If the crying is not reinforced by the mother's attention, it will theoretically extinguish. This reduction of response is more an inhibition than a direct loss of response, since the behavior can reappear spontaneously, as any parent can attest.

Nonreinforcement does not usually produce an immediate decrease in the frequency of response. The course of extinction varies with the strength of the initial conditioning. This initial learning in turn varies with the schedule of reinforcement. Different schedules result in different resistances to extinction.

Spontaneous Recovery

During extinction trials, responses decrease, usually continuously, during a given experimental session. At the start of the next session, however, the rate of response will be higher than the rate obtained at the end of the previous session.

For example, at the end of extinction session A, a pigeon might reduce its responses to ten per second; at the beginning of the next extinction session, the rate might be fifteen per second. This is called *spontaneous recovery* because the rate of response seems to return spontaneously.

Generalization

A response that has been reinforced in the presence of one stimulus may be emitted when a similar stimulus is present. A child who has learned the word *dog* might say "dog" when she sees any four-legged animal. A reinforced response can also generalize to similar responses. A baby reinforced for saying "dada" might generalize to saying "baba."

Discrimination

If an organism responds the same way to two stimuli, it does not discriminate between them. When the response is different in the presence of two stimuli, there is *discrimination*. If the discrimination task becomes too difficult, the subject will become confused and exhibit bizarre behavior. This is called *experimental neurosis*.

INSIGHT LEARNING

Wolfgang Köhler, a leading Gestalt psychologist, reported a model of learning that could not be readily explained by operant conditioning. Köhler was studying a bright chimpanzee named *Sultan*. The chimp had to get some food that had been placed outside of his cage. He had two sticks but each stick alone was too short to reach the food. As he was sitting with two sticks in his hand, the ape seemed to have a sudden insight. He quickly fitted the sticks together, so that with this elongated stick he was able to get his food. Sultan exhibited what Köhler called *insight learning*—the process by which the solution to a problem suddenly becomes clear.

SIGN LEARNING

Edward Tolman contended that learning was not the result of conditioning alone; cognitive understanding was also necessary. For him learning was the acquisition of a *cognitive structure* or *cognitive map*.

According to Tolman, a rat learns to run a maze by understanding the spatial relationships within the maze, not just by learning a chained sequence of turning and movement responses. A rat will take shortcuts or will detour around obstacles in a maze. These responses might never have been conditioned. Tolman called this *place learning*. The animal learns the location of paths or places rather than movement habits.

Latent learning is another of Tolman's constructs. A rat will learn to run a maze even if it is not reinforced for the response. As a person walks or drives around town, he or she might notice a store that he would later frequent if it proved advantageous. The person is not reinforced but still learns.

BEHAVIORAL CONTRAST

Behavioral contrast occurs when two behaviors are reinforced on different schedules, and then one of the behaviors is extinguished. When this is done, the behavior that has not been extinguished increases in frequency.

The classic experiment used pigeons that were reinforced for pecking at two different colored buttons. When reinforcement for pecking at one of the colors was withheld, pecking at that color diminished but pecking at the second color, which was still reinforced, actually increased.

DRIVE REDUCTION LEARNING

An influential learning theory developed by **Clark Hull** stresses *drive reduction* as a motivation for learning. Hull predicted that the probability of a behavior's occurring depends on the strength of the learning habit and the motivation, or level of drive. The drives that Hull had in mind are most of the basic human needs, such as hunger, thirst, aggression, and sex. A hungry rat runs faster to the food box than does a sated one.

Central to Hull's thesis is the notion that the desire to reduce drives motivates learning. Hull's *drive reduction theory* influenced other researchers **(Dollard, Doob, N. Miller, Sears)** who in the 1940s and 1950s applied these principles to the learning of maladaptive behavior by humans.

Miller and Dollard investigated the learning of aggressive responses. In their famous study *Frustration and Aggression* (1930), they showed that prior to any manifestation of hostility by an organism, there was always some frustration. The aggression is either expressed directly or, if the organism learns that this is socially unwise, it is *displaced*.

Miller, along with Dollard, later (1950) proposed that psychopathic symptoms, such as hysterical responses, are learned behaviors. They attempted to correlate learning theories with psychoanalysis. Following Hull's work on drive reduction as a motivating force, they predicted that if a drive such as fear is induced, its reduction will serve as a reward. Anything the organism does that reduces the fear drive becomes the likely action when the fear recurs. Thus the organism learns responses in order to reduce the drive. These are the *coping responses*.

Certain neurotic and psychotic disorders, according to Miller and Dollard, are learned coping responses to drives such as fear. They believe that the psychotic or neurotic symptoms allow escape from the original fear and thereby serve to reinforce the symptom behavior.

Drives can be divided into two categories—those that lead an organism to approach a situation (the goal) and those that lead it to avoid the goal. The *approach* and *avoidance drives* depend on the distance to the goal. The nearer the organism is to the goal, the more intense the drive. But the avoidance drive is stronger than the approach drive as the goal is approached. The closer one gets to a feared object, the more intense becomes the drive to avoid it. The approach and avoidance drives, called *gradients,* can be seen in the following graph:

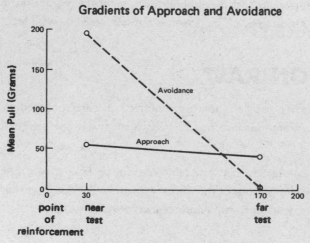

Gradients of Approach and Avoidance

Distance (cm) from Point of Reinforcement

The strength of each gradient was measured in experiments by the pull on the restraining harness attached to the rat. The goal for the approach gradient was getting food. The goal for the avoidance gradient was avoiding a shock. The point at which the two gradients crossed is called the *point of maximal conflict*.

OTHER ISSUES IN LEARNING

Yerkes-Dodson Law

The level of drive has a bearing on learning. Increased drive level facilitates learning only up to a point. Increasing drive or arousal beyond that point interferes with learning. This is known as the *Yerkes-Dodson law*. For optimal performance, high arousal is most appropriate for relatively simple tasks. For more complex tasks, lower levels of arousal have been found to be more facilitative.

Transfer of Training

The *doctrine of formal discipline* was at one time a popular construct in education. This doctrine teaches that formal study of certain academic subjects, such as Latin and mathematics, strengthens intellectual functioning in general. It was thought that the benefits of training in one subject, say Latin, could be transferred to the study of other subjects. The doctrine was used to rationalize teaching subjects that had no immediate practical value in the school curriculum. Investigations by **Thorndike and Woodworth** (1901) demonstrated that *transfer of training* is caused by similarity of concepts and techniques, not by any generalized improvement in brain or intellectual functioning as a result of mental exercise. It is now accepted that mental functioning in one academic area rarely brings about equal improvement in any other academic area.

Curiosity

It is possible that behavior can be elicited without reinforcement if the nature of the task itself is rewarding enough. **Harlow** (1950) has shown that monkeys will solve a complicated puzzle for the intrinsic reward of working it. Harlow (1954) also found that monkeys are motivated by curiosity. Monkeys confined in a closed box with two doors learned to open the door that allowed them to look out on an interesting scene. The more interesting the scene, the more rapid was the learning.

Massed Versus Spaced Practice

Research indicates that given equal practice time, spacing the practice sessions for a learning task produces faster learning than practicing without a break. An explanation is that the neural processes have time to consolidate if the learning is spaced. (See Theories of Forgetting under MEMORY AND FORGETTING.)

Programmed Learning

Following earlier work by **Skinner,** *teaching machines* and *programmed texts* briefly became popular. With these devices, the student proceeds at his or her own rate, and the material is programmed so there is immediate feedback about the correctness of responses. Results obtained using these once-promising techniques, as well as with other attempts to teach without a human teacher present (such as television instruction), have been disappointing.

CONDITIONING THROUGH SELF-STIMULATION

J.A. Olds (1954) found that electrodes implanted in the hypothalamus of a rat can stimulate the animal to such a degree that it would rather have the stimulation than eat. Rats learned to press a bar in order to get the reinforcement of the electrical stimulation. Some animals were pressing at the phenomenal rate of thousands of responses an hour for 15 or 20 hours, until they finally dropped from exhaustion.

Neal Miller (1969) reported that by using electrical stimulation of the pleasure centers of the brain as a reward, he could control certain visceral functions of rats. He could condition the rats to increase or decrease heart rate, blood pressure, intestinal contractions, amount of blood in the stomach wall, and formation of urine by the kidneys. In other words, the rats could learn to alter their autonomic processes by being reinforced. Miller's finding suggests that responses previously thought to be involuntary and automatic are susceptible to conditioning.

SOCIAL LEARNING

The *social learning* paradigm is illustrated by the work of **Rotter, Bandura,** and **Mischel.** The operant learning theory emphasizes that a person imitates a behavior because his imitation has been reinforced in the past. Bandura, however, contends that reinforcement is not necessary for *observational learning*. The observer can acquire novel responses without being directly rewarded for this action. Bandura and others (1963) studied the effect of *models* on children's behavior. Generally, they found children learned certain aggressive behaviors by first observing and then imitating a powerful adult. High-status and nurturant models were more likely to be imitated than low-status or nonnurturant ones.

FOR FURTHER READING

Reynolds, G.S. *A primer of operant conditioning.* 3rd ed. Glenview, Ill.: Scott, Foresman and Company, 1987.

Perception

INTRODUCTION

What we perceive is a construction. External stimuli are first registered by the peripheral receptors (such as the eye), then relayed to the brain, and finally they become our perceptions. Perception is the culmination of a synthesis of what our senses, our past experiences, our particular cognitive styles, and our expectations tell us. Perception is therefore an active process of interpretation.

For example, when we focus on something *(fixate)*, our eyes naturally wander. These small drifts can occur as often as five times a second. Because of these quick movements, called *saccadic eye movements* or *nystagmus*, we receive stimulation from more than the fixated object. Yet the object remains a constant perception. What we perceive does not precisely correspond to the retinal stimulation.

Gibson (1966) explains perception by postulating a system of information processing at the sensory level. The senses extract the invariant properties of the object, process this information, and transmit it to higher cortical centers. This view eliminates the need to assume a brain function that organizes discrete sensations into a perceptual configuration. Gibson thus criticizes the structuralist idea that perception is the aggregate of independent sensations.

Some perceptual processes are inherent in the organism. Investigations of the visual systems of frogs and cats (see EYE PHYSIOLOGY) show that neural responses to various stimulus patterns do not require previous training. The visual cliff experiments of **Gibson and Walk** (1960) show that neonates of all species, including humans, are able to discriminate depth (see EARLY DEVELOPMENT).

Other research has demonstrated that some visual experience is necessary for the development of normal perceptual functions. **Von Senden** (1960) reported that subjects blinded from birth by cataracts who later had their cataracts removed not only weren't able to "see" without training, but at first weren't even sure the sensations were coming through their eyes. About all they could make out were figure-ground relationships and color. **Riesen** (1947) raised chimpanzees in a dark environment and found that complex perceptual behaviors were seriously impaired. He also found that rearing them in diffuse light, for instance by placing goggles over their eyes, resulted in impaired visual-movement coordination.

PATTERNS

We perceive stimuli as patterns, such as *figure-ground* patterns. Objects are always seen against a background that serves to give them contour and boundary. In ambiguous situations, figure-ground reversals occur. The figure-ground pattern seems to be basic. Blind people whose sight is restored are able to perceive figure-ground relationships. Likewise, infants can make a figure-ground distinction.

STRUCTURE

We tend to structure stimuli within a context that is to some degree culture-specific. Geometric shapes are often perceived according to the following principles: *similarity*—objects of similar shape, size, color, etc., tend to be grouped together; *contiguity* or *proximity*—things tend to be patterned or grouped if they are near to each other; *closure* or *good continuation*—when part of a familiar figure is seen, it tends to be perceived as the completed closed figure; *common fate*—a group of objects that appear to move together are perceived as forming a whole; and *pragnanz*—a pattern is perceived in such a way as to make it the best or most correct pattern possible, as when a misspelled word is read as correct.

ILLUSIONS

Sometimes the perceptual process plays tricks and we perceive things that are grossly unreal. We thus experience an illusion. Illusions vary with cultures and with age. The more commonly studied illusions are:

The *Müller-Lyre illusion*—two lines of equal length are seen as unequal depending on what surrounds them.

The *phi phenomenon*—lights going off and on at a certain optimal rate give the illusion of movement. (Neon advertising arrows illustrate the phi phenomenon.)

The *ponzo illusion*—equal lengths will appear unequal if placed between converging lines. (The Ponzo illusion increases with age, suggesting that the illusion depends on learning.)

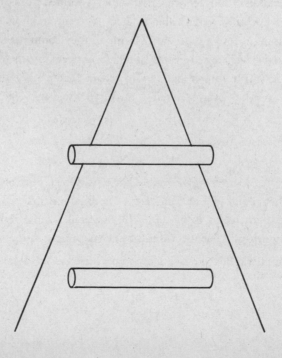

The *autokinetic effect*—a simple spot of light in a darkened room will appear to move erratically. This apparent motion occurs when there is no *frame of reference.*

DEPTH PERCEPTION

The retinal image is only two-dimensional. Although it has no third dimension to give depth, we perceive depth nevertheless. Depth perception comes from various cues. The perception of these cues is either *monocular* (one eye) or *binocular* (two eyes).

Monocular Cues to Depth

The size of the retinal image is larger for nearby objects and smaller for distant objects. We perceive an object as farther away when its retinal image is smaller.

An object that seems to obscure part of another object is perceived to be closer. This is called *interposition.*

Representational artists frequently take advantage of *linear perspective,* in which it appears that both distant objects and parallel lines converge at the horizon; the more distant an object, the higher on the horizon it appears to be. According to *gradient perspective,* closer objects seem to have more texture.

To a moving observer, distant objects appear to move in the same direction, while nearer objects appear to move in the opposite direction. Nearer objects seem to move more rapidly than more distant objects. This is called *motion parallax.*

Binocular Cues to Depth

Because the two eyes are located at different places, each eye receives a slightly different stimulus. The difference in views is the *retinal disparity* or *stereoscopic effect.*

As an object moves closer to the perceiver, the eyes *converge.* This means that the eyes rotate so that the image of the object remains focused on the fovea.

HEBB'S CELL ASSEMBLIES

Some perceptual phenomena appear to be innate (such as figure-ground patterns). Others, especially illusions, appear to be learned. **D.O. Hebb** (1949) considers perception to be largely learned. His most fundamental postulate is the concept of *cell assemblies.* A cell assembly is a group of cortical neurons that make up a circuit in the cerebral cortex. These functionally associated assemblies are developed through practice early in life—a neurological equivalent of learning. Cell assemblies come about through the development of synaptic knobs on cell endings that are in close proximity to active cell bodies. The active cell and associated cells form a circuit that operates as a unit.

For example, a sensory neuron excites a localized area of the cortex. The activity spreads to adjacent associated areas. With repeated excitation, the associated nerves become assemblies that are fixed as a unit. Thus, simple figures like triangles are perceived as triangles and not as three discrete lines.

SENSORY DEPRIVATION

During the 1930s, **Metzger** studied the effects of exposure to a structureless visual field. His apparatus, called a *Ganzfeld*, was a square surface with wings extended toward the observer on three sides. The field was illuminated with a neutral light. After 20-minute exposures to the Ganzfeld, subjects showed extreme fatigue, feelings of great lightness of body, poor motor coordination, and disturbed time perception. One-third of the subjects experienced complete disappearance of the faculty of vision for short periods of time. Metzger's conclusion was that persistent uniform stimulation without a *structured field* results in failure of the perceptual mechanism to produce a *phenomenal field*.

Research by **Hebb** at McGill University during the 1950s concentrated on total *sensory deprivation*. Subjects were deprived of visual, auditory, and tactile stimulation for periods of up to seven days. Under these conditions, reactions included hallucinations, anxiety, confusion, somatic complaints, feelings of depersonalization, inability to concentrate, and increased suggestibility. A later investigation at Boston City Hospital studied subjects immersed in a tank of tepid water. Symptoms like the ones described above occurred, except they happened earlier and more intensely.

One explanation for the effects of sensory deprivation is that the innate need for stimulation makes the lack of incoming stimuli a need-drive condition. Where there is not enough input, fantasies, sleep, boredom, and displeasure occur.

PERCEPTUAL DEFENSE

Perception can vary with the meaning the stimulus has for the perceiver. In other words, perception is mediated by *cognition*. Studies of *perceptual defense* (called at the time the *"new look in perception"*) have shown that the recognition threshold for emotionally charged stimuli is different from the threshold for neutral stimuli. For instance, children overestimate the size of coins as compared with equal-sized paper discs. Also, subjects tend to have a higher perceptual threshold for certain sex-related words as compared with neutral words.

FOR FURTHER READING

Kaufman, L. *Sight and mind: An introduction to visual perception.* 2nd ed. New York: Oxford University Press, 1987.

Cognition

MEMORY AND FORGETTING

Pioneer Work of Ebbinghaus

Using himself as a subject and *nonsense syllables* (such as VOL, RIZ, and TAV) as the material to be learned, **Ebbinghaus** developed methods of measuring both learning and retention. He worked so carefully that the results of his experiments have never been seriously challenged.

His *savings method*, or *method of relearning*, was the measure of the time it took to relearn a previously learned list. How much was saved from the first learning was reflected in how much less time it took to learn the list a second time. One finding was that original *overlearning*—repeating the list beyond a minimal standard—resulted in both a saving of time and a reduction of errors upon relearning.

Ebbinghaus's *retention curve* is classic. It depicts the general nature of forgetting—an initial drop-off, followed by slower forgetting with increased time.

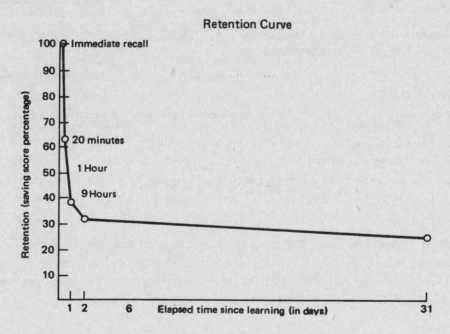

Retention Curve

About 63% is remembered after 20 minutes, 38% after 1 day, 31% after 2 days, and 25% after 31 days.

Short-Term Memory

Recent experiments have concentrated on fine distinctions of the memory system. Studies have found that immediate memory fades much more quickly than Ebbinghaus had thought. This led to the notion

143

of two memory systems, *long-term memory* (LTM) and *short-term memory* (STM). Short-term memory is similar to James's concept of the *primary memory system*. Short-term memory is the material that can be retained without rehearsal.

An important study by **Peterson and Peterson** (1959) introduced a new technique that prevents the subject from rehearsing material in STM. Subjects were exposed to three consonants, then asked to count backward by threes from a given number, then asked to recall the original series of letters. After 3 seconds, recall was about 80%; after 18 seconds of this distractive activity, the material could be correctly recalled only 10% of the time.

In a classic article, **George Miller** (1956) reported that the amount of information that can be apprehended on one exposure to new material is between five and nine items, depending on the kind of material used. Miller called this the *"magic number 7, ± 2."* The seven items may be seven sentences or phrases as well as seven words or letters. However, if the information is grouped or organized into *chunks*, the amount of information can be greatly increased.

The short-term memory system is actually two systems—STM and a briefer *very-short-term memory* (VSTM). Miller's magical number seven can be divided into five chunks retained in STM and two chunks retained in VSTM. If the information is auditory, the VSTM system is called *echoic memory;* if the information is visual, the VSTM system is called *iconic memory*.

A famous experiment by **George Sperling** (1960) demonstrated that the iconic memory system is a rapidly fading visual image preserved on the retina. The iconic image is believed to be an unprocessed "picture" retained at this peripheral retinal level. This is supported by findings that subjects exposed to a very bright light immediately following a presentation cannot report any of the information presented. It is as if the intense light wiped out the iconic memory.

Span of Attention

How much incoming information a person can attend to has been investigated through a technique called *shadowing*. The subject wears a set of headphones that allows a different message to be sent to each ear. This is called *dichotic listening*. **Cherry** (1953) found that if the subject repeats, or shadows, what he hears in one ear, he has difficulty making out what he hears in the unshadowed ear. About all that gets through is the gender of the speaker. All the other incoming channels seem to be blocked by the shadowing of the designated message.

Broadbent (1958) also employed a dichotic listening task, presenting three spoken digits simultaneously to each ear. He found that subjects reported the incoming digits in sequence—first the three from the left ear, then the three from the right ear. Broadbent felt these findings supported the notion of a *filter system* at the input level that holds incoming information until the processing channels are free to absorb and use it.

A later shadowing experiment by **Treisman** (1960) found that information from the unshadowed ear can be perceived if it is relevant to the shadowed message or if it is an important word, such as the subject's name. This finding raised questions about the Broadbent filter model.

The Broadbent model was also shown to be an incomplete explanation by the investigations of **Gray and Wedderburn** (1960). They gave their subjects a dichotic listening task modelled on "Dear-7-Jane" in the left ear and "3-Aunt-2" in the right ear. Presentations were too rapid for a filter system to switch back and forth, yet the subjects could report in pairs, serially, or backward. Apparently, as Treisman found, attention depends on the meaningfulness to the subject of the incoming information.

Eidetic Imagery

Some people are able to maintain a kind of mental picture of a stimulus even after it is removed. They are able to retain visual images that are almost photographic in clarity. These individuals can very accurately describe a scene as if they were still looking at it. This is called *eidetic imagery*. It is much more common in children than in adults and is most common with visual information.

Tip-of-the-Tongue Phenomenon

The common phenomenon of being unable to recall a word while simultaneously feeling the word is on the tip of one's tongue *(TOT)* has been investigated. The words that come to mind when one is searching for a word have some common connection to the target word, either through the sound or the lexical meaning. It seems we can selectively forget certain characteristics of a word yet retain other information about it. (See THEORIES OF FORGETTING.)

Mnemonics

Mnemonics is the term used to describe the system a person uses to encode information. *Mnemonic devices* are idiosyncratic systems that aid in memory and recall. Associating a newly encountered bit of information with something already familiar will facilitate learning the more recent item.

Reminiscence

An initial improvement on a memory task with the passage of time is called *reminiscence*. This phenomenon is contrary to the classical forgetting curve. However, reminiscence is only temporary; it is followed by the expected loss of retention.

Recall

Recall has been investigated using lists of words as the stimuli to be memorized and recalled. When recall in the order of presentation *(serial recall)* of the list is required, subjects exhibit a *primacy effect* and a *recency effect*. This means that more words at the beginning and/or the end of the presented list are recalled, while the greatest number of errors occur with words in the middle of the list. If certain items are distinguished from the others, as by using different typefaces or different colors, these items tend to be learned faster than the others. This is known as the *Von Restorff effect*.

Masking

Sometimes a tone or a visual image can mask another tone or image. For instance, radio static can mask the program's signal. An unusual situation occurs when a tone or image cannot be perceived because of a stimulus whose presentation follows it in time. This is termed *backward masking*. The explanation of this phenomenon assumes that an intense stimulus can initiate neural activity which, in a sense, "overtakes" the activity caused by the previous stimulus.

Theories of Forgetting

Decay

It is assumed that a *memory trace* deteriorates unless used. This principle was first espoused by Thorndike, who posited a *law of disuse*. The assumption that decay *alone* accounts for forgetting has never been popular among psychologists except when explaining STM.

Interference

Interference effects are currently believed to be more important than decay as an explanation of forgetting. According to this theory, forgetting arises because of competing experiences. The kinds of interference studied have been *retroactive* and *proactive inhibition*.

Retroactive Inhibition

When a new experience or amount of information interferes with recall of an earlier experience or unit of information, *retroactive inhibition* is said to have taken place. Forgetting is due to the interference of new learning on the recall of older material. To test for the presence of retroactive inhibition, a subject might be asked to learn a list of nonsense syllables, then to learn a second list, then to recall the first list. This paradigm can be sketched as follows: learn A—learn B—recall A. A control group can be told to learn the first list, rest, then recall the original list: learn A—rest—recall A. Retroactive inhibition is demonstrated if the experimental group does worse than the control group on recall of the original list. If this is the case, learning the second list has interfered with earlier learning.

Retroactive inhibition commonly occurs when ordinary waking life experience intervenes. Sleep, however, has been shown not to have an inhibiting effect on memory.

Proactive Inhibition

The second type of forgetting due to interference is called *proactive inhibition*. In this case, material learned earlier interferes with recall of material learned later. An example of this occurs when a student who learned Spanish in high school finds herself using Spanish vocabulary in a college French class. To test this hypothesis, the experimental group would: learn A—learn B—recall B. The control group would: rest—learn B—recall B.

Repression

Both scientific psychologists in the laboratory and Freudians in the consulting room use the term *repression* to explain how some memories are not easily recalled because of the emotional significance of the memory. The memory that is repressed is, in principle, recoverable, but its appearance in consciousness is prohibited or delayed. For example, a severe fright or trauma is repressed because recall of the experience is disturbing. Even minor lapses in memory, such as forgetting an appointment or a name, can be motivated by repression.

Obliteration of the Memory Trace

As information gets transferred from short-term to long-term memory, there is a *consolidation* period during which changes in the nervous system occur. If the *memory trace* is disrupted during this period, memory loss occurs.

A demonstration of this hypothesis is given when people with brain concussions experience amnesia for events that occurred immediately prior to the injury. Another term for this experience is *retrograde amnesia.*

Disruption of the memory trace has been produced in animals by using electroconvulsive shock (ECS) following a learning experience. If the shock is administered shortly after the learning experience, the animal shows little recall of the learned task. The assumption is that the shock interferes with the consolidation process and causes the loss of the memory.

Accessibility or Retrievability

Some psychologists believe that the problem of information retrieval is related to the way in which information was originally encoded. It is frequently found that a person who uses an efficient strategy for encoding (a useful mnemonic) will find that the information is more accessible when needed.

Long-Term Memory Storage: See Brain Physiology

PSYCHOLINGUISTICS

Introduction

The study of language and psychology, called *psycholinguistics,* was given a major boost upon the publication of a classic work by **Whorf** (1950) on Native American languages. Whorf found that language not only serves a communicative function, but also embodies and perpetuates a particular world view. Whorf went on to hypothesize that the language one learns and uses directs the formation of one's perception and thought. Specifically, the *Sapir-Whorf hypothesis* asserts that different linguistic communities perceive and conceive reality in different ways. Even *lexical* and *rhythmic features* (the actual words and inflection) of a language convey more than one level of meaning. For example, the Inuit or Eskimo people, who live in cold and stormy climates, have many more words for snow than do dwellers in more temperate climates, such as English-speaking people.

Semantic Differential

Denotative meaning refers to the specific object or event or phenomenon that a word describes. *Connotative* meaning refers to additional dimensions of meaning carried by a word, such as a word's emotional meaning. The *semantic differential,* developed by **Osgood** (1957), is a measure of the *connotative* meaning of words. Osgood found that people fit words into an internal semantic structure that evaluates meaning on three basic dimensions—*evaluative* (good-bad), *potency* (strong-weak), and *activity* (active-passive). Osgood found that these dimensions exist across different languages and cultures. This suggests that these three dimensions represent the basic information humans need to understand people, objects, and events in their environment. Of the three, evaluation seems the most important. According to Osgood, the tendency of people to evaluate on the good-bad dimension is so powerful that once a word is seen as describing something "good," additional information cannot reduce people's attraction to that object. On the other hand, if something or someone is connoted to be "bad," all other attributes, no matter how positive, won't increase people's attraction to that person or thing.

Lexical Markings

A measure of the way verbal concepts are organized and understood is called *lexical markings*. Certain words or phrases are basic and "unmarked," such as *greater than, tall,* and *heavy*. Other words and phrases are "marked," such as *less than, short,* and *light,* and are presumed to be derived from the unmarked form. Children understand unmarked forms at an earlier age than marked forms, and adults can remember unmarked forms more easily than the marked forms. Also, an unmarked form can represent the entire dimension. If you ask "How tall is she?" she could be tall or short. But asking "How short is she?" implies that she is short.

The Structure of Language

Elements

Psycholinguists assume there are three basic constituent elements of language—*phonemes, morphemes,* and *syntax*.

All languages are composed of various sounds, called *phonemes*. Phonemes are the meaningful sound units that can be distinguished in a language. For example, the word *cat* has three phonemes—*k, a,* and *t*.

Phonemes are combined in various ways to form *morphemes,* which are the smallest language units having distinct and separate meanings. For example, *handful* has two morphemes—*hand* and *ful*.

Morphemes are arranged in certain ways to form phrases, clauses, and sentences. The set of rules for forming such arrangements is called *syntax*. The rules of syntax taken together constitute the *grammar* of the language.

Transformational Grammar

Noam Chomsky investigated the properties of grammar shared by all languages. He called these rules *generative transformational grammar* because they can generate an infinite number of sentences. According to Chomsky, each person possesses some competence for language. That is, each person possesses some internal capacity both to generate and to interpret sentences according to rules. While actual speech is determined by habit and learning, grammar rules seem innate.

Basic to the study of grammar is the sentence. Chomsky identified two structures of sentences—*deep structure* and *surface structure. Deep structure* is the intended meaning; *surface structure* is the actual series of words and sounds. For example, the two sentences "John is eager to please," and "John is easy to please," have similar surface structures but different deep structures. The rules governing these transformations compose the *grammar* of the language.

Teaching Language to an Animal

Recent attempts to teach language to chimpanzees seem to have been having only mild success. The chimp **Washoe** was raised to use American sign language. Washoe was reported to have mastered over 100 signs and seemed to be able to use them conceptually.

Terrace (1979), reviewing data he collected on his own chimp at Columbia University, questions whether chimps can use language conceptually at all. This issue seems to have lost scientists' attention in recent years and is considered unresolved.

Primary and Secondary Thought

The two thought processes described by Freud are *primary* and *secondary* process thinking. The mental life of children is characterized by primary process thinking. Children are much more spontaneous than are adults. Among adults, primary process thinking might be so impermissible that it occurs only in dreams, if then. Primary process thinking is primitive, irrational mental functioning with no negatives and no sense of time. Secondary process thinking is organized, rational, and controlled. Primary process thinking corresponds to an early level of cognitive development described by Piaget as *preoperational processing*. (See Cognitive Development in the Developmental Psychology section of this book.)

FOR FURTHER READING

Neisser, U. *Cognitive psychology*. New York: Appleton-Century-Crofts, 1967.

Developmental Psychology

PHYSIOLOGICAL DEVELOPMENT

Development corresponds to *biogenetic law,* which is the principle that states that the development of each individual recapitulates the evolution of the species. Stated another way, *ontogeny recapitulates phylogeny.*

Development is a continuous process that begins at conception. The sperm cell from the father penetrates the wall of the ovum, or egg, from the mother. Immediately the process of *mitosis,* or cell division, begins: the fertilized ovum divides and subdivides into millions of cells. These cells assume special functions and differentiate into the various body systems. This is the *ontogenesis* of the organism—the individual's developmental process.

The fertilized *ovum,* called a *zygote,* begins to grow immediately. Between 24 and 36 hours after fertilization, the zygote makes its first cell division. Within two weeks the zygote is firmly implanted in the wall of the uterus.

Once the growing egg is successfully lodged in its new home, development is rapid. This is the period of the *embryo,* from two to eight weeks. The embryo even at two weeks has begun to take some shape. It has a discernible head and tail, front and back, and left and right sides. By the third week, a primitive heart has developed and has begun to beat. All the major organs, nervous system, and body parts are developed during this period. The embryo is about one inch long.

From the second month, the embryo phase gives way to the period of the *fetus.* The rudimentary body systems established in the embryo become more developed and begin to function. The reproductive system begins to develop and unprovoked spontaneous movements occur. The fetus period lasts until birth.

The sequence of development in these prenatal phases is fixed and invariable. The body parts and internal organs develop in the same order and at about the same age in all fetuses. Development is *cephalocaudal,* or from head to foot. The head of the fetus develops much earlier than its legs. Development is also *proximodistal,* meaning that the more central body parts, such as the arms, develop earlier than the peripheral parts, such as the fingers. Activities are from mass to specific or from large, gross movements to small, fine ones. Development is differentiated by sex, with girls being more advanced at birth than boys.

HEREDITY

Hereditary characteristics are transmitted by the *chromosomes.* Each sperm cell has 23 rodlike bodies, or chromosomes; each ovum cell likewise has 23 chromosomes. From conception on, each human cell contains 23 pairs of chromosomes. On the chromosomes are thousands of *genes,* the carriers of hereditary traits. The gene is composed of a chemical called DNA, which contains the genetic code and is in effect

151

the "program" for the body's cells. With so many genes available on each chromosome, the possible combinations are infinite, thus accounting for the differences in individuals even with the same parents.

One of the 23 pairs of chromosomes in the fertilized cell determines the sex of the organism. The ovum always contains an X chromosome; the sperm can contain either an X or a Y. The union of an X from the ovum with an X from the sperm produces a female. An XY combination results in a male.

Abnormalities in the combinations of chromosomes lead to genetic defects, emotional and behavioral dysfunctions, and sexual abnormalities. In some cases, the genital appearance *(phenotype)* does not coincide with the genetically determined sex *(genotype)*. *Teratogens* are substances from the environment that invade the developing fetus and cause abnormalities.

Klinefelter's syndrome occurs with an XXY combination. The person is phenotypically male but there is no masculinization at puberty. Tests for the genotype show up female.

Turner's syndrome occurs when one sex chromosome is lacking, producing an XO combination. The person is phenotypically female but there are no gonads and no sex hormones are secreted.

Down syndrome, mistakenly called *mongolism* in the past, is caused by aberrations in chromosomes other than sex chromosomes. It is characterized by mental retardation, a broad skull and slanted eyes, physical deformities, and reduced activity.

Phenylketonuria (PKU) is an inherited disorder caused by a defective gene that affects metabolism. Toxic chemicals are not properly metabolized in the brain. This disorder is characterized by severe mental deficiency. If the problem is detected at birth through a simple diagnostic urine test, babies can be put on special diets that neutralize the effects of the disorder and permit normal mental development.

A predisposition to *schizophrenia* is likely to have some genetic basis which, in turn, becomes exacerbated through excessively strong physiological reactions to mild stress, slow recovery from autonomic imbalance, and excessive stimulus generalization (**Mednick,** 1958).

EARLY DEVELOPMENT

The newborn infant *(neonate)* continues to grow according to the cephalocaudal developmental principle. During the first year, relative increases in size and weight are greater than at any later time. Birth weight doubles during the first six months and almost triples in the first year.

Girls develop faster than boys, beginning even in the fetal period. Infant girls have more fat and less water than boys, and girls' growth is less variable than that of boys.

Perceptual Development

In circumstances in which the mother is the primary caretaker, the mother's face is a primary organizer of the infant's perceptual experience. By four weeks, the infant can follow the mother's face with its eyes. By two months, the child will smile when a face (or even a mask resembling a face) is presented. Social smiling to any human face continues until around eight months. At this age, the baby begins to discriminate friend from stranger, and an unfamiliar face generally elicits *stranger anxiety* (**Spitz,** 1965). It is at this age, according to Piaget, that the baby begins to acquire the cognitive structure of recognition of an object.

Some perceptual systems are innate in the neonate. Besides the seemingly prewired response to the face configuration, especially to the eyes and forehead region, the infant appears to have innate depth perception.

Experiments by **Gibson** (1960) with a *visual cliff* indicate that infants avoid what seems to be a drop-off in the floor beneath them. Infants were placed on a glass sheet. Under the glass was a textured pattern. Half the pattern could be lowered to produce a visual illusion of depth. Infants did not cross over to the side that seemed to drop off. Even infants who could not crawl showed changes in autonomic processes, such as exhibiting an increased heart rate when placed on the deep side. The effect lessened as the visual cliff became less deep.

Motor Development

At birth the neonate is capable of a large number of responses independent of those acquired through learning or practice. Reflexes such as sucking and grasping are evident at birth. The neonate responds to sudden stimulation by throwing its arms apart and extending its legs (the *startle reflex*).

Motor responses generally develop in a uniform pattern, although there is variation in the speed of development. Most locomotor behaviors depend upon maturation, not learning. Infants bound to cradleboards for the first three or four months of life, as in the Hopi culture, nevertheless show appropriate walking behavior at about the same ages as children not so confined in infancy. Likewise, practice will not accelerate a motor skill (such as shoelace tying) that the child is not mature enough to possess.

Speech Development

Early vocalizations are largely motor responses and show a definite sequence of development. Infants of all nations and cultures tend to make the same sounds in the same sequence. Later, sounds not used in the infant's language disappear—presumably through extinction—while useful sounds are strengthened through reinforcement.

On the average, babies pronounce recognizable syllables by the third month. The first word is spoken around the end of the first year. These single words soon express complex meanings. One- and two-word phrases, called *holophrases* (like "Daddy go" or "more juice"), occur between 18 and 24 months. By the fourth year, the child understands rules of syntax and grammar well enough to construct any kind of sentence.

Speech can be accelerated or retarded through the environment. Babies reared in unstimulating orphanage environments vocalize less than babies reared in homes. Babies reared in middle-class homes show more frequent and varied sounds than babies reared in working-class homes.

First language acquisition involves a standard developmental sequence. The child's speech tends to be *egocentric;* that is, he talks overwhelmingly of his intentions and is not able to take another's point of view. Initial talk is about the way in which objects relate to each other or function; it is not just a naming of the object. The first nouns spoken stand for things that move, such as pets, persons, toys. The beginning language of the baby seems to be structure for encoding action events.

By about two or three years of age, the child is usually talking to himself or herself as well as to others. Eventually this constant talking becomes internal and the child develops *covert speech*.

Social Interaction

The neonate comes to life with a functioning nervous system, with orienting reflexes, and with certain survival responses. Yet, to make him or her a socially adaptive human requires interaction with another person, usually an adult caretaker.

The infant's interaction with the parent or caretaker provides the stimulation needed for further development of the emotional, cognitive, and motor processes. In turn, the caretaker's or parent's attitude—warmth, responsiveness, interest—is critical for the baby's growth.

Experiments with chimpanzees by **Harlow** (1959) illustrate some important issues concerning childrearing. Chimps reared with stark *wire surrogate mothers* and furry *terry cloth surrogate mothers* showed marked differences. Chimps preferred the feel of the cloth mothers and spent more time clinging to them even though the wire mothers had been the source of adequate food and nutrition. When the chimps were frightened experimentally, they fled to the terry cloth mothers for security.

In other experiments Harlow found that monkeys placed in isolation during the first few months of life showed extremely abnormal and autistic social and sexual behaviors. However, Harlow found that placing the isolate with normally reared but younger monkeys would cause significant remission of the pathological behaviors.

Spitz (1946) found that nursery babies deprived of maternal attention at some point between the sixth and eighth month of life exhibited a syndrome of weepiness, withdrawal, some insomnia, and a general decline in health and affect. Spitz called this state *anaclitic depression*.

Similar results were found by **Bowlby** (1960). In Bowlby's phylogenetic view, the bond between infant and mother ensures both safety and species reproductivity. If this attachment bond is broken by separation, the child reacts to this *object loss* by a typical sequence of protest, despair, then detachment. Bowlby posits that much of psychopathology can be accounted for by faulty attachment-separation processes.

An important contemporary approach to the study of early social bonds is **Mahler**'s work on *separation* and *individuation*. She calls the child's early absolute dependence upon the mothering one a *social symbiosis*. It is from this symbiotic bond, together with inborn constitutional factors, that the psychological makeup of the child is derived. Distortions in the symbiotic relationship lead to infantile as well as adult psychosis.

At the height of the *symbiotic stage,* generally in the third quarter of the first year, the child begins his or her *separation* and *individuation*. The first process refers to the infant's emergence from *symbiotic fusion* with the mothering one to the development of *object constancy*. The individuation process refers to the internal formation of a *self-representation*.

The separation process is facilitated by the child's achieving locomotion during the toddler stage. However, early separation results in anxiety, so the infant returns to the mothering one for support and security. This is called the *rapprochement phase*. The child is able to tolerate more separation as he or she substitutes the actual symbiotic object for an internalized representation of her. The child gives up the symbiotic partner by taking the mothering one in, identifying with this person, and thereby assimilating this representation into the psychic structure as part of his or her *self-identity*.

Sex Role Socialization

The empiricist tradition points to the role of socialization in a child's learning his or her gender identity and sex roles. **Maccoby and Jacklin,** in reviewing the research, contend that there are very few biologically determined differences: boys are more active and aggressive, probably due to the effects of the male androgen hormones; boys have better visual-spatial perceptual abilities; girls have better verbal skills, at least through high school.

John Money found in his studies that sex assignment is more powerful than genotypic influences in determining gender identity and sex-typed behaviors.

Two other researchers support the idea that sex roles are socialized. **Homer** posited that the stereotypic female attitudes of caution, dependency, and timidity are part of a socialized behavior pattern she termed "fear of success." **Sandra Bem** wrote that *gender-stereotyped* individuals have rigid stereotyped cognitive constructs that lead to stereotyped perceptions. Bem feels it is the stereotyped individual who is out of sync with the modern world not the *androgynous* individual who is able to combine attributes of both sexes and use whatever is appropriate at any specific moment. The scale she developed to assess how stereotyped or androgynous a person is is the *Bem Sex Role Inventory* (BSRI).

Psychologists who disagree with Bem's position claim that gender-specific hormones make more of a difference than the empiricists want to admit and that anatomical structures and functions contribute as much as, if not more than, social influences in determining how the individual perceives his or her gender identity and sex role.

Imprinting and Critical Periods

Imprinting is an phenomenon observed in certain animals in which a newborn will follow a moving object, presumably its mother. Research by **Lorenz** (1950) has shown that there are *critical periods* for imprinting. During the critical period, the animal will follow a model. Lorenz imprinted graylag geese between 12 and 17 hours after birth so they would follow him, even if there later were other geese available as models. The attachment is not reversible—the original learning persists.

Critical periods for the establishment of primary social relationships probably occur in human development, although the process is not as well researched as with Lorenz's geese. It is probably impossible to conduct controlled laboratory experiments on the development of human infant social relationships, so this matter may never be resolved by rigorous scientific experimentation.

Enriched Environment

The effects of an enriched environment on growth and development have been studied at Berkeley by **Rosenzweig** (1960). In these experiments, rats were reared in either enriched or impoverished environments. The results indicated that the enriched animals were significantly superior in total brain weight, cortical thickness, number of neuroglial cells, and size of cortical cell bodies. The implications of this study for human development scream out loudly and clearly.

COGNITIVE DEVELOPMENT

Cognition is the process of organizing, representing, storing, recalling, connecting, and abstracting information. The study of cognition also includes processes such as thinking, speaking, and problem solving. Another term for cognition is *higher mental processes.* Children come equipped with potentials for cognition that develop and evolve with age. Some cognitive processes are innate, others are learned, and most result from an interaction between the organism and the environment.

Piaget's Developmental Concepts

The most systematic and well-known theory of cognitive development was developed by **Jean Piaget** of Geneva. To Piaget, the child is an active organism who tries to make sense of the environment by dealing actively with it. The child exhibits adaptive behavior that facilitates coping with and eventually mastering the environment. Piaget called himself a *genetic epistemologist,* meaning that it was his aim to study the genetics, or development, of children's epistemology, or the study of how people know what they know. He staunchly maintained the position that each child is a budding scientist experimenting on the world and eventually developing an understanding of the world based primarily on his or her own experiments.

Adaptation begins with random, diffuse, mass reflexes, and progresses through invariant developmental stages to the formal, logical reasoning of adulthood. The basic unit of adaptation is the *operation.* Children master operations appropriate for each cognitive level. An operation is a kind of mental routine, a rule. The acquisition of more and more cognitively sophisticated operations is the heart of intellectual growth.

The two processes of cognitive growth are *assimilation* and *accommodation.* They are functionally invariant, inborn, and universal.

When a child *assimilates,* he or she incorporates and interprets new information based on pre-existing cognitive structures, or *schema.* He thus achieves a balance *(equilibrium)* between himself and his environment. As his experience widens, however, the application of the assimilation function creates a disorganization *(disequilibrium)* since the new information no longer fits the old schema. The child thus *accommodates* to the new stimuli by changing his schema.

Cognitive development thus proceeds sequentially in discrete stages, with each new stage built upon an earlier one. The child develops the structural invariants that underlie the operations of intelligent thought—time, speed, space, logic, number, geometry, and movement.

There are four major stages of cognitive development in the Piagetian model: the *sensorimotor,* the *preoperational,* the *concrete operational,* and the *formal operational* stages.

The *sensorimotor period* lasts from birth to about two years of age, before the appearance of language and the symbolic function. This stage is characterized by a logic of actions starting with reflexes and proceeding through habits, imitation, then delayed imitation. Two major developments of the sensorimotor child are *object permanence* and *object constancy.* Learning that objects continue to exist even when they are out of the sight of the child is called *object permanence.* Learning that objects maintain their sizes and shapes despite changes of location is called *object constancy.*

From about one-and-a-half to seven years of age, the child experiences the *preoperational* period. It is during this period that the beginning of symbolic schemas (including, but not limited to, language) and pretend fantasy activities occur. The language developed during this stage is characteristically *egocentric*. Piaget uses the term *egocentric* to mean that the child experiences the world through himself, as if he is the center of the experienced universe. Reasoning is based overwhelmingly on what the child perceives in his immediate situation. What does not exist in the child's "here-and-now" barely gets concern. The preoperational child has only a very limited capacity to engage in abstract thought. For example, while a preoperational child may play games and think he is doing what the rules require, in fact the child may not be playing by the rules at all!

From about 7 to 12 years of age, the child goes through the period of *concrete operations*. This is characterized by the achievement of true *operations*. The child understands the principles of *reversibility* (some changes in the appearance or constitution of objects can be reversed) and *conservation* (changing an object's shape will not change its mass), and can classify objects on more than one dimension. The concrete operational child acquires a social character and is able to cooperate with others. He is able to understand and adhere to rules.

From 12 years of age on, the child is in the period of *formal operations*. During this period the child masters abstract reasoning and becomes capable of problem solving through *deduction*. Genuine cooperation and a fascination with rules result in the settling of problems through rule invoking. According to Piaget, the child of this period is almost capable of becoming a member of adult society.

Moral Development

Piaget theorized that a child's moral development passes from an initial *heteronomous* stage—in which rules are believed to be absolute and transgressions are thought always to result in punishment *(moral realism)*—to a more relativistic, *autonomous* stage. At around eight years of age, the child discovers that infractions of rules can be examined on the basis of the intentions of the actor. Actions are judged according to their relative justness or unjustness. During the earlier heteronomous period, the child believed that rules exist independently of people; during the autonomous stage the child understands that rules are made by people and can be altered or adjusted by people.

A popular formulation of moral development based on Piaget's cognitive developmental sequence has been presented by **Kohlberg,** who posits six stages of moral development grouped into three levels. According to Kohlberg, children pass through the sequence in an invariant progression, although the more advanced levels are generally not reached by most people. The stages relate to moral judgments rather than to moral conduct, so there is a low correlation between assessed moral level and manifest behavior.

Kohlberg's stages of moral development are: (1) *premoral*—(a) orientation toward punishment and obedience, (b) naive, egotistic orientation; (2) *morality of conventional rule* (conformity)—(a) "good boy/good girl" attitude or social approval, (b) reliance on precepts of authority or "law and order"; (3) *morality of self-accepted moral principles*—(a) adherence to contractual obligations and democratically accepted law or "social contract," (b) adherence to principles of individual conscience and universal ethical principles.

FREUDIAN DEVELOPMENTAL THEORIES

In the Freudian developmental paradigm, the person passes through a sequence of stages of emotional growth culminating in the mature individual who is capable of love and work free of anxiety and conflict.

Freud postulated a basic biological energy with which each person is born. The amount of energy is fixed, and it gets channeled in uniform ways. The energy takes the form of instincts or drives—pleasure drives, life-preserving drives, and aggressive drives. The energy becomes attached to objects in the interest of satisfying these drives. This attachment is called *cathexis*.

As the child grows, his pleasure-seeking drive, called his *libido*, gets attached *(cathected)* to different parts of his body. Later, at maturity, the libido becomes attached to another person, and a love relationship evolves.

The *psychosexual* stages the child passes through correspond to the parts of the body *(erogenous zones)* that are cathected and give him pleasure.

During the *oral* stage, in infancy, pleasure is derived from the mouth by sucking and eating, thumbsucking, and putting objects into the mouth.

During the *anal* stage, between two and three years of age, pleasure is derived from the anal area through defecation and through anal masturbation. Fantasies at this stage are often sadistic in nature.

During the *phallic-Oedipal* stage, from about age three, the genitals are cathected and pleasure is derived from manipulation and masturbation of the penis or clitoris. Fantasies at this stage revolve around sexual relations with the opposite-sex parent. This presents a conflict for the child since he or she soon realizes that the desired mate is unobtainable. This desire is termed the *Oedipus complex* and, like the Greek myth, the fantasy involves killing the rival in order to possess the loved parent. Resolution of the Oedipal conflict comes when the child gives up longing for the loved parent and instead resolves to find his or her own mate. When the child figures this out, he or she *identifies* with the same-sex parent. In identifying with the same-sex parent, the child *internalizes* the parental values and thus develops a *superego*. This internal structure becomes the child's *conscience*.

In the elementary school years, the sexual interests become quiescent. During this *latency period,* the child directs his or her energy toward social development and learning.

The *genital* stage begins in early adolescence, when the child begins pursuing external sexual interests.

If the development does not progress normally, if the child experiences a trauma or a severe fright or just imagines one, his or her development is *arrested* and the person can become *fixated* at a given stage. Though his cognitive and physical skills might develop appropriately for a given chronological age, emotional development could be stuck at an earlier stage.

ERIKSON'S DEVELOPMENTAL MODEL

Following Freud, the psychoanalyst **Erik Erikson** formulated a paradigm of development that stresses social aspects in addition to sexual aspects. For Erikson, growth occurs in *psychosocial stages* in which the child interacts with his or her environment. Each stage presents a specific socially related problem that must be resolved if development is to continue on schedule.

Erikson's Developmental Stages

Age	Freudian Stage	Social Problem
I. birth through first year	oral-sensory	basic trust vs. mistrust
II. second year	anal-muscular	autonomy vs. shame and doubt
III. third through fifth year	phallic	initiative vs. guilt
IV. sixth year to onset of puberty	latency	industry vs. inferiority
V. adolescence	genital-puberty	identity vs. role confusion
VI. early adulthood		intimacy and solidarity vs. isolation
VII. young and middle adulthood		generativity vs. stagnation
VIII. maturity		ego integrity vs. despair

FOR FURTHER READING

Ginsburg, H., and Opper, S. *Piaget's theory of intellectual development.* 2nd ed. Englewood Cliffs, N.J.: Prentice-Hall, 1978.

Hurlock, E.B. *Developmental psychology.* 5th ed. New York: McGraw-Hill, 1980.

Family Systems Therapy

The family systems approach looks at the total interaction of all individuals in a *system*. The model differs from traditional therapy and counseling, which focuses on the individual as the unit of treatment. And it differs from traditional group therapy in which groups rarely have a history together and are not connected to each other outside of the therapy situation.

The major family systems theories are: *Structured,* associated with **Minuchin;** *Strategic,* associated with **Haley;** *Systems,* associated with **Bowen;** *Experimental,* associated with **Satir** and **Whittaker;** and *Psychodynamic,* associated with **Ackerman.**

General tenets of all these approaches include the idea that the system is an organized whole. The behavior of any one member is seen in the context of the whole system. Behavioral patterns are manifestations of the family structure. For example, a child might have more power than is optimal because the relationship between the parents is faulty. So the goal of an intervention would be to re-align the power by restructuring the family dynamics. The restructuring is done first by joining the family system and then unbalancing it to create a more viable system.

Recent Psychotherapies

Primal Therapy

Primal therapy was developed by **Arthur Janov.** He posited that neurotic behavior is the result of extremely early—meaning, around the time of birth—experiences of deprivation. This nonfulfillment of basic needs causes the child to repress his *true self* and substitute his *neurotic self.* The therapeutic process requires the patient to re-experience early situations directly, at first in marathon individual sessions and later in regularly scheduled group sessions. The cathartic effect of re-experiencing these primal scenes leads, according to this model, to remission of neurotic behaviors.

Thomas Szasz

Szasz contends that nonorganic psychic disturbances are a myth and that deviations from the norm are not medical problems but social and legal ones. He feels that only physical abnormalities can be classified as diseases. Consequently mental illness is a *myth,* and the term should be abandoned.

MAJOR PERSONALITY STUDIES

Authoritarianism

Authoritarianism refers to the attitude system of antidemocratic sentiments, ethnic prejudice, political conservatism, rigid moralistic rejection of the unconventional, and low tolerance for ambiguity. The classic study of the authoritarian personality was undertaken by **Adorno, Frenkel-Brunswik, Levinson, and Sanford.** The work was carried out in the late 1940s and published in 1950. The scale they developed to measure authoritarianism is the *Fascist Scale,* or *California F-Scale.* The items are worded so that agreement indicates an authoritarian attitude. This type of construction and scoring method has led to criticisms that the F-Scale is confounded by acquiescence or yea-saying response biases.

The study, based on psychoanalytic theory, describes the authoritarian as a person who uses **repressive defenses to control sexual and aggressive needs and who develops** conforming, submissive, and conventional patterns of interpersonal behavior. Repressed hostility and sexual impulses are projected outward, and the person feels surrounded by depraved and dangerous individuals.

The studies of the so-called authoritarian personality have been criticized as politically motivated and politically biased. The original work on the authoritarian personality was done during the heyday era of trait theory, an approach no longer in favor.

Need for Achievement

The need for achievement is a learned drive to compete and to strive for success. The need to achieve was postulated originally by **Henry Murray.** Research with the *n-Ach* variable was begun by **David McClelland** and his associates using responses to TAT cards. The assumption was that expressed achievement fantasies reflect the strength of the achievement motive. Later studies indicated that high parental expectations and early independence training are positively correlated with high achievement motivation. People who are achievement oriented prefer reasonably challenging tasks to tasks that are too easy or too difficult.

Field Dependency and Independency

Witkin and his colleagues (1954) were concerned with the way personal characteristics influence perceptions. They developed a battery of orientation tests that discriminated subjects who could locate objects and themselves without regard to the environment from subjects who relied on the environment for location cues. One test was the *Rod-and-Frame Test.* A vertical rod was presented against a rotating frame. Some subjects were able to perceive the rod as vertical no matter what the position of the frame. These subjects were called *field independent.* Others relied on the frame as a reference. These subjects were called *field dependent.* These assessments correspond to clinical assessments using Rorschach, MMPI, and interview measures. For instance, the inability to separate the stimulus from its context (field dependency) is associated with relative immaturity, submission to authority, poor impulse control, and low display of initiating activity.

Anxiety and Learning

A number of studies have investigated the relationship between anxiety level and learning. High-anxious people tend to learn simple conditioned responses more readily than low-anxious people. For instance, they will acquire a conditioned eyeblink to a puff of air sooner. High-anxious people tend to do less well on complex learning tasks—there is a negative correlation between anxiety level and school performance. Girls seem to have higher test anxiety than boys.

PSYCHOLOGICAL DISORDERS

The common distinction between relatively mild mental disorders—once called neuroses—and psychosis dates from psychiatry's first attempts during the latter part of the nineteenth century to categorize psychological disorders.

What follows is based on this classical nosological system. Keep in mind, though, that there is a current diagnostic system that is different from this one. The current system is based on the American Psychiatric Association's *Diagnostic and Statistical Manual Fourth Edition* (DSM-IV). We will review the DSM-IV later.

Neurosis

Charcot was the first to make a systematic study of the disorder he called *neurosis*. **Janet** followed with the first attempt to classify neuroses on the basis of their dynamics. The theory of neurosis developed by **Freud** is probably the most widely accepted and complete explanation to the present.

In the Freudian scheme, neuroses are chronically ineffective ways of dealing with personal problems and are caused by unconscious conflicts. Neuroses develop under the following conditions: (1) There is an inner conflict between drives and fears that prevents drive discharge. (2) Sexual drives are involved in this conflict. (3) The conflict has not been worked through to a realistic solution. Instead, the drives that seek discharge have been expelled from consciousness through repression or through another defense mechanism. (4) Repression merely succeeds in rendering the drives unconscious; it does not deprive them of their power and make them innocuous. Consequently, the repressed tendencies fight their way back to consciousness, but these repressed tendencies are now disguised as neurotic symptoms. (5) An inner conflict leads to neurosis in adolescence or adulthood only if a neurosis or a rudimentary neurosis based on the same type of conflict existed in early childhood.

In a neurosis, only part of the personality is affected. Reality for the person is not qualitatively changed, although its value might be diminished.

Conversion Hysteria

Conversion hysteria is characterized by bodily symptoms that resemble those of physical disease, such as paralysis, anesthesia, blindness, convulsions, or headaches. Anxiety is "converted" into an organic or bodily symptom that has no somatic basis.

Phobic Neurosis

Phobias are abnormal fear reactions. The psychoanalytic interpretation explains phobic reactions as caused by paralyzing conflict due to an increase in sexual excitation attached to an indifferent object. The individual unconsciously displaces anxiety, which is too disrupting and pervasive to be dealt with appropriately. The result is an irrational fear that is so intense as to interfere with the person's functioning. Since the fear is directed toward a specific object, the person hopes to reduce anxiety by avoiding the "phobic" object.

Obsessive Neurosis

The obsessional or *obsessive-compulsive* neurosis is characterized by persistent or urgently recurring thoughts *(obsessions)* and repetitively performed behaviors *(compulsions)* that bear little relation to the patient's realistic requirements.

Post-Traumatic Stress Disorder

Post-Traumatic Stress Disorder is a type of anxiety disorder following a severe, unusual, and unexpected trauma, such as being in a plane crash. The person will have some type of recurrent reexperiences of the trauma. There can be, for instance, intrusive painful recollections or recurrent painful dreams and nightmares. The person could experience dissociative states during which the trauma is relived in a very real way. These reactions can begin shortly after the trauma or months or even years later.

Psychosis

Psychotic reactions are more serious behavior disorders, almost inevitably requiring some period of hospitalization and/or treatment with drugs. The personality is disorganized, and normal social functioning is greatly impaired. There is a loss of contact with reality, language is distorted, and the unconscious often comes to direct verbal expression. The psychotic often experiences *delusions* and *hallucinations*. The psychotic adjustment utilizes primitive and fragmentary types of defenses such as regression to infancy and social withdrawal.

Psychotic reactions can be *process* (long-term and chronic) or *reactive* (acute with remission of symptoms usually occurring).

Manic-Depressive Psychosis

The *manic-depressive* psychotic manifests a particular kind of infantile, narcissistic dependency on a love object. To offset feelings of worthlessness, he or she requires a constant supply of love and moral support from a highly valued and idealized love object. As long as the object gives this support, the manic-depressive is able to function with enthusiasm and effectiveness. But because of strong self-punitive tendencies, the manic-depressive is bound to be disappointed by his or her object choice. Consequently, when the individual is disappointed by the idealized love object, ego functioning is impaired at every level. Behavior is then characterized by recurrent and exaggerated deviations of mood from the *manic* phase (strong excitement and elation) to the *depressive* phase (extreme fatigue, despondency, and sadness).

Schizophrenia

Schizophrenia is the most common of the psychotic disorders. Estimates are that half of all neuropsychiatric hospital beds are occupied by patients diagnosed as schizophrenic. Since the introduction of antipsychotic medication in the mid-1950s, the population of mental hospitals has been reduced by about two-thirds. However, this reduction has been accompanied by at least a two-fold increase in admissions, indicating that patients return quite often after release.

The word *schizophrenia,* first used by **Bleuler,** literally means "splitting the mind." It replaced the earlier term, *dementia praecox,* which means "youthful insanity." Although the linguistic root of the word "schizophrenia" suggests a split into parts, it is not the case that schizophrenia means or a schizophrenic exhibits "multiple personality." Schizophrenia is marked by disturbances in thinking, mood, and behavior. The thought disorders typical of schizophrenia have been termed *paleologic,* indicating the primitiveness of these mental processes. There are four classic categories of schizophrenia—*simple, hebephrenic, catatonic,* and *paranoid.*

Simple Schizophrenia

Simple schizophrenia is a dull and colorless reaction. Individuals with simple schizophrenia lack obvious interests and social assertiveness and develop a simple and secluded way of life. They appear introverted and preoccupied, and except for infrequent signs of irritability, they show little emotion.

Hebephrenic Schizophrenia

The hebephrenic state is characterized by wild excitement alternating with tearfulness and depression, vivid hallucinations, and absurd or bizarre delusions. Hebephrenics sometimes regress to very immature levels and display illogical and infantile thinking.

Catatonic Schizophrenia

Catatonic schizophrenics alternate between brief periods of uncontrolled excitement and much longer periods of immobility. In a controlled environment like a mental institution, a catatonic schizophrenic may go for weeks or months simply staring into space, rigidly resisting any change in position.

Paranoid Schizophrenia

Paranoid schizophrenia is the most common and the most vivid schizophrenic reaction. The thought processes of paranoid schizophrenics are dominated by the defense mechanism called *projection:* guilt and blame are projected outward to other people or institutions, while the individual professes innocence and unjust persecution. These individuals speak quite lucidly, and often quite convincingly, about an unreal world. *Hallucinations* and especially *delusions* frequently are present. Thinking in this state is more systematized than in the other schizophrenic categories. Often the themes have to do with delusions of grandeur and persecution.

Childhood Psychosis

Early Infantile Autism

This syndrome, first described by **Kanner,** includes withdrawal, obsessive desire to maintain the status quo, self-absorption, perseverative play, stereotypic movements, and many language disturbances or no language at all. Autism is present from early infancy. Although at one time autism was considered an early death sentence, people who suffer from autism are now capable of living a long life—and a productive life if they are cared for in a protective environment, such as a sheltered living facility.

Symbiotic Psychosis

This term is used by **Mahler** to describe a pathologic syndrome resulting from a faulty symbiotic relationship between infant and mother. The child is unable to progress beyond the closeness and complete dependency of the symbiotic union. Mahler feels this condition probably has some constitutional basis.

Korsakov's Psychosis

This syndrome is associated with chronic alcoholism and is characterized by *confabulation,* marked loss of memory, impaired attention, disorientation, and *emotional lability*.

Diagnostic and Statistical Manual, Fourth Edition (DSM-IV)

The DSM-IV is a multiaxial system. A patient or client is evaluated along five dimensions:

Axis I—clinical syndrome

Axis II—developmental disorders and personality disorders

Axis III—physical disorders and conditions

Axis IV—severity of psychosocial stressors

Axis V—global assessment of functioning

The DSM-IV does not attempt to infer causation; hence the term *neurosis* is omitted completely, since neurosis is based on the Freudian model of an unconscious conflict between psychic structures. Instead the term *disorder* is used.

The DSM-IV is the standard of diagnosis across North America. In other parts of the world a different classification system is in common use: *ICD-9.*

DRUG THERAPY

Major Tranquilizers (Neuroleptics)

Major tranquilizers, earlier called *neuroleptics,* produce a tranquilizing effect with little overall effect on consciousness. They are primarily used in treating schizophrenia and manic states. Major tranquilizers act to reduce the levels of certain neurotransmitters in the brain (especially dopamine); it is believed that schizophrenic reactions are related to an imbalance of *dopamine.* The major tranquilizers include *phenothiazine* derivatives, such as *chlorpromazine* (brand name: Thorazine). A long-term, irreversible side effect of phenothiazine use is *tardive dyskinesia,* a motor rigidity that results from depleted dopamine in certain parts of the brain. Chronic use of these drugs reduces dopamine to the point where the motor system becomes affected.

Another kind of tranquilizer, used mostly in treating manic-depression, is lithium carbonate. Unlike the phenothiazines, lithium carbonate can be quite toxic.

Antidepressants

Antidepressant drugs are used to correct an abnormal condition; they do not generally alter a normal condition into a euphoric or stimulated state. These drugs are most effective with *endogenous depressions,* those that are not merely reactions to simple precipitating circumstances. The three main classes are *tricyclic antidepressants, monoamine oxidase (MAO) inhibitors,* and *serotonin enhancers* (e.g., Prozac).

A treatment for severe depression that is not a drug treatment is *electro-convulsive therapy* (ECT). Electrodes are placed on either side of the forehead, and an electrical current is passed between them for one or two seconds. A series of about eight to ten treatments is administered over a period of a few weeks. Even though ECT seems inherently objectionable, its positive results make it an accepted treatment method for depression.

Antidepressants function by increasing the amount of effective neurotransmitters in the central nervous system. The antipsychotic medications do the opposite—they reduce the amount of active neurotransmitters.

Severe anxiety disorders, such as panic attacks, have been shown to be responsive to antidepressant treatment. The mechanism is not fully understood, but this treatment works for many people with panic attacks.

Sedatives, Tranquilizers, Hypnotics

These drugs act to depress cellular activity. They produce sedation at low doses, hypnosis at intermediate doses, anesthesia at higher doses, and death at extremely high doses. *Barbiturates* are the most widely used of this class. Nonbarbiturate hypnotics include *methaqualone* (Quaalude), tranquilizers such as Miltown, and alcohol.

Antiepileptics

Epilepsy is a chronic disease characterized by the occurrence of seizures during which there is a loss or disturbance of consciousness, at times accompanied by convulsions. In most cases epilepsy is related to some organic pathology in the brain. The current drug of choice to treat epilepsy is *Dilantin*.

Antiparkinsonian Agents

Parkinson's disease is a chronic, progressive disease of the central nervous system. Symptoms include muscular rigidity, spontaneous tremor, fixed facial expression, bizarre walk, and stereotyped hand and arm movements. A new treatment for this disease is *L-dopa*, a drug that is converted to dopamine in the brain; Parkinson's disease patients are deficient in this neurotransmitter.

PERSONALITY INVENTORIES

Psychological Assessment

MMPI (Minnesota Multiphasic Personality Inventory)

Perhaps the most popular objective test of personality in the US, the MMPI measures the nature and extent of emotional maladjustment. The test was standardized on a hospital population and is designed to detect pathological trends within the personality. The MMPI profiles psychiatric classifications such as paranoia, schizophrenia, depression, and hysteria. The test also contains a scale to measure faking and other scales to check on the respondent's answering biases. The MMPI, which has been revised and is now available as the MMPI-2, is designed to be computer-analyzed. Once scores on the MMPI scales have been obtained, results can be interpreted by computer, although most professionals who use this test do not rely exclusively on computer-generated interpretations.

Taylor Manifest Anxiety Scale (MAS)

The MAS is the classic technique for measuring anxiety. Fifty items from the MMPI are used for this scale. The items discriminate chronic anxiety reactions from more normal reactions.

Gough's CPI (California Psychological Inventory)

This inventory is similar to the MMPI, but the questions are not geared as much toward assessing pathology. Because of this, the CPI is sometimes called "the sane person's MMPI."

Q-Sort

The technique of the Q-Sort is similar to that of the Likert scale (see ATTITUDE STUDY). It is a way of assessing an individual's self-perceptions. The subject is given a set of statements and asked to distribute them in a set number of piles representing a continuum from "most like me" to "least like me." The subject is then asked to do the same with reference to an ideal self. The difference between self-perception and ideal-perception is an indication of self-esteem or self-value.

Cattell 16 Personality Factor Scale

Cattell's work in factor-analyzing personality into a number of basic source traits resulted in a test of 16 personality factors. The scales are 16 relatively independent personality dimensions such as dominance-submission, radicalism-conservatism, high ego strength-low ego strength.

Eysenck Personality Inventory (EPI)

Eysenck's theory of personality assumes there are two main dimensions of the nonpsychotic individual— stable-unstable and introverted-extraverted. His scale is constructed to yield a profile of these characteristics.

Projective Tests

Projective tests assume that a person projects his or her psychological characteristics onto relatively neutral stimuli. It is used more in a psychodynamic framework than in, say, a behavioral paradigm. The major criticism of projective tests is that the scoring system is unreliable. That is, different scorers tend to get different results.

Rorschach Test

The **Rorschach** test is the most frequently used individual test. This is a standardized set of ten inkblots of various amorphous shapes. The subject describes what he or she sees. The responses are scored for such variables as movement, animal and human imagery, number, use of form, shape, or color, and originality. A more-or-less objective scoring system for the Rorschach developed by **Exner** is now in use.

Thematic Apperception Test (TAT)

Subjects tell stories using a standardized set of pictures as stimuli. Subjects are asked to tell the antecedents of the pictured situation, what the characters in the pictures are thinking and feeling, and what the outcome will be. Once used quite frequently in the experimental laboratory, the TAT is fading in importance, in part because the scenes depicted in the pictures appear dated to the modern observer.

Sentence Completion Test

The sentence completion test is designed to tap the subject's associations. The test is composed of a series of sentence stems that the subject completes, such as "I like . . . ," "Sometimes I wish . . . ." The term "sentence completion test" is now considered a generic method, since there is no one agreed-upon list of sentence stems used in a standard way in all testing situations. For this reason, it is virtually impossible to make broad statements about the validity and reliability of sentence completion tests.

Draw-a-Person Test

This technique was first used by **Goodenough** as a measure of children's intelligence. It is now used as a projective technique. The assumption is that the drawing of a person represents the expression of the self or the body image. A frequently used variation on the Draw-a-Person test is the House-Tree-Person test, in which the subject is asked to draw a house, a tree, and a person. The validity and reliability of these tests is in question.

Word Association Tests

Many forms of this technique have been used, an early one having been developed by **Jung.** Commonly, the subject is asked to respond to a stimulus word with the first word that comes to mind. The responses, as well as such behaviors as reaction time, are analyzed.

Motor Tests

The *Bender Visual-Motor Gestalt Test* is useful as a measure of organic brain defects and retardation in children and adults. The subject is asked to copy nine geometric figures. From these drawings, maturational levels and the degree of visual-motor coordination can be assessed.

Tests of Special Abilities

The *Seashore Measure of Musical Talents* is used by schools to select musically inclined individuals. The test assesses the child's abilities to distinguish pitch, rhythm, timbre, and tone.

Interest Inventories

The *Strong-Campbell Vocational Interest Blank* and the *Kuder Preference Record* assess an individual's interest in a wide range of occupations and activities. On the Strong-Campbell test, a person responds with "like," "dislike," or "indifferent" to a wide range of occupations, amusements, and other activities. The Kuder test asks the subject to indicate which of three activities he or she likes best and which he or she likes least. The results of these three-item choices indicate the person's interests and preferences.

These interest inventories are quite reliable. They tap a part of a person's basic character that counseling psychologists call *interests.* Our interests are fairly well established by the time we are in junior high school and, given the opportunity to make choices in educational and vocational situations, we tend to follow our interests.

A feature of the Strong-Campbell test that is important to note is that it was derived by asking people who were happy and successful in different occupations what they were interested in. Profiles were established in this empirical way by defining interests that are associated with persons currently in various occupations. If a test-taker's profile of interests matches the interest profiles previously established, the counselor tells the client that he might like to choose that occupation.

Tests of Cognitive Style

Embedded Figures Test

This test, based on **Witkin**'s work, assesses the degree of field dependency and independency. Figures are embedded in other figures and subjects are asked to find the hidden stimuli. Those that can locate the embedded figures in the short time allowed are judged *field independent,* while those who cannot are judged *field dependent.*

Internal-External Locus of Control Test

This test, developed by **Rotter,** assesses the subject's locus of control, i.e. where he or she feels the control of behavior lies. There are 23 forced-choice items, such as: (a) "What happens to me is my own doing," versus (b) "Sometimes I feel I don't have enough control over my life." Items are scored for externality; thus the more externally controlled the person feels, the higher the score.

Role Construct Repertory Test (REP Test)

This test was developed by **George Kelly** to measure a person's organization of personal constructs (see THEORIES OF PERSONALITY). Sets of three roles—such as spouse, boss, friend—are presented. The subject is asked to describe how two of these are alike and how they differ from the third. This process is repeated for a variety of sets. The most frequently named characteristics or constructs indicate the person's cognitive style.

Dogmatism Scale

The Dogmatism Scale developed by **Rokeach** is similar to the F-Scale, but instead of measuring only right-wing authoritarianism, it attempts to measure attitudes of intolerance and rigidity no matter which end of the political spectrum is chosen. Rokeach found that dogmatic people are more likely to give simple answers to complex questions and less likely to search for additional information than are more open-minded people.

FOR FURTHER READING

Mischel, W. *Introduction to personality.* 4th ed. New York: Holt, Rinehart and Winston, 1986.

Intelligence

INTRODUCTION

Intelligence is the ability to think abstractly, to reason deductively and inductively, and to use appropriate skills to gain mastery over the environment. Intelligence can be seen as a single generalized and unitary characteristic or as an amalgam of different types of cognitive processes.

THEORIES OF INTELLIGENCE

Francis Galton

Galton pioneered the measurement of individual differences more than a century ago. He concluded that intelligence is a unitary faculty and that it is an inherited trait distributed normally in the population from high to low in the same way other characteristics such as height are distributed.

Henry Goddard

Goddard, in tracing the family ancestry of a mentally retarded subject, Deborah Kallikak, concluded that intelligence and the lack of it are inherited global characteristics.

Charles Spearman

Spearman published his two-factor theory of intelligence in 1904. Spearman's basic assumption was that all mental tasks require two kinds of ability, a general ability, G, and a specific ability, S. G is common to all intellectual tasks while S is specific to a given task.

Louis Thurstone

Thurstone believed that a single unitary intelligence index is inadequate to describe mental endowment. He postulated instead a group of independent intellectual factors. These are the *primary mental abilities,* which include word fluency, memory, spatial relationships, and reasoning. Thurstone developed the method of factor analysis, which he used to isolate these primary factors.

J.P. Guilford

Using factor analysis, **Guilford** isolated a matrix of 120 elements that in sum compose intelligence. Two of Guilford's more frequently used dimensions are *divergent* thinking, which is the facility to generate new, creative, and different ideas, and *convergent* thinking, which is the ability to group divergent ideas and synthesize them into one unifying concept.

David Wechsler

Wechsler viewed intelligence in a global way, feeling that high ability on one intellectual reasoning task will fairly well predict high ability on another. Intelligence for Wechsler centers on the ability to adapt. The different subsets of the Wechsler scales are different measures of intelligence, not measures of different kinds of intelligence. They merely imply the different ways intelligence manifests itself.

Raymond Cattell

A useful theory of the factors underlying intelligence is **Cattell**'s idea that there are really two types of intelligences. One is called *fluid.* This intelligence depends on the neurochemistry of the nervous system. Such abilities as psychomotor speed, short-term memory, and inductive reasoning depend on fluid intelligence. It is the intelligence that is given, that is unschooled. The other type of intelligence is the application of fluid factors to formal socialized education. This results in *crystallized* intelligence. Crystallized intelligence is seen in such formal abilities as vocabulary, deductive reasoning, and long-term memory. Normally we don't distinguish between the two factors; however, sometimes we can. Aging people, for example, show decrements in fluid intelligence (such as longer reaction times) while they maintain crystallized intelligence (for example, vocabulary and language remain intact). Certain brain injuries will also affect the two factors differently.

STUDIES OF INTELLIGENCE: HEREDITY VERSUS ENVIRONMENT

The inherited nature of intelligence continues to be debated. There is no consensual agreement on the relative influence of heredity or the relative influence of environment.

Support for the hereditary hypothesis has been inferred from correlational studies of IQ scores of identical twins and from correlations of scores of parents and children. Some of the data show that identical twins reared apart have a higher correlation coefficient of intelligence test scores than fraternal twins reared together. Children raised by foster parents have a higher test correlation with their natural parents than with their foster parents. Children's scores resemble their biological parents' scores to a significantly greater degree than foster children's scores resemble their foster parents' scores. It is therefore suggested that heredity sets the limits of intellectual growth within which the environment can foster or retard development.

The influence of heredity on intelligence has been studied experimentally, using rats as subjects. Rats that learned to run a maze well were mated. The poorer-performing rats were also mated. Within a few generations two distinct strains were produced—bright rats and dull rats. Many years later the descendants of these rats were tested. The bright strain still performed better than the dull strain.

Early childrearing practices and extreme environmental conditions can affect intellectual development. Upper-class and middle-class children have consistently higher scores than lower-class children. It should be kept in mind, however, that these differences in intelligence test scores merely predict school performance. Their predictive validity for life experiences outside of school is not great.

MEASURES OF INTELLIGENCE

Tests of intelligence were originally developed by **Alfred Binet** in collaboration with **Theodore Simon** during the period 1905–1908. The tests were administered to Parisian schoolchildren in order to systematically discriminate normal from retarded children. The test was a series of school-related tasks scaled for difficulty and designed to measure judgment, comprehension, and reasoning. An age-seven task, for instance, would be one that at least 50% of the seven-year-olds tested could answer correctly, such as naming the days of the week, repeating three digits backwards, or describing differences between a fly and a butterfly. At succeeding age levels, the items included more verbal problems requiring abstract reasoning and problem solving. This test is the forerunner of all intelligence tests, and it displays the underlying assumption that intelligence can be equated with performance on school material and verbal abilities.

Intelligence on these early tests was described by the IQ *(intelligence quotient)* score. The *mental age* divided by the *chronological age* then multiplied by 100 yielded the IQ. This computation was derived by **William Stern.** An eight-year-old passing items for six-year-olds but failing items for those above six would have an IQ of $6/8 \times 100 = 75$.

Presently a deviation IQ score is used instead of the old ratio IQ. This is because the ratio IQ has inherent psychometric problems that need not be described here. The deviation IQ is computed by comparing the obtained score of the individual with a norm. The resulting computation shows how far the person's obtained score deviates from the average (mean) of the normative or standard set of scores. If, for example, the obtained score of the test-taker is one standard deviation above the average score of the normative group, the test-taker is assigned an IQ score of 115 (116 if it is the Stanford-Binet test).

Through the years, the normative samples have been improved so that all recent revisions of the standard IQ tests (and other tests) have become more representative in their norming groups.

The Stanford-Binet Test

In 1916, **Lewis Terman** of Stanford University adapted the Binet test for American use. The result was the *Stanford-Binet Intelligence Scale,* revised in 1937, in 1960, and again in 1986. This test includes verbal and performance items, grouped by age levels, beginning with age two years and running to "superior adult." The Stanford-Binet test is appropriate to administer to individuals from age two years to adult (32.5 years). In administering this test, *basal* and *ceiling* levels are derived. The basal is the level at which four tests are passed at two consecutive levels from an "entry" point. The ceiling is the level at which three of four tests are failed at two consecutive levels.

Major changes were included in the 1986 revision of the Stanford-Binet test. Now the term *standard age score* (SAS) is used instead of the term IQ. Another change is that similar items are grouped together as subtests, much like the Wechsler scales. And the subtests are grouped into content areas that reflect the distinction between crystallized and fluid intelligence.

Because the Stanford-Binet test discriminates well at the extremes of the intelligence dimension, it is a better test than the Wechsler tests for very high- and very low-functioning individuals.

The Wechsler Scales

David Wechsler developed the *WISC-R (Wechsler Intelligence Scale for Children Revised)*, designed for children 6 to 17; the *WPPSI (Wechsler Preschool Primary Scale of Intelligence)*, designed for ages 4 to 6 ; and the *WAIS-R (Wechsler Adult Intelligence Scale Revised)*, designed for ages 16 and above. These tests are individually administered.

The Wechsler tests are divided into two scales, *verbal* and *performance*, with subtests for each scale. Results are given in terms of a *verbal IQ*, a *performance IQ*, and a *full-scale IQ*. Scores are standardized for each subtest, and the IQ is the obtained score in comparison with the standardized score. The standardized mean for each age is 100, and the standard deviation is 15. This standardization procedure eliminates the need for calculating the IQ.

The Stanford-Binet IQs correlate about +.80 with the WISC verbal, +.65 with the WISC performance, and +.80 with the WISC full-scale IQ. The WISC-R vocabulary subtest is the best single predictor of school performance.

Group IQ Tests

The need to test large numbers of people efficiently and cheaply required the development of group tests. This sudden necessity arose during wartime when the military faced massive emergency staffing needs. The earliest of the well-known and widely used tests were the *Army Alpha*, for literate subjects, and the *Army Beta*, for illiterate subjects. These tests were developed by **Robert Yerkes** to test recruits during World War I.

During World War II, the test used was the *Army General Classification Test* (AGCT). From 1950 until the mid-1970s, the military used a uniform screening test called the *Armed Forces Qualification Test* (AFQT) to meet the mandate of the Selective Service Act of 1948. The test currently in use is the *Armed Services Vocational Aptitude Battery* (ASVAB). As its name implies, much of this exam is designed to seek out special aptitudes for vocational training placement to best meet needs of both recruit and the service. Scores of the four "basic" intellectual skills subtests are combined to give an AFQT score. Recruits must meet a specified AFQT cutoff score in order to be inducted.

The military group tests are the most used and the best known. However, there are many independently developed group tests in use as well. A group test for children is the *Lorge-Thorndike Intelligence Test*.

Infant Tests

Infant intelligence tests are poor predictors of later IQ scores. They are useful, however, in early identification of intellectual retardation. The major tests are *Gesell Developmental Schedules, California First-Year Mental Scale, Bayley's Scale of Infant Development, Cattell Intelligence Test for Infants and Young Children*, the *Merrill-Palmer Scale of Mental Tests*, and the *Minnesota Preschool Scale*.

Terman's Study of Gifted Children

In 1921, **Terman** began a longitudinal investigation of very bright individuals. Over 1500 children with IQs of 140 or more were selected and followed through their adulthood. Terman found the group to be generally better adjusted, higher in achievement, and more accomplished than the population at large.

Culture-Fair Tests

In the 1960s and early 1970s, test designers attempted to create standardized tests that were relatively free from middle-class American culture, that is, tests that did not emphasize verbal abilities. It was thought at the time that lower-class and minority children did poorly on IQ tests because these tests were culturally biased; but attempts at creating culture-free tests (such as the SOMPA—System of Multicultural Pluralistic Assessment) have failed. It is impossible to take culture out of the exam process. Further, minority children actually do worse on nonverbal tests than on verbal tests. Finally, it turns out that standardized tests such as the Stanford-Binet and the Wechsler scales are good predictors of success: those who score high do well in life and those who score low do not do well in life. This is true no matter who is being assessed. These tests are not biased because they predict equally for all groups. While it is true that average scores differ on these tests so that members of minority groups and of the lower class tend to do worse on the average than those from the dominant culture and middle-class people, the predictions we make from the scores are the same. Hence from the point of view of psychometric theory, they are not biased.

FOR FURTHER READING

Anastasi, A. *Psychological testing*. 5th ed. New York: Macmillan, 1982.

Social Psychology

INTRODUCTION

Social psychology is the study of how the thoughts, feelings, and behavior of people are influenced by the actual, imagined, or implied presence of other people. The origins of social psychology lie with the European theorists of the late nineteenth and early twentieth centuries—**Tarde, Durkheim, LeBon, Freud**—who introduced the concept of an *emergent group mind*. In America, social psychology was introduced in 1908 with the publication of two books—*Introduction to Social Psychology* by **McDougall** and *Social Psychology* by **Ross**.

American social psychology has tended to emphasize the hypothesis-testing experimental approach. Research has generally clustered around specific theories or themes. In the early twentieth century, *attitudes toward ethnic groups* were a chief concern of social psychology (**Thurstone, Likert, Bogardus**). By the 1950s, attitude study was focused on *attitude change* (**Hovland, Feshbach, Janis, McGuire**). In mid-century, the Gestalt school generated research on *conformity* (**Asch, Sherif, Schacter**), *group dynamics,* and *field theory* (**Lewin, Zeigarnik**). *Cognitive dissonance* and *cognitive balance* became major themes in the late 1950s (**Festinger, Heider, Osgood, Newcomb**). Behaviorism influenced research in *S-R learning* (**Hovland, Miller, Dollard, Doob**), *social learning* (**Bandura, Mischel, Rotter**), and *social exchange* (**Kelley, Thibaut**). The popular contemporary themes are *attribution* (**Heider, Kelley, Thibaut, Riecken, Valins, DeCharms, Bem, Jones, Nisbett, Zimbardo**), *obedience to authority* (**Milgram**), *affiliation* (**Singer, Schacter**), *helping behavior* (**Latané, Darley**), *role theory* (**Sarbin**), *urban behavior* (**Milgram**), and *environmental psychology* (**Proshansky, Ittelson**).

HISTORY

European Antecedents

Emil Durkheim (1858–1917) was one of the founders of modern sociology and one of the first European thinkers to stress the significance of the group in determining human conduct. He felt that a social aggregate generates a psychic unity that is more than the sum of its parts.

Gustav LeBon (1814–1931), author of *The Crowd* (1895), considered a group to be governed by an *emergent collective mind* characterized by inhibition of intellect, intensification of emotion, submission to authority, and extreme suggestibility.

Sigmund Freud (1856–1939), who wrote *Group Psychology and the Analysis of the Ego* (1921), presented a metapsychological explanation for the kind of group behavior LeBon had previously described. Freud contended that the force holding the group together is the attachment the group members feel for the group leader. Members invest their *libido* in the leader the way a patient does with a doctor or a subject does with a hypnotist. The prototype for this libido attachment is the family relationship. As in the family

189

constellation, the group members (children) feel brotherly toward the other members (siblings). The leader (parent) in turn is obliged to treat all members equally. The libido attachment and the giving up of the rational ego—similar to what exists in a love relationship except without the sexual component— explain the blind allegiance and irrational behavior groups display. Freud, who leaned toward the pessimistic in his social psychological thinking, was strongly influenced by the sad events of World War I.

Early American Social Psychologists

William McDougall's social psychology was strongly influenced by contemporary ideas concerning the power of *instincts*. He contended that individual and group behavior springs from innate or inherited tendencies that are the motive force behind all thought and action, individual and collective. He called his view *hormic psychology*. McDougall was very popular after the publication of his *Introduction to Social Psychology* (1908). His Darwinian instinct approach lost favor, however, after the 1920s because it ran counter to the behaviorist views that were popular at that time.

Floyd H. Allport promulgated the concept he called *social facilitation,* which he used to explain the facilitating effect others have on an individual's performance. An earlier study by **Triplett** (1897) demonstrated that a person's rate of winding a fishing line improved when in competitive conditions. Allport found that rote task performance, such as reporting word associations, improved when the individual performed in a group.

ATTITUDE STUDY

Attitudes have historically been an extremely significant area of study in American social psychology. *Attitudes* are defined as relatively stable and enduring predispositions to act, think, or feel in a certain way toward a certain object.

Attitude studies began in the 1920s. **Bogardus** (1925) developed a *social distance scale,* which rated how a person felt about different ethnic groups. There were seven items denoting varying degrees of social acceptability, such as admission to kinship, admission as a neighbor, as a co-worker, and to citizenship. At the time, American ethnic attitudes were most favorable toward the English, Canadians, Irish, Scotch, and French. The least favorable attitudes were toward Jews, Negroes (the contemporary term), Greeks, Mexicans, and Turks.

Katz and Braly (1933) had 100 Princeton students assign traits to ten different nationalities. There was high *stereotype* agreement, even when students had never had contact with the target groups. **Guilford** (1931) assessed ethnic prejudices of over 1000 students at universities across the country and also found striking stereotypical agreement in the attitudes of students.

More recently, **Rokeach** (1960) studied ratings of the friendliness toward racial groups as well as toward others who differ in beliefs on important issues. It was found that liking was based more on similarity of beliefs than on similarity of race or religion.

Attitude Measurement

The pioneer work in attitude measurement was undertaken by **Thurstone, Likert, Guttman, Stevens,** and **Coombs.**

The *Thurstone Scale* (1929) was an elaborate affair that asked subjects to rate an item on an 11-point scale. A large number of judges were given many statements concerning the topic in question, such as capital punishment. The statements, as many as 300, ranged from pro ("people who shoot cops should be given the electric chair") to anti ("murderers are basically mentally ill and should be given psychiatric help"). The judges put the items in a number of piles, typically 11, according to pro- or anti- feelings. After the rated statements were sorted, scaled values for each statement were calculated. The most unambiguous statements, those with the least variability, were then used to construct the final scale. Subjects were administered the final scale and asked to indicate agreement or disagreement. An individual subject's attitude score was then arrived at.

The *Likert Scale* (1932) is easier to administer than the Thurstone scale. Subjects are asked to rate individual statements on a 1-to-5 or 1-to-7 scale from "strongly agree" to "strongly disagree." The attitude score is the sum of the individual values for each response. The Likert scale does not use intermediaries to judge each statement. The statements are given directly to the subjects.

Guttman (1944) proposed a unidimensional ordinal, cumulative scale. That is, items are arranged in order so that an individual who agrees with any particular item also agrees with all items of lower-rank order. For example, when asking about height, the items might be: (a) "I am more than 5'0" tall," (b) "I am more than 5'3" tall," (c) "I am more than 5'6" tall," etc. Anyone who chooses item (c) also automatically agrees with items (a) and (b). The social distance scale by Bogardus is a Guttman-type scale; it assumes that accepting a group to kinship also means accepting the same group to more distant social relationships.

Problems in Attitude Measurement

Sometimes the responses that people give to attitude scale items reflect the test-taker's desire to be seen as socially desirable rather than the true expressions of the test-taker's attitude or feelings. The *Edwards Social Desirability Scale* and the *Marlow-Crowne Scale* measure this bias. People also tend to respond in set ways regardless of what they are responding to. Common response sets are yea-or-nay saying, gambling, extremism and anti-extremism, and acquiescence. The phrasing of questions, including subtle semantic nuances, may also bias responses. Different people have different understandings of the meaning of words such as "sometimes," "often," or "moderately."

Attitude Change Studies

Attitude change research is primarily associated with **Carl Hovland** and the Yale Communication Research Program. The Yale group studied attitude change as a function of the communicator, the communication, and the audience.

Communicator

If a communicator is highly regarded, his or her conduct and views will likely be judged favorably. Positions advocated by highly creditable and prestigious sources will more readily be adopted than opinions expressed by less creditable sources.

The *sleeper effect* holds that after a period of time people forget the source of the communication but remember the message. The effect of the message remains relatively constant. Recent reevaluation of this research has shown that the sleeper effect is not as powerful as originally contended.

Communication

The relative value of *one-sided* versus *two-sided communications* as influences on the morale of US soldiers was studied by Hovland. Hovland concluded that presenting both sides of an argument is most effective for changing attitudes when the listener is initially opposed to the issue and is relatively well informed and intelligent. If the listener is initially favorable, poorly informed, and relatively unintelligent, a one-sided communication is more effective.

Fear-arousing communications produce results dependent on the level of fear aroused. High fear-arousal communications tend not to produce a great deal of change. **Janis and Feshbach** (1953) found that high school students given high-fear-arousal messages about tooth decay were less likely to change their attitude about toothbrushing than students given low- or medium-arousal messages. It was explained that high-fear-arousal communications may be so overwhelming that the subjects tune out completely to the message. However, if along with the high-arousal message comes a means of doing something about what is feared, the message is more likely to be effective.

Another explanation for the negative reaction to high-arousal communications is that the listener feels threatened by such an assault and reacts negatively. **Brehm**'s *reactance theory* predicts this reaction. When one feels his options are being limited, the reaction is to assume the opposite attitude.

The *inoculation theory* of **McGuire** uses the medical analogy that the most effective way of increasing resistance is to build up defenses. Weakly attacking an individual's attitude requires him to think of counterarguments. McGuire argued that it is possible to inoculate people against persuasive attacks the way we inoculate them against diseases.

Social judgment theory predicts that the degree of attitude change is a function of the difference between the subject's initial attitude and the new position advocated. A communication that falls at or near the listener's position is within his *latitude of acceptance* and will be accepted. A new position that the listener finds unacceptable is within his *latitude of rejection.*

When subjected to attitude change communications in the laboratory, independent, high self-esteem people show less change than dependent, low self-esteem people. Intelligence seems to have little bearing on attitude change.

Conformity to Group Norms

A little more than a decade after Allport published his *theory of social facilitation,* **Sherif** (1935) published his classic study on the formation of social norms in a group. In his studies, Sherif took advantage of the *autokinetic effect,* which consists of the apparent—though illusory—movement of a pinpoint of light in a dark room. Sherif asked observers in groups to judge the length of movement of the pinpoint of light. He found that an individual's estimation of the length of movement very often depended on the announced judgment of the rest of the group. Subjects were first tested when alone, then tested in a group. The majority of subjects tended to modify their estimates the second time around to conform to the group norm. Subsequent tests indicated that subjects retain the group standard as a basis of judgment rather than reverting to their previous standards.

More recent research on conformity to group norms measures the effect of *confederates* (stooges) on the behavior of a naive subject. In these studies, there is only one real experimental subject while, unbeknownst to the real subject, all the rest of the participants in the study are confederates of the experimenter. The purpose of these experiments is to study the influence of the group on the single experimental subject.

Solomon Asch (1946, 1956) presented the classical paradigm in this field. A naive subject was seated in a semicircle with seven others, actually confederates of the experimenter. The task was to find matches of lines projected on a screen in front of the room. The confederates gave obviously false responses. It was shown that many, if not most, subjects tend to alter their answers to conform to the false responses of the majority, even when the subject knows that the answer being given by the majority is wrong.

Asch varied the size of the group and found that beyond three there was little increase in conformity. He also found that if the confederates' responses were not unanimous, conformity was reduced.

Crutchfield (1955) and **Deutsch and Gerard** (1955) automated variations on the Asch experiment. The subject was alone in a cubicle but was made to believe there were other experimental subjects. After hearing the others' opinions, the subject anonymously expressed a judgment about the projected lines by pressing a button. The confederates' responses were actually manipulated by the experimenter. In this more private condition, the subject's responses were not as conforming as in the live Asch experimental situation.

Conformity to False Emotions

A classic experiment by **Schacter and Singer** (1962) showed how emotions are related to social reality. The experimenters gave some subjects the drug *epinephrine,* which produces strong emotional arousal. The subjects were then put in rooms with confederates who, depending on the experimental design, acted either euphoric or angry. The aroused subjects, who were not informed beforehand of the effect of the drug, took on the emotion of the confederate. Those in the room with the euphoric stooge became euphoric; those in the room with the angry stooge became angry. It was concluded that when people find themselves in an ambiguous, undefined emotional state, they tend to look to others in their environment to define their emotions.

Conformity and Deviancy

When a member of a group disagrees with the group consensus, the group makes various efforts to get that person to conform. The other members argue, present support for their position, and use whatever methods they can think of to pressure the deviate to change his mind. If the disagreer does change, he is accepted and is treated as a regular member without prejudice. If, however, the disagreer maintains his deviant position, after a while the group just stops communicating with the disagreer. Those people the group cannot influence are eventually ignored.

Conformity and Risk Taking

The *risky-shift* phenomenon was observed in investigations of risk taking. It was found that, contrary to the popular notion that groups are inherently conservative, group decisions are actually more risky than the decisions of the individual group members. By means of group discussions, alternatives previously rated as unacceptably risky by the individuals when questioned alone seemed less risky to the individuals when they were in the group. More recent research indicates that the shift is actually to the social norm, not necessarily to a more risky position.

Theory of Social Comparison

The theory of *social comparison* developed by **Festinger** has been presented as an explanation of these conformity findings. When physical reality becomes uncertain, people rely more and more on social reality. Hence, the more ambiguous the stimulus the more conformity there is likely to be.

OBEDIENCE TO AUTHORITY

Studies of obedience to authority by **Stanley Milgram** (1963, 1965) are classic and frequently cited, although they are subject to criticism as too volatile for contemporary experimental standards. Milgram told his subjects that they were participating in an investigation of learning and they were to administer a shock to a student when he gave a wrong answer. The subject could hear but not see the student. Actually, the student was a confederate, and all the authentic-looking instruments were not really hooked up. The subject was instructed by the experimenter to administer more and more intense shocks. The confederate feigned pain, and as the shock seemed to reach fatal levels, the confederate stopped responding altogether. The dependent variable was how much shock a naive subject would administer. Milgram had previously surveyed 40 psychiatrists who predicted only 1% of the subjects would administer the highest voltage. The amazing results were that 62% of the subjects went all the way to the "fatal" level!

Later experiments varied the conditions of the experiment. In one variation, the laboratory was in a seedy downtown warehouse building instead of the original prestigious Yale campus building. The percent of subjects administering the maximum shock dropped down to 48%. This indicates that the prestige of the experimenter has an influence on the behavior of subjects.

It was also found that the proximity of the experimenter to the subject had an effect. With the experimenter out of the room issuing orders by telephone, less than 25% of the subjects gave the maximum shock. Interestingly, under this telephone condition, several subjects lied; they said they were giving the shocks when they really were not.

Milgram's conclusion from his series of controversial studies was that most people in our culture accede to the demands of what they perceive to be legitimate authority. Following authority's demands to inflict pain on others is not the exclusive domain of the followers of Hitler in the 1940s.

Another form of obedience is elicited by the application of the *foot-in-the-door* technique. Door-to-door salespeople have been using this method for ages. The notion is that to increase compliance, one first gets the subject to agree to a less odious request. In one field study by **Freedman and Fraser** (1966), a group of housewives was asked to sign a safe driving petition. Some time later, the same women were asked if they would allow a large "Drive Carefully" sign to be placed in their front yards. Compared to a control group who were not previously polled, the experimental group was much more ready to have the sign placed in their yard. It is assumed that prior commitment to support safe driving created a tendency to consistent future commitment.

INTERPERSONAL ATTRACTION

We tend to like and associate with people based on three variables that have been identified by social psychologists: how physically close we are, how physically attracted we are, and how similar we are in attitudes and beliefs. We tend to like people we are in proximity of, other things being equal. For instance, if one sees the same people each morning on one's way to work, one tends to have a familiar and positive feeling toward them. The second variable is obvious: we are all attracted to attractive people. Even though we tend to end up with mates of about the same level of attractiveness as ourselves, our fantasies are toward more attractive persons. How else to explain movie stars. And, finally, we tend to associate with those who share our beliefs.

AFFILIATION

The hypothesis that affiliation reduces fear was studied by **Schacter** (1959). Schacter told subjects they were going to participate in an experiment in which they would receive a shock. For half the subjects, the shock was described as quite painful (high-fear); for the others, it was described as nothing more than a tingle (low-fear). The subjects were then told they had to wait 10 minutes before beginning. They were given a choice of waiting alone or waiting with other subjects. As predicted, 62.5% of the high-fear subjects chose to wait with others, while only 33% of the low-fear subjects chose that alternative.

In a group of high-fear subjects, some people show stronger affiliation needs than do others. Schacter found birth order is an important variable in relation to need for affiliation. First-born and only children show a stronger tendency to affiliate. The affiliative tendency decreases progressively for later-born children.

Zimbardo and Formica (1963) expanded Schacter's model. They gave the high-fear subjects the choice of waiting with others who, like themselves, were about to take part in the study or waiting with others who had just completed the study. Subjects showed a preference for waiting with those who had not yet done the study. The more similar the others, the stronger the drive to affiliate. The researchers' conclusion was that misery doesn't love just any company, it prefers to love miserable company.

One theory that attempts to explain affiliation and attraction is called the *social exchange theory*. According to this theory, a relationship between two people will continue if the rewards for maintaining it are greater than the costs.

FIELD THEORY

Kurt Lewin has had great impact on social psychology. His concept of *field theory* rests on the notion of *cohesiveness* (the forces that bind the parts of the group together and that resist disruption). Cohesiveness depends upon the *positive valence* or attractiveness among members of the group. Lewin's equation is $B = f(P \times E)$; that is, behavior is a function of the interaction of the person and the environment.

Lewin's theory begins with the idea he called an individual's *life space* (the totality of all possible events that influence him or her). A person's needs give rise to tension, which is reduced by action toward or away from an object in the life space. Objects that satisfy needs have *positive valence,* while objects that threaten the individual have *negative valence*. The direction and strength of attraction of the objects can be represented by lines called *vectors*.

In graphic form, the following box represents the life space of a person (P) at the moment. The vector indicates that the person is motivated to approach an object (O), which has positive valence. The barrier is shown with negative valence. This barrier presents a *conflict*.

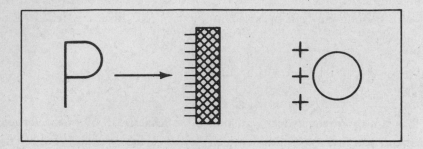

A person moves toward positive objects and away from negative objects. However, conflicts arise when there are competing objects within the life space. Lewin's analysis of these conflict situations is classic.

The *approach-approach conflict* exists between two positive goal objects of approximately equal attractiveness. For example, when a person gets accepted by two top-ranked graduate schools, an approach-approach conflict ensues. Initially, it is likely that the response is ambivalence. As the person moves toward one of the goals, that one becomes more attractive and the approach toward it is continued.

The *avoidance-avoidance conflict* exists when the person has to choose between two negative alternatives. The solution is either to choose the lesser of the two evils or to escape by *leaving the field* altogether.

The *approach-avoidance conflict* is extremely disruptive since the person is drawn to and repelled by the same situation at the same time. This conflict has a stable equilibrium at the point where these positive and negative forces are balanced.

Neal Miller (1944) adapted Lewin's basic model to investigate the approach-avoidance conflict. Miller trained rats to run along an alley to a food box, then shocked them with an electroconvulsive shock (ECS) as they were eating. On the next trial, the animals ran to the goal more slowly and stopped short of the goal itself. The point at which rats stopped was the *point of balance* where an equilibrium between approach and avoidance tendencies (gradients) was reached (see DRIVE REDUCTION LEARNING).

An important experimental application of the field theory is the *Zeigarnik effect*. Interrupting a subject in the middle of a task has the effect of leaving him in a state of tension and disequilibrium: to reduce the tension the subject wants to complete the task. **Zeigarnik** (1938) assigned her subjects simple puzzle-like problems. The subjects were allowed to finish half the problems but were interrupted and kept from finishing the other half. Later the subjects were asked to recall all the tasks. About 50% of the tasks could be recalled. However, 68% of the unfinished tasks were recalled versus 43% of the finished tasks. The Zeigarnik effect has been found to vary with the amount of ego involvement associated with the task.

Another classic field theory study was the work on *group leadership styles* by **Lewin, Lippitt, and White** (1939). The authors tested the effects of different kinds of group leadership (authoritarian, democratic, laissez-faire) on productivity and the behavior of small groups of boys. The democratic groups were found to be the most productive, less dependent on the leader, more friendly, and less internally divided. The authoritarian group tended to be either more aggressive or more apathetic than the democratic group.

COGNITIVE CONSISTENCY

The balance theories of **T.M. Newcomb, Charles Osgood,** and **Leon Festinger** center on the postulated natural tendency of people to achieve a balanced cognitive state, also called *cognitive balance*. These theories assume that there is a tendency for the cognitive system to move from a state of inconsistency to a state of consistency. This concept is expressed by the Gestalt notions of *pragnanz* and *closure* (see PERCEPTION).

Balance Theory

Newcomb (1953) applied balance theory to interpersonal communications. The theory presents a person (P) in communication with another person (O) about an object or activity (X). The three elements are in some kind of relationship to each other, positive (+) or negative (–).

Newcomb felt that people tend to want others whom they like to have the same attitudes toward issues. They thus act to bring the elements into a balanced state. If P likes O and is in favor of X, but thinks O opposes X, the relationship is said to be unbalanced. The theory predicts that P will communicate with O in order to persuade O to change his mind, thus reducing the imbalance. In the three-element network, the balanced and unbalanced conditions are as follows:

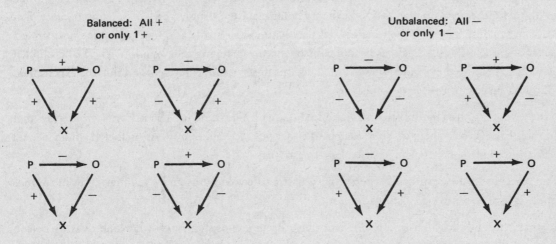

Osgood's Congruity Theory

The congruity theory of **Osgood and Tannenbaum** (1953) deals with one person's cognition of two objects. It assumes that a person's feelings toward an object or person will generalize to things associated with that object or person. For instance, a communication from a well-liked source will be more readily accepted than a communication from a disliked or distrusted source. A state of balance *(equilibrium)* exists if equally evaluated concepts are associated; imbalance exists if they are disassociated.

For example, if a person feels positively toward the Governor and also perceives himself as a "good law-abiding American," he probably will feel unbalanced if the Governor chooses to advocate legalization of marijuana. The person will thus attempt to correct the imbalance. The theory predicts that the Governor will lose some positive regard and legalization of marijuana will gain some positive regard. The attitude that changes the most is the one that was initially least extreme. If a person feels very strongly about something, that person's attitude is less likely to change than if he feels only moderately about it. The closer one's attitude is to neutral, the more it will change.

Festinger's Cognitive Dissonance Theory

The most popular and dramatic balance theory is *cognitive dissonance theory*, described by **Leon Festinger** (1957). The theory states that if a person is committed to a belief or action that is inconsistent with other views held or actions the person has taken, he will seek to resolve the dissonance by changing cognitions. States of dissonance create tension and anxiety and motivate a person to do something that will alleviate the tension.

The amount of dissonance is never measured directly; it is only inferred by the attempts to reduce it. The two ways to reduce dissonance are to deny the importance of the elements ("I don't care anyway!") or to change the balance by seeking new cognitions that are more consistent ("Even though my work is boring, at least it gets me out of the house"). Cognitive dissonance has stimulated much laboratory research.

The classic dissonance experiment was developed by **Festinger and Carlsmith** (1959). Subjects were recruited to perform a very dull and repetitive motor task. After an hour's boring work, the subject was asked to explain the task to a new subject and to stress how fascinating and worthwhile it was. Subjects were paid either $1 or $20 to do this. Later, the subjects filled out a questionnaire that included a question asking how interesting they thought the original task was. As the theory predicted, the $1 subjects showed higher liking for the experimental task. The theory holds that the $1 subjects felt dissonance because their actions were inconsistent with their beliefs and they had no real justification for telling the next subject how enjoyable the task was. They resolved the dissonance by changing their opinion. The $20 group felt no dissonance because they could attribute their actions to the money they got for doing the experiment. The $20 was sufficient justification for lying.

This study was replicated by **Brehm and Cohen** (1962) with Yale students. The students wrote essays that ran counter to their basic beliefs. They were paid either 50¢, $1, $5, or $10. As predicted, students paid the least showed more belief change when later questioned.

Dissonance seems to arise especially when subjects participate voluntarily and when they know in advance that there is little incentive or justification for their actions.

Dissonance theory holds that one looks for things that are consistent with what one does. A person making a choice among different automobiles would tend to ignore information about the models not selected and would maximize exposure to information about the car actually selected. The theory also predicts that the negative features of the unchosen alternatives will be magnified.

An alternative dissonance theory proposed by **Bem** (1967) is called *self-perception*. Bem contends that behavior causes attitudes. In other words, we observe ourselves doing something and from that we infer our attitudes. This is similar to the James-Lange theory of emotions and is supported by the Schacter and Singer study described above.

COMPETITION VERSUS COOPERATION

The classic *Robber's Cave* experiment by **Sherif** et al. (1961) dealt with the development and mitigation of group hostility through competition and cooperation. Boys at a summer camp near Robber's Cave, Oklahoma, were unknowingly subjects for this study. The boys were housed in two cabins and manipulations were introduced to encourage competition between the two groups. This led to intergroup hostility and intragroup cohesiveness. Later manipulations that introduced *superordinate goals* requiring joint efforts seemed to reduce the rivalry and stereotyping previously engendered.

Cooperation has been investigated using *non-zero-sum* games, games in which gains and losses do not sum to zero. In these games, one side's winning need not mean the other side's losing. If the players cooperate, they minimize their losses and maximize their total gains. The findings indicate that even though it is in the players' interest to cooperate, most people compete anyway.

The best-known game of this kind is *prisoner's dilemma.* Subjects role-play being suspects in a criminal case. They get interrogated separately by the district attorney and are given two alternatives—to confess or to remain silent. The game is worked out so that if both remain silent there can be only minor charges lodged against both of them. If one confesses and the other remains silent the confessor receives lenient treatment and the other gets the severe punishment. If both confess, they both get severe sentences. The best strategy is for both to be cooperative and not confess. The results, however, show that both players tend to confess in the hope of beating each other. But since both confess, they both lose.

AGGRESSION

Innate Aggression

Instinct theorists (**McDougall, Freud**) and ethologists (**Lorenz**) postulate that humans have an innate drive or instinct to fight. **Lorenz** (1963) observed that certain tropical fish seem to have instinctive needs to be aggressive and, when the ordinary targets are removed, they attack whatever target is available.

Frustration-Aggression Theory

A generally accepted hypothesis is that frustration leads to aggression. The classic studies of this theory were done by the Yale group—**Dollard, Doob, N. Miller, Mowrer, and Sears** (1939). These authors proposed that frustration is displaced elsewhere as aggression when it is impossible or dangerous to direct aggression toward the frustrating object. **Mintz** (1946) showed that a strong relationship exists between poor economic conditions and aggression. In the South during the years 1882 to 1930, when cotton prices declined, lynchings increased.

Barker, Dembo, and Lewin (1941) showed that children frustrated by not being allowed to play with very desirable toys later acted destructively toward the toys when they were allowed to have them.

Learned Aggression

According to the social learning theorists, aggression is greatly influenced by learning. The classic examples of learned aggressive responses are the experiments of **Bandura** and his associates, showing the effect of witnessing aggression from either live or filmed models. The studies showed that children tend to imitate the aggressive behavior of adults. The more important, powerful, successful, and well-liked the adults, the more the children will imitate them.

Diffusing Aggression

Catharsis is the construct that predicts that expressing aggression in socially acceptable ways reduces the aggressive drive. **Feshbach** (1955) studied this by first getting subjects angry, then letting them express their anger through fantasy (responding to TAT cards), and then measuring their aggression through analysis of their verbalizations. The control group that did not get the TAT cards later showed more aggression than the experimental group.

In another study, **Feshbach** (1961) allowed half the angered group to watch a boxing film while the other half viewed a neutral film. The neutral film was not as cathartic, and these subjects later showed more aggression than the group that had viewed the boxing film. The conclusion was that when an individual is angry, releasing aggression in other than overtly physical ways reduces the anger and makes it less likely that physical aggression will occur immediately afterward.

A series of studies by **Berkowitz** (1965) and others, however, suggested that under certain circumstances overt aggression is increased following the viewing of an aggressive film. Berkowitz found that aggressive behavior is a likely consequence if the action in the film seems justified (i.e., the guy deserved the beating), if the depicted situation is close to the viewer's actual life situation, or if there are other aggression-eliciting cues in the environment (e.g., guns lying on a nearby table).

Aggression and TV Violence

The controversial issue of the effects of television violence on children's behavior has been studied by a presidential commission. The commission concluded that TV violence makes children more aggressive and in general has a negative effect. This is consistent with Bandura's thesis described previously (see LEARNED AGGRESSION).

HELPING BEHAVIOR (ALTRUISM)

The study of the variables involved in helping behavior is an important contemporary concern. **Latané and Darley** (1970) have found that the presence of other bystanders exerts an inhibiting influence on altruistic behavior of any given bystander. They proposed that the nonintervention of witnesses to the infamous **Kitty Genovese** murder in Queens, New York, was attributable to the diffusion of felt responsibility; the pressure to intervene did not focus on any of the observers individually. These investigators found that the number of subjects responding to a victim's distress decreases and the response time increases as the number of bystanders increases.

When a victim is obviously in distress and the problem is not ambiguous, the likelihood of the occurrence of altruistic behavior is increased. **Piliavin, Rodin, and Piliavin** (1969) found that a confederate feigning illness on a New York subway car was aided in almost every trial. Even when the confederate appeared to be drunk, he was aided in half the trials.

ATTRIBUTION

Attribution is an approach to understanding how people perceive and think about the causes of things that happen to themselves and to others. It deals with the rules the average individual uses in attempting to infer the causes of observed behavior.

Causal Attribution

One important area studied is how people attribute causation for events. A person is perceived as acting either because of some internal motivation or because of some external force. For instance, if people see a worker with his supervisor nearby, they tend to think the worker is externally motivated. They attribute the worker's productivity to the fact that he is supervised. The supervisor begins to think the worker will produce only if constantly watched, and even the worker himself will tend to attribute behavior to this external motivation since the supervisor is always there.

A classic study by **Thibaut and Riecken** (1955) shows this distinction. A subject was asked to convince two other subjects (actually confederates) to give blood. One confederate was introduced as a high-status (Ph.D.) person; the other as a low-status (undergraduate) person. Both confederates agreed to donate blood. Later, the real subject was asked why he thought these two had been influenced to give blood. In almost all cases the subject reported that the high-status confederate wanted to do it anyway (was internally motivated) while the low-status confederate yielded to the pressure (was externally motivated). A second finding was that the subject came to view the high-status person more favorably.

Jones and Nisbett (1971) consider attribution a function of whether the person is an actor or an observer. Actors tend to attribute their failures to external circumstances, while observers tend to attribute the same actions to underlying personality characteristics. For example, if an individual does not get accepted by a graduate school, he is more likely to believe the rejection was because the admissions procedure was faulty in some way. Another person observing the unsuccessful applicant's situation would tend to attribute the failure to the applicant's lack of satisfactory qualifications (perhaps low GRE scores?).

Attribution of responsibility has been studied by **Lerner** (1966). Lerner concluded that there is a tendency for people to attribute responsibility for an unlucky event to the actor involved, even if they know it was an accident. Lerner calls this a *belief in a just world*. It seems that most people have an attitude that people deserve what they get. The explanation is that people have an interest in believing the world is ordered and rational and just. If it were not, if it were capricious and threatening, then the same ill fate which befell the individual observed could befall the observer. The defense against this thought is to attribute the individual's ill luck to his own doing.

An individual's general orientation toward the causes of events can be measured by **Rotter**'s *Locus of Control Scale,* also called the *Internal-External Scale.* This scale assesses how individuals view the causes of things they do—whether they feel self-motivated and self-responsible *(internal)* or whether they see most of the things that happen to them as outside their control *(external).*

Attribution has been used as an explanation for the labeling of emotions. The **Schacter and Singer** (1962) epinephrine study described earlier showed that an emotional state depends both upon the state of physiological arousal and upon an attribution appropriate to this state of arousal. The cognition determines the name of the emotion.

In a famous study of misattribution, **Valins** (1967) gave subjects false feedback information on heart rate. The subjects viewed slides of seminude women while supposedly listening to their own heartbeats. Actually they were listening to randomly assigned recordings. The pictures associated with a speed-up of heartbeat were later judged to be more attractive. The attribution of causation for heartbeat response determined how the pictures were perceived.

Person Perception

There is a tendency for people to infer a whole personality from the perceived presence of only one trait. For example, knowing someone is intelligent leads most people to expect that the person is clever, active, and reliable. The explanation is that people see others in limited ways and tend to fit their perceptions into preconceived molds.

Central Traits

An early study by **Asch** (1946) tested this hypothesis. Asch postulated that certain characteristics imply more about a person than do others. These are called *central traits*. For example, the warm-cold trait seems central because it is associated with many other traits. The experimental design was to give subjects a description of an individual that contained seven traits including the trait "cold." Other subjects got the same list except "warm" was used in place of "cold." The subjects' impressions of the person described were vastly different even though only one word was changed.

Kelley (1950) replicated this study. He introduced a guest lecturer to two groups of students and presented them with two sets of descriptions of the lecturer. The sets were identical except that one used the trait "warm" while the other used "cold." The students later rated the lecturer and, as predicted, the two groups' impressions were markedly different even though the lecturer's performance was the same before both groups.

Semantic Differential

The phenomenon of seeing people in terms of "good" and "bad" is the *halo effect.* **Osgood** et al. (1957) studied this evaluative tendency and developed the concept of the *semantic differential.* They found that there are three basic dimensions that people use in describing things and people—*evaluation* (good-bad), *potency* (strong-weak), and *activity* (active-passive). The evaluative dimension appears to be the most important, especially in the description of persons.

ROLE THEORY

For role theorists, the concept of a person is equivalent to that of a role. A role typically refers to the behaviors usually expected of a person occupying a given social position or to the actions actually carried out by the person in this position. The self is thought of as an internalization of social roles. Social conduct is considered to be regulated by the part the individual has in a stabilized system of relationships.

Unclear roles are sources of tension and dissatisfaction. Poor crew performance in the Air Force has been traced to unclear role expectations.

Role theorists include **Mead, Heine,** and **Sarbin.**

SOCIAL CUES AND EATING HABITS

Studies of the effect of social and environmental cues on eating habits have shown that certain people respond more to external stimuli and others respond more to internal stimuli. **Schacter** found that people who are overweight tend to be led to eat by external stimuli, such as presence of food, social example, and time of day. People of normal weight with regular eating habits are primarily influenced by the need for food and by feelings associated with hunger. In the study, the subjects were deceived into thinking it was mealtime. Fat people tended to want to eat even though it was not, in reality, time to eat. Subjects who were not overweight tended to wait until they were hungry before they ate. Schacter predicted a relationship between fat-thin and internal-external cues.

FOR FURTHER READING

Freedman, J.L., Carlsmith, J.M., and Sears, D.O. *Social psychology*. 5th ed. Englewood Cliffs, N.J.: Prentice-Hall, 1985.

References

HISTORY AND SYSTEMS

Ebbinghaus, H. *Memory*. Translated by H.A. Ruger and C.E. Bussenius. New York: Teachers College, Columbia University, 1913.

EXPERIMENTAL METHODOLOGY

Rosenthal, R., and Jacobson, L. *Pygmalion in the classroom*. New York: Holt, Rinehart and Winston, 1968.

PHYSIOLOGY

Bakan, P. The eyes have it. *Psychology Today*, 1971, *4*, 64–67.

Dewey, J. The reflex arc concept in psychology. *Psychological Review*, 1896, *3*, 357–370.

Hubel, D.H., and Wiesel, T.N. Receptive fields, binocular interaction, and functional architecture in the cat's visual cortex. *Journal of Physiology*, 1962, *160*, 106–154.

McConnell, J.V. Memory transfer through cannibalism in planarians. *Journal of Neuropsychiatry*, 1962, *3*, 542–548.

Olds, J. Pleasure centers in the brain. *Scientific American*, 1956, *193*, 105–116.

Ornstein, R.E. *The psychology of consciousness*. New York: Viking Press, 1972.

Sherrington, C.S. *The integrative action of the nervous system*. New Haven: Yale University Press, 1906.

LEARNING

Bandura, A., Ross, D., and Ross, S.A. A comparative test of the status envy, social power, and secondary reinforcement theories of identificatory learning. *Journal of Abnormal and Social Psychology*, 1963, *67*, 527–531.

Cowles, J.T. Food-tokens as incentives for learning by chimpanzees. *Comparative Psychology Monographs*, 1937, *14*, No. 71.

Dollard, J., Doob, L.W., Miller, N.E., Mowrer, O.H., and Sears, R.R. *Frustration and Aggression*. New Haven: Yale University Press, 1939.

Dollard, J., and Miller, N.E. *Personality and psychotherapy: An analysis in terms of learning, thinking, and culture.* New York: McGraw-Hill, 1950.

Harlow, H.F., Harlow, M.K., and Meyer, D.R. Learning motivated by a manipulation drive. *Journal of Experimental Psychology,* 1950, *40,* 228–234.

Krasner, L. On the death of behavior modification: Some comments from a mourner. *American Psychologist,* 1976, *5,* 387–388.

Miller, N.E. Learning of visceral and glandular responses. *Science,* 1969, *163,* 434–445.

Olds, J., and Milner, P. Positive reinforcement produced by electrical stimulation of septal area and other regions of rat brain. *Journal of Comparative and Physiological Psychotherapy,* 1954, *47,* 419–427.

Thorndike, E.L. Animal intelligence: An experimental study of the associative processes in animals. *Psychological Monographs,* 1898, *8,* 1–109.

Thorndike, E.L., and Woodworth, R.S. The influence of improvements in one mental function upon the efficiency of other functions. *Psychological Review,* 1901, *8,* 247–261, 384–395, 553–564.

PERCEPTION

Gibson, E.J., and Walk, R.D. The visual cliff. *Scientific American,* 1960, *202,* 64–71.

Gibson, J.J. *The senses considered as perceptual systems.* Boston: Houghton Mifflin, 1966.

Hebb, D.O. *The organization of behavior.* New York: Wiley, 1949.

Riesen, A.H. The development of visual perception in man and chimpanzee. *Science,* 1947, *106,* 107–108.

von Senden, M. *Space and sight: The perception of space and shape in the congenitally blind before and after operations.* Translated by P. Heath. London: Methuen, 1960.

COGNITION

Broadbent, D.E. *Perception and communication.* London: Pergamon Press, 1958.

Cherry, C. Some experiments on the perception of speech with one and with two ears. *Journal of the Acoustical Society of America,* 1953, *25,* 975–979.

Gray, J.Q., and Wedderburn, A.A. Grouping strategies with simultaneous stimuli. *Quarterly Journal of Experimental Psychology,* 1960, *12,* 180–184.

Miller, G.A. The magical number seven, plus or minus two: Some limits on our capacity for processing information. *Psychology Review,* 1956, *63,* 81–97.

Osgood, C.E., Suci, G.J., and Tannenbaum, P.H. *The measurement of meaning.* Urbana, Ill.: University of Illinois Press, 1957.

Peterson, L.B., and Peterson, M.J. Short-term retention of individual verbal items. *Journal of Experimental Psychology,* 1959, *58,* 193–198.

Sperling, G. The information available in brief visual presentations. *Psychological Monographs,* 1960, *74,* (Whole No. 498).

Treisman, A.M. Contextual cues in selective listening. *Quarterly Journal of Experimental Psychology,* 1960, *12,* 242–248.

Whorf, B.C. *Four articles on metalinguistics.* Washington: Foreign Service Institute, 1950.

DEVELOPMENTAL PSYCHOLOGY

Bowlby, J. Separation anxiety. *International Journal of Psychoanalysis,* 1960, *41,* 89–113.

Gibson, E.J., and Walk, R.R. The visual cliff. *Scientific American,* 1960, *202,* 2–9.

Harlow, H.F., and Zimmerman, R.R. Affectional responses in the infant monkey. *Science,* 1959, *130,* 421–432.

Lorenz, K. The comparative method of studying innate behavior patterns. In *Physiological Mechanisms in Animal Behavior.* New York: Academic Press, 1950.

Mednick, S.A. A learning theory approach to research in schizophrenia. *Psychological Bulletin,* 1958, *55,* 315.

Rosenzweig, M.R., Krech, D., and Bennett, E.L. A search for relations between brain chemistry and behavior. *Psychological Bulletin,* 1960, *57,* 476–492.

Spitz, R.A. Anaclitic depression. *The Psychoanalytic Study of the Child,* 1946, *2,* 313–342.

Spitz, R.A. *The first year of life.* New York: International Universities Press, 1965.

Whiting, J.W.M., and Child, I.C. *Child training and personality: A cross-cultural study.* New Haven: Yale University Press, 1953.

PERSONALITY AND CLINICAL PSYCHOLOGY

Adorno, T.W., Frenkel-Brunswik, E., Levinson, D.J., and Sanford, R.N. *The authoritarian personality.* New York: Harper and Row, 1950.

Breuer, J., and Freud, S. *Studies on hysteria.* Standard Edition, *2.* London: Hogarth Press, 1955.

Erikson, E.H. *Childhood and society.* New York: W.W. Norton, 1950.

Freud, S. *The interpretation of dreams.* Translated by James Strachey. New York: Basic Books, 1955.

Fromm, E. *Escape from freedom.* New York: Rinehart, 1941.

Fromm, E. *Man for himself.* New York: Rinehart, 1947.

Fromm, E. *The sane society.* New York: Holt, Rinehart and Winston, 1955.

Fromm, E. *The art of loving.* New York: Harper and Row, 1956.

McClelland, D.C. *The achieving society.* Princeton, N.J.: Van Nostrand, 1961.

Rozenzweig, S. A transvaluation of psychotherapy: A reply to Hans Eysenck. *Journal of Abnormal and Social Psychology,* 1954, *49,* 298–304.

Sarason, I.G. Empirical findings and theoretical problems in the use of anxiety scales. *Psychological Bulletin,* 1960, *57,* 403–415.

Witkin, H.A., et al. *Personality through perception.* New York: Harper and Row, 1954.

SOCIAL PSYCHOLOGY

Asch, S.E. Forming impressions of personality. *Journal of Abnormal and Social Psychology,* 1946, *41,* 258–290.

Asch, S.E. Studies of independence and submission to group pressure: A minority of one against a unanimous majority. *Psychological Monographs,* 1956, *70.* (Whole No. 416).

Asch, S.E. Effects of group pressures upon the modification and distortion of judgments. In *Group leadership and men.* ed. Harold Guetzkow. Pittsburgh: Carnegie Press, 1956.

Barker, R.G., Dembo, T., and Lewin, K. Frustration and regression: An experiment with young children. *University of Iowa Studies in Child Welfare,* 1941, *18,* No. 1.

Bem, D.J. Self-perception: An alternative interpretation of cognitive dissonance phenomena. *Psychological Review,* 1967, *74,* 183–200.

Berkowitz, L. Some aspects of observed aggression. *Journal of Personality and Social Psychology,* 1965, *2,* 359–369.

Bogardus, E.S. Measuring social distance. *Journal of Applied Sociology,* 1925, *9,* 229–308.

Brehm, J.W., and Cohen, A.R. *Explorations in cognitive dissonance.* New York: Wiley, 1962.

Deutsch, M., and Gerard, H.B. A study of normative and informational social influences upon individual judgment. *Journal of Abnormal and Social Psychology,* 1955, *51,* 629–636.

Dollard, J., Doob, L.W., Miller, N.E., Mowrer, O.H., and Sears, R.R. *Frustration and aggression.* New Haven: Yale University Press, 1939.

Feshbach, S. The drive-reducing function of fantasy behavior. *Journal of Abnormal and Social Psychology,* 1955, *51,* 3–12.

Feshbach, S. The stimulating versus cathartic effects of a vicarious aggressive activity. *Journal of Abnormal and Social Psychology,* 1961, *63,* 381–385.

Festinger, L. *A theory of cognitive dissonance.* Stanford: Stanford University Press, 1957.

Freedman, J.L., and Fraser, S.C. Compliance without pressure: The foot-in-the-door technique. *Journal of Personality and Social Psychology,* 1966, *4,* 196–202.

Jones, E.E., and Nisbett, R.E. *The actor and the observer: Divergent perceptions of the causes of behavior.* Morristown, N.J.: General Learning Press, 1971.

Lerner, M.J., and Simmons, C.H. Observer's reaction to the "innocent victim." *Journal of Personality and Social Psychology,* 1966, *4,* 203–210.

Miller, N.E. Experimental studies of conflict. In *Personality and behavior disorders,* ed. J.M. Hunt. New York: Ronald, 1944.

Mintz, A. A re-examination of correlations between lynchings and economic indices. *Journal of Abnormal Social Psychology,* 1946, *41,* 154–160.

Newcomb, T.M. An approach to the study of communicative acts. *Psychological Review,* 1953, *60,* 393–404.

Osgood, C.E., and Tannenbaum, P.H. The principles of congruity in the prediction of attitude change. *Psychological Review,* 1953, *62,* 393–404.

Osgood, C.E., Suci, G.J., and Tannenbaum, P.H. *The measurement of meaning.* Urbana, Ill.: University of Illinois Press, 1957.

Piliavin, I.M., Rodin, J., and Piliavin, J.A. Good Samaritanism: An underground phenomenon? *Journal of Personality and Social Psychology,* 1969, *13,* 289–299.

Rokeach, M. *The open and closed mind.* New York: Basic Books, 1960.

Ross, E.A. *Social psychology: An outline and source book.* New York: Macmillan, 1908.

Schacter, S. *The psychology of affiliation.* Stanford: Stanford University Press, 1959.

Schacter, S. Obesity and eating. *Science,* 1968, *161,* 751–756.

Schacter, S., and Singer, J.E. Cognitive, social, and physiological determinants of emotional states. *Psychological Review,* 1962, *69,* 379–399.

Sherif, M. *The psychology of social norms.* New York: Harper, 1936.

Sherif, M., Harvey, O.J., White, B.J., Hood, W.E., and Sherif, C.W. *Intergroup conflict and cooperation: The Robber's Cave experiment.* Norman, Okla.: University of Oklahoma Book Exchange, 1961.

Thibaut, J.W., and Riecken, H.W. Some determinants and consequences of the perception of social causality. *Journal of Personality,* 1955, *24,* 113–133.

Thurstone, L.L., and Chave, E.J. *The measurement of attitudes.* Chicago: University of Chicago Press, 1929.

Triplett, N. The dynamogenic factors in pacemaking and competition. *American Journal of Psychology,* 1897, *2,* 507–533.

Valins, S. Emotionality and information concerning internal reactions. *Journal of Personality and Social Psychology,* 1967, *6,* 458–463.

Zeigarnik, B. On finished and unfinished tasks. In *A sourcebook of Gestalt psychology,* ed. W.D. Ellis. London: Routledge, 1938.

Zimbardo, P.C., and Formica, R. Emotional comparison and self-esteem as determinants of affiliation. *Journal of Personality,* 1963, *31,* 141–162.

53. Aggression in animals, such as the charging of a bull, may be controlled by electrical stimulation to which area of the brain?

    (A) Basal ganglia

    (B) Cerebellum

    (C) Pons

    (D) Superior colliculi

    (E) Limbic system

54. The typical male has

    (A) 23 pairs of XY chromosomes

    (B) an extra Y chromosome

    (C) an extra X chromosome

    (D) one more Y chromosome than the typical female

    (E) 50% X chromosomes and 50% Y chromosomes

55. An experimenter following the example of Tryon's selective breeding of maze-bright rats wishes to selectively breed dogs for the ability to do entertaining tricks. Which method would the experimenter most likely follow?

    (A) Compare performance of sets of twins, then breed twins with each other

    (B) Breed performance-bright dogs with other performance-bright dogs, regardless of the performance of their siblings

    (C) Enrich the environments of the dogs that will be selectively bred for performance-brightness

    (D) Enrich the nutrition of the dogs that will be selectively bred for performance-brightness

    (E) Select out dogs who show high *general intelligence* in most skills and breed them with each other.

56. Research on the effects of early environments on animals has demonstrated that

    (A) early *enriched* environments may improve performance, but have no other effects

    (B) inheritability of skills acquired in early environments can be selectively inbred

    (C) the physical development of the nervous system can be influenced by early environments

    (D) the effects of early environments are temporary only

    (E) emotional characteristics are uninfluenced by early environments, although intellectual characteristics may be influenced

57. One of the benefits of using computers in brain research is that we can now

    (A) simulate most measurable brain activity on the computer

    (B) measure activity in the nervous system without the use of electrodes

    (C) study synaptic transmission without chemical intervention

    (D) measure evoked potentials

    (E) count the number of nerves involved in a circuit

58. Imagine that the lower half of a person's somatosensory motor area is destroyed in an accident. The result of such damage would likely be

    (A) loss of control over facial movements and speech

    (B) loss of control over bodily movements

    (C) loss of control over ambulatory functions (legs and feet)

    (D) partial loss of control over a wide range of bodily functions, including speech and large muscle movement

    (E) lack of coordination between sensory and motor activity

59. Disorders characterized by intense, unrealistic, irrational fears are called

    (A) schizotypal disorders

    (B) schizoid disorders

    (C) anxiety disorders

    (D) hysteria

    (E) affective disorders

60. When an individual is concentrating on a spatial-visual problem, eye movements are most likely to be

    (A) minimal

    (B) to the right

    (C) to the left

    (D) up

    (E) down

61. One of Penfield's most important discoveries about the brain was that

    (A) the speech area of right-handed people is on the left side of the brain, while the speech area of left-handed people is on the right

    (B) symbolic memory is consolidated in Broca's area

    (C) electronic stimulation of the brain can evoke some otherwise long-forgotten memories

    (D) epilepsy involves the destruction of the permanent memory record

    (E) brain functioning can be controlled by techniques such as biofeedback

62. Which of the following is not a method used in the study of brain functioning?

    (A) GSR

    (B) CAT scan

    (C) ESB

    (D) EEG

    (E) EMG

63. In comparison to humans, lower animals have a much less highly developed

    (A) hindbrain

    (B) forebrain

    (C) pons

    (D) midbrain

    (E) medulla

64. A nerve that commands a hand to move a pencil is

    (A) afferent

    (B) efferent

    (C) sympathetic

    (D) parasympathetic

    (E) autonomic

65. Which of the following is a part of the telencephalon?

    (A) Cerebral cortex

    (B) Inferior colliculi

    (C) Cerebellum

    (D) Hypothalamus

    (E) None of the above

66. Short-term memories are converted into long-term memories in which part of the brain?

    (A) Frontal lobe

    (B) Parietal lobe

    (C) Temporal lobe

    (D) Association areas

    (E) Fissure of Sylvius

67. From sound wave to perceived sound, which is the path for hearing?

    (A) Auditory canal, cochlea, eardrum, semicircular canal, auditory nerve

    (B) Eardrum, semicircular canal, cochlea, auditory nerve

    (C) Eardrum, cochlea, semicircular canal, auditory nerve

    (D) Eardrum, auditory canal, semicircular canal, auditory nerve, cochlea

    (E) Auditory canal, eardrum, cochlea, auditory nerve, semicircular canal

68. The Apgar scoring system

    (A) measures exposure of pregnant women to teratogens

    (B) measures visual responses of newborns

    (C) measures reflexes of the newborn, such as plantar, Moro, and Babinski

    (D) assesses condition of the newborn immediately after birth

    (E) measures the infant's reaction to visual cliff

69. The Yerkes-Dodson law, one of the principles espoused by early twentieth-century psychologists, is updated in modern

    (A) arousal theory

    (B) signal-detection theory

    (C) human factors theory

    (D) feature-detection theory

    (E) field theory

70. Zajonc's theory of emotions concludes that

    (A) what we don't know (cognition) won't affect us (emotion)

    (B) if we don't have a word for it (encoding), it's not important (emotion)

    (C) if it doesn't show on the face (catharsis), it's not important (emotion)

    (D) even if we don't know (cognition) we can react (emotion)

    (E) the unconscious (cognition) always controls the conscious (emotion)

71. Fatality is most likely to result from damage to which of the following?

    (A) Medulla

    (B) Spinal cord

    (C) Reticular formation

    (D) Forebrain

    (E) Midbrain

72. Studies of rates of maturation among boys and girls indicate that

    (A) late maturing boys and girls undergo emotional "growth spurts," causing them to overcompensate for their early deficiencies

    (B) early maturity tends to be advantageous in boys, but is less so for girls

    (C) age of menarche and growth of pubic hair are genetically determined

    (D) late maturing boys and girls become social isolates and participate less in social activities

    (E) maturity rates are the same for boys and girls in most cultures other than North American and European

73. Under the influence of alcohol, the activities of the cerebellum can be _____, possibly causing _____.

    (A) accelerated . . . loss of inhibitions

    (B) accelerated . . . double vision

    (C) depressed . . . slurred speech

    (D) depressed . . . depression

    (E) unaffected . . . no change in cerebellum activity, though other parts of the brain may react

74. The genetic disorder associated with an extra chromosome in the 21st chromosome pair and usually with advanced age of the mother is

    (A) cretinism

    (B) Klinefelter's syndrome

    (C) Down syndrome

    (D) hydroencephaly

    (E) microencephaly

75. A patient with Parkinson's disease

    (A) is now commonly treated with artificial dopamine

    (B) suffers from memory lacunae (blank spaces) and hallucinations

    (C) must avoid L-DOPA and MPTP

    (D) does not use dopamine properly because of the death of the axons that use this substance

    (E) shows a deficiency of Vitamin B-1 which assists the brain's use of glucose

76. In Selye's General Adaptation Syndrome (GAS), the final stage is

    (A) adaptation

    (B) actualization

    (C) exhaustion

    (D) death

    (E) balance

77. Scarr and Weinberg found IQ scores of African-American children raised by white, middle-class adoptive parents

    (A) were poorer than IQ scores of other African-American children because of racial identity confusion

    (B) were equal to other African-American children, but not as good as other whites

    (C) were equal to other white, middle-class adopted children

    (D) were invalid because the tests were culturally unfair and/or biased

    (E) were equal to the scores of whites on verbal but not on mathematical skills

78. The most widely used medication for treatment of pain is

    (A) alcohol

    (B) phenobarbitol

    (C) salicylates

    (D) Prozac

    (E) paregoric

79. Compared to the decisions of juries, judges

    (A) disagree with juries about two-thirds of the time

    (B) concur with juries about four times out of five

    (C) tend to be much more harsh in their evaluations of defendants

    (D) tend to be much more likely to acquit than to convict

    (E) tend to have great disdain for the jury system

80. According to Bowlby,

    (A) sexual identification is cognitively determined

    (B) birth trauma is a major determinant of later personality

    (C) the role of fathers in successful development has not been sufficiently stressed by most researchers

    (D) early separation leaves deep scars on the infant that cannot be overcome

    (E) maternal attachment is essential in human development

81. Patient compliance with medical treatment instructions

    (A) is highest among patients who ask the fewest questions and make the fewest demands on the physician

    (B) is only around 50% for patients on prescribed medication

    (C) is highest among patients with long-term conditions, such as breast cancer or high blood pressure

    (D) is related to socio-economic status

    (E) is highest when treatment is perceived as a good monetary bargain

82. The standard of competency for a defendant to stand for trial was reviewed by the US Supreme Court. The results of this case have been used subsequently to determine the minimal level of mental competence of defendants. This case was

    (A) Brown v. Board of Education

    (B) Tarasoff

    (C) Daubert

    (D) Frye

    (E) Dusky

83. A regular smoker is presented with data on the relationship between smoking and cancer. Under which circumstance would the smoker be *most* likely to stop smoking?

    (A) If the data are extremely dramatic and anxiety-provoking

    (B) If the data are ambiguous and mildly anxiety-provoking

    (C) If the smoker has to give an oral presentation of the data to a group of smokers

    (D) If the data are balanced on both sides of the question

    (E) If the data are endorsed by prestigious medical authorities

84. Worker satisfaction has been found to be higher when the communication network is

    (A) fluid

    (B) invariant

    (C) centralized

    (D) decentralized

    (E) unidirectional

85. A frequent objection to political polls is that the sample size is small, averaging around 1200 or fewer respondents, but its results are supposed to represent the millions of voters in the United States. If you were in charge of a polling organization, what would you do to increase the reliability of your poll results by 50%?

    (A) Double the size of the sample to 2400

    (B) Quadruple the size of your sample to 4800

    (C) Divide the 1200 person sample into smaller, equal-sized groups, and question them at different times, months apart

    (D) Poll the 1200 person sample several times, months apart, and pay special attention to trends

    (E) None of the above

86. Although structuralism, which played an important role in the development of experimental psychology early in the twentieth century, has for the most part ceased to be an important school in psychology, its closest philosophical descendant among modern schools of psychology is

    (A) information-processing theory

    (B) physiological psychology

    (C) transactional analysis

    (D) phenomenology

    (E) psychoanalysis

87. Friends seeking to adopt a child are told the next available child is one year of age. The friends are worried about whether a one-year-old is too old to bond with them as adoptive parents. You would advise them that:

    (A) bonding by female children is more likely than bonding by males

    (B) bonding to adoptive parents at one year of age is no problem for most children

    (C) bonding to adoptive parents is difficult after the early critical period has elapsed

    (D) cross-racial bonding is difficult after the early critical period has elapsed

    (E) bonding to adoptive parents is dependent on IQ; only higher IQ adoptees bond as late as one year of age

88. Astrology is a systematic body of thought. Most scientists nowadays, however, denigrate astrology because they feel it is unscientific. They say that in order to be more scientific, astrology would have to meet the test of

    (A) falsifiability

    (B) verifiability

    (C) time

    (D) laboratory experimentation

    (E) hypothetico-deductive reasoning

89. Which of the following sets of symptoms appears commonly in newborns suffering from fetal alcohol syndrome (FAS)?

    (A) Subtle impairments of motor and cognitive development

    (B) Blindness, deafness, brain abnormalities, heart abnormalities

    (C) Mental retardation, abnormal facial characteristics, behavior problems

    (D) Overall growth retardation, problems in labor, retardation of learning in early life

    (E) Premature separation from placenta, premature birth, respiratory problems

90. In one system of derived scores, the mean is expressed as 50 and the standard as 10. This is the

    (A) Z-score

    (B) T-score

    (C) half-time score

    (D) standard score

    (E) smoothed score

91. Attribution theory predicts that

    (A) people judge others by the same criteria on which they judge themselves

    (B) certain professionals, such as psychologists, are better judges of character than are others

    (C) with age and experience, people become more adept at judging the causes of others' behaviors

    (D) only a minority of observers attribute causation to independent personality factors

    (E) others are judged based on both situational and dispositional causes

92. Levinson found job satisfaction in men between 20 and 60 years of age

    (A) tends to decrease with age

    (B) shows no clear relationship with age

    (C) increases for married men, but decreases for single men

    (D) increases for single men, but decreases for married men

    (E) tends to increase with age

93. According to the Hering opponent-process theory, blue stimulation increases one's sensitivity to

    (A) violet

    (B) yellow

    (C) red

    (D) green

    (E) white

94. The terms *factor analysis, trait theory, introversion-extroversion,* and *neuroticism-stability* are associated with

    (A) Mischel

    (B) Kelly

    (C) Eysenck

    (D) Minnesota Multiphasic Personality Inventory

    (E) Anastasi

95. The perceived size of a moving frisbee is

    (A) predicted by the Weber-Fechner law

    (B) predicted by Stevens' law

    (C) a relative constant

    (D) orthogonal to the retinal image

    (E) subject to the Doppler effect

96. The leading cause of death in most age, race, and sex categories and the leading cause of pre-retirement years of lost life is

    (A) traumatic brain injury

    (B) heart attack and hypertension

    (C) sexually transmitted disease

    (D) cancer

    (E) smoking

97. Studies of the linguistic abilities of primates

    (A) support Skinner's theories of reinforcement

    (B) have fallen out of favor because of serious experimenter-bias issues

    (C) find ape language as syntactically complex as that of human three-year-olds

    (D) find chimpanzees cannot use linguistic symbols meaningfully

    (E) find the critical period for language development in apes is 14 days

98. Edwards, Crowne, and Marlowe found that

    (A) people with a high need to be socially desirable report that they enjoy monotonous tasks more than people with a low need

    (B) people with a high social desirability need answer personality questionnaires more reliably

    (C) people with a low social desirability need tend to be less cautious in their social behavior

    (D) people high on need for social desirability also are more popular with their peers

    (E) social desirability is a transient personality characteristic that can easily be changed

99. Fear and anger are controlled by the

    (A) peripheral nervous system

    (B) amygdala

    (C) pons

    (D) sympathetic nervous system

    (E) pineal gland

100. In going over old experimental research reports you notice that Jones in 1907 accepted as true a hypothesis that was later demonstrated by Smith in 1920 and Johnson in 1955 to be false. It appears that Jones

    (A) obviously falsified the data

    (B) used the wrong level of statistical significance

    (C) used the wrong statistical test

    (D) committed a Type I error

    (E) committed a Type II error

101. You are in charge of a charity fund-raiser. Rather than using the usual thermometer-style bar chart, you plot a curve of money collected on a graph so that the amount of money is measured on the ordinate and time in months on the abscissa. Your curve

    (A) approaches a normal distribution

    (B) is an ogive

    (C) is skewed to the left

    (D) is skewed to the right

    (E) is leptokurtic

102. Of the following, which method of conditioning holds the least likelihood of success?

    (A) Fixed-interval

    (B) Vicarious reinforcement

    (C) Secondary drive reduction

    (D) Shaping

    (E) Backward conditioning

103. A patient in therapy begins to mock the therapist, to show up late for sessions, and to withhold payment. A psychoanalyst would call this behavior

    (A) negative valence

    (B) countertransference

    (C) ego defense

    (D) regression in the service of the ego

    (E) negative transference

104. The therapist in the above example reacts to the patient's behavior by teasing the patient, by giving misleading advice, and by reporting the patient to a collection agency. A psychoanalyst would label the therapist's behavior

    (A) reaction formation

    (B) identification with the aggressor

    (C) displacement

    (D) countertransference

    (E) negative transference

105. People who are color-blind can correctly identify the color white. This is explained by the color vision theory of

    (A) Kolmogorov-Smirnov

    (B) Young-Helmholtz

    (C) Hurvich-Jameson

    (D) Weber-Fechner

    (E) H.B. Barlow

106. The performance of your favorite athlete is severely penalized by a game official during a game you are watching on TV. According to social learning theory, as a consequence of seeing the athlete penalized your identification with the athlete will

    (A) increase because vicarious punishment causes paradoxical shift

    (B) increase because of identification with the victim

    (C) hardly change, since vicarious punishment has less effect on the observer than does vicarious reinforcement

    (D) decrease because vicarious identification has less effect on the observer than secondary reinforcement

    (E) decrease because of identification with the aggressor

107. The inability to retain information in memory storage for more than a brief period of time is called

    (A) fugue

    (B) agnosia

    (C) retrograde amnesia

    (D) anamnesis

    (E) transient global amnesia

108. Studies of successful brain-surgery patients have found

    (A) near-death and "other-world" experiences are common

    (B) a high incidence of postoperative addiction to pain-killing drugs

    (C) in most modern patients from industrial societies, the brain's immune responses have been impaired by artificial food ingredients

    (D) REM sleep does not return to its prior levels after the operation

    (E) no need for general anesthetic; only local anesthetic for the scalp is needed

109. Which of the following statements about the MMPI-2 is *not* true?

    (A) Its scales are construct valid.

    (B) It is not radically different from the original MMPI.

    (C) All races are normed in the same way.

    (D) It is normed on a normal population.

    (E) It attempts to measure lying and other forms of deception by the test-taker.

110. *Halstead-Reitan* and *Luria Nebraska* are standard tests

    (A) of intelligence

    (B) in neuropsychology

    (C) of personality

    (D) in clinical psychology

    (E) in career counseling

111. A group of airline pilots is instructed to pay attention to moving triangles on a video screen, but to disregard moving circles. The pilots' N100s and P300s for triangles are greater than for circles. This is an experiment in

    (A) autokinetic effect

    (B) receiver operating characteristic curves

    (C) evoked brain potentials

    (D) signal detection theory

    (E) motion parallax

112. According to cognitive dissonance theory, a person is most likely to read automobile advertisements

    (A) after reading about automobile accidents

    (B) before going on a long trip by car

    (C) after buying a new car

    (D) before bringing up the topic of buying a new car to his or her spouse

    (E) after paying taxes

113. The term "aura" is used to describe

    (A) the special properties of folk medicine practitioners that enables them to be effective

    (B) the capacity of suggestion to elicit physiological symptoms among asthmatics

    (C) a foreign, "non-self" substance introduced into the autoimmune system

    (D) a warning sign of a heart attack

    (E) the first phase of a migraine headache

114. Extensive physical contact between newborn and mother immediately after birth

    (A) must be accomplished within a brief critical period for normal development

    (B) is unrelated to later infant development

    (C) can be delayed no more than a day or two for normal cognitive development

    (D) can be delayed no more than a day or two for normal emotional development

    (E) may be harmful to later infant development if excessive

115. Research on the effects of day-care indicates that

    (A) day-care has a mildly negative effect on attachment formation

    (B) the clearest documented benefit is in increased intellectual performance of children from impoverished backgrounds

    (C) day-care children show superior social and intellectual performance compared with home-raised children

    (D) day-care children show superior social skills but weaker attachment to parents

    (E) IQ scores tend to increase the longer a child is in day-care

116. Studies of alcohol and alcoholism have shown

    (A) support for genetic causation of alcoholism is so strong that other explanations are no longer given scientific credence

    (B) hard liquor, when measured by percentage of alcohol in the blood, has a significantly more deleterious effect than beer

    (C) alcohol has a different effect on the walls of neurons of alcoholics than on those of non-alcoholics

    (D) while it was once thought alcoholics must be "dry" for life, modern techniques make social drinking possible

    (E) antabuse is now the treatment of choice in medical recovery programs

117. Jean withdraws his hand from a hot radiator pipe even before his brain receives a pain signal, demonstrating

    (A) a basal reflex

    (B) a reflex arc

    (C) a spinal reflex

    (D) an automatic reflex

    (E) a peripheral reflex

118. DSM : psychiatric diagnosis : :

    (A) MMPI : projective testing

    (B) computer : Windows

    (C) APA : PsychInfo

    (D) Freud : defense mechanism

    (E) MMY : psychological testing

119. An industrial psychologist varies the payoff matrix of an experiment to compensate for systematic false alarms. The experimenter is studying

    (A) unconscious inferences

    (B) Type I error

    (C) signal detection

    (D) social attribution theory

    (E) workplace harassment

120. The .05 level of statistical significance was adopted by most psychology journal publishers because

    (A) it is the level of significance used in most of the *hard* sciences

    (B) it is mandated as the minimally acceptable standard in government research

    (C) it can be mathematically proven to be valid

    (D) it can be mathematically proven to be reliable

    (E) of historic convention, primarily

121. Steinberg found that as adolescents mature their relations with their parents change. He found that adolescents

    (A) gained more power over same-sex parents than over opposite-sex parents

    (B) became more secretive with parents until rebellion became manifest

    (C) were more conforming to social role expectations if the same-sex parent lived at home

    (D) gained more power over opposite-sex parents than over same-sex parents

    (E) were more conforming to social role expectations if the opposite-sex parent lived at home

Questions 122 and 123 are based on the following paragraph:

The ideal of many experimental psychologists is to study behavior without having the experimental procedures artificially alter the *natural* occurrence of the behavior. However, many psychologists are concerned about how experimentation influences the behavior being studied.

122. The theory or principle of physics, frequently cited by psychologists and philosophers of science, claiming that the act of observing a phenomenon often changes some aspect of its nature is known as

    (A)   The Theory of Relativity

    (B)   The Heisenberg Principle

    (C)   Gödel's Proof

    (D)   The Law of Thermodynamics

    (E)   Bernoulli's Principle

123. A psychologist who conducted extensive research on the effects of experimenter bias in behavioral research is

    (A)   Allport

    (B)   Festinger

    (C)   Rosenthal

    (D)   Aronson

    (E)   Freedman

124. It has been observed that there is little convergence of cones, bipolar cells, and ganglion cells. This is because

    (A)   cones play a minor role in vision

    (B)   cones require an even more elaborate set of nervous pathways than rods

    (C)   some cones are directly connected to the brain

    (D)   cones compete with rods for access to ganglion cells

    (E)   clusters of cones occupy the same nervous pathway

125. Motion parallax is

    (A)   a symptom of tardive dyskinesia

    (B)   a development of the concrete operational period

    (C)   a form of inner ear disturbance

    (D)   a binocular depth cue

    (E)   a hypochondriacal disorder

126. Cross-cultural studies of sexual behavior show that

    (A) older females initiate sexual contact in European societies, but not in African societies

    (B) female initiation of sexual contacts and relations is more common in more primitive, "natural" societies

    (C) with rare exceptions, in most societies males initiate sexual contacts and relations with females

    (D) when there is a disproportionate number of females, as in post-war societies, females initiate sexual contacts with men more frequently than the reverse

    (E) male initiation of sexual contacts and relations is the ideal in most societies, although poorly practiced in many cases

127. A likely reason why users of marijuana have short-term memory problems is

    (A) the influence of marijuana on serotonin receptors

    (B) the influence of marijuana on endorphins

    (C) behavior in response to past studies that were influenced by anti-marijuana social attitudes; recent studies have shown there are, in fact, no memory problems associated with marijuana.

    (D) the influence of marijuana on anadamides

    (E) reduction of absorption of vitamin B

128. When the wavelength of electromagnetic radiation of a source of light changes from 500 to 600 millimicrons, the pupil of the eye

    (A) constricts

    (B) dilates

    (C) varies in size depending on the observer's location

    (D) remains constant

    (E) changes pigmentation minutely

129. One of the primary goals of a person who is meditating is to

    (A) stop the "inner voice"

    (B) achieve wealth and health

    (C) achieve focused insight

    (D) regularize heart rate

    (E) detach from the world

130. Teratogens are usually

    (A) environmental

    (B) genetic

    (C) least damaging late in pregnancy

    (D) resistant to nutritional intervention

    (E) least damaging early in pregnancy

131. Birds do not appear to experience periods of drowsiness equivalent to the states of semi-wakefulness humans experience before or after sleep. This is because of

    (A) the more highly developed forebrain of the bird

    (B) hormonal secretions, apparently from the pituitary gland of the bird

    (C) the structure of the visual system of the bird, which is directly connected to the brain

    (D) the absence of a reticular formation in the brain of birds

    (E) conditioning

132. A driver stops on the road to ask for directions. The directions include the names of seven streets. As a psychologist familiar with research on human memory, you would predict that

    (A) the driver would probably get to the destination expediently because Miller has shown that humans can easily store eight units of information

    (B) the driver would be able to get only the first few streets right because of the primacy effect

    (C) the driver would get only the last few streets right because of the recency effect

    (D) the driver might get the first couple of streets or the last couple of streets right, but not the middle few because of the serial order effect

    (E) the bystander would lead the driver astray on purpose because of the fear of intervention

133. Sensitivity to a constant olfactory stimulus, when plotted as a function of time of onset, has been found to be

    (A) a positively accelerated rising curve

    (B) a negatively accelerated rising curve

    (C) orthogonal to time

    (D) a negatively accelerated falling curve

    (E) a positively accelerated falling curve

134. A Z-score of 50 (mean = 40, standard deviation = 5) could be converted into what raw score of a distribution whose mean = 212, standard deviation = 36?

    (A) 284

    (B) 130

    (C) 320

    (D) 250

    (E) 50

135. A person diagnosed as phobic differs from a person diagnosed as obsessional in that the phobic is

    (A) more likely to be preoccupied with thoughts about the object of his or her disorder

    (B) more likely to be subject to many phobias, whereas an obsessional is more likely to have only single, discrete obsessions

    (C) likely to cover up his or her disorder better than the obsessional

    (D) more likely to identify his or her phobias, whereas the obsessional tends to have more diffuse anxiety

    (E) more likely to seek help than the obsessional

136. A scattergram is plotted and a regression line drawn to describe the best fit to the given data. If the distance from each point to the mean and the square of each distance is measured, the sum of the squares is equal to the

    (A) correlation coefficient

    (B) variance

    (C) square root of the t-test

    (D) variance squared

    (E) analysis of variance

137. A researcher is trying to design a computer program that emulates the sensory input of airplane pilots flying in foggy weather. The computer program that accurately accounts for the sensory evidence attempts to achieve

    (A) mental imagery

    (B) constraint satisfaction

    (C) spatial integration

    (D) artificial intelligence (AI)

    (E) visual expectation

138. A survey differs from a focus group in that

    (A) survey participants are usually members of a stratified random sample, while focus group participants are usually members of an accidental sample

    (B) a survey is experimental, while a focus group is naturalistic

    (C) focus group members are usually chosen for their greater interest in and knowledge of politics

    (D) focus group participants are usually more dedicated consumers than survey participants

    (E) survey participants can easily be replaced, while focus group participants are chosen with greater care

139. Research following Friedman and Rosenman's work has shown

    (A) Type As and Type Bs have similar reactions under stress, but Type As cannot relax when not under stress

    (B) Type As are not only more prone to heart attacks, but to cancer and gastrointestinal disorders as well

    (C) Type Bs become just as angry as Type As, but they suppress their anger more effectively

    (D) Type Bs are more productive than Type As

    (E) Type As produce higher levels of stress hormones when under stress than do Type Bs

140. To achieve equal levels of performance, massed practice, when compared to distributed practice, requires

    (A) less warm-up

    (B) more practice time

    (C) more incentive

    (D) less knowledge of results

    (E) more transfer of training

141. In order to reduce the negative effects of retroactive inhibition, a student preparing for an examination should do which of the following between sessions?

    (A) Sleep

    (B) Socialize

    (C) Study another subject

    (D) Do physical activity

    (E) Eat low-fat food

142. An infant turns its head and begins sucking when its cheek is touched. This is called

    (A) rooting reflex

    (B) Babinski reflex

    (C) Moro reflex

    (D) sucking reflex

    (E) plantar reflex

143. The process of converting sensory information into neural activity is

    (A) input

    (B) detection

    (C) coding

    (D) transduction

    (E) evoked potential

144. If an investigator wishes to develop norms for a test, the best procedure is to

    (A) administer the test to representative groups

    (B) do an item analysis of each question

    (C) do a factor analysis of the test

    (D) compare the test with established tests

    (E) administer the test repeatedly to the same group

145. The item that *least* belongs among the following is

    (A) catecholamines

    (B) serotonin

    (C) acetylcholine

    (D) glucose

    (E) GABA

146. Which test is the most empirically oriented in that it makes the fewest assumptions about intervening abilities or traits?

    (A) Primary Mental Abilities Test

    (B) Embedded Figures Test

    (C) Culture-Fair Intelligence Test

    (D) Wechsler Adult Intelligence Scale

    (E) Strong Vocational Interest Blank

147. Suicide is most likely to occur

    (A) in medical settings, in big cities, during the day

    (B) among ethnic minority women after divorce or social abandonment

    (C) with minimal forewarning and out of a desire for social revenge

    (D) three times more frequently among men than among women

    (E) after inter-generational conflict

148. A therapist instructs a patient to ignore the past, try not to make predictions about the future, concentrate on his own thoughts rather than the motivations of others, and concentrate on his own conscious experience. The therapist is most likely a(n)

    (A) psychoanalyst

    (B) phenomenologist

    (C) transactional analyst

    (D) idiographologist

    (E) personologist

149. Which of the following tests is most likely to be used by a psychologist who wishes to categorize people into psychiatric categories based on forced-choice answers?

    (A) MMPI

    (B) CPI

    (C) Rorschach

    (D) TAT

    (E) 16 PF

150. If an investigator does a study to discover the use of defense mechanisms in the personalities of a typical class of students, he or she is likely to find that

    (A) defense mechanisms are most likely to be used by the least successful students

    (B) the most successful students use defense mechanisms most frequently

    (C) the students who use denial as a defense mechanism are most likely to be the best adjusted

    (D) projection is likely to be used most at moderate levels of anxiety

    (E) even the best students find it impossible to avoid using defense mechanisms

151. A spurned lover just cannot seem to get her former boyfriend out of her mind. This is an example of

    (A) a fugue state

    (B) dissociative reaction

    (C) compulsive reaction

    (D) undoing

    (E) obsessive reaction

152. The number of psychiatric illnesses identified in the DSM-IV (published in 1994) is

    (A) 99

    (B) 410

    (C) 26

    (D) 145

    (E) 1215

153. When a child gives a gift to a parent, the parent scolds the child for wasting money. When the child gives only a birthday card to the same parent on the parent's birthday, the parent becomes sullen. The parent's behavior is an example of

    (A) a dyssocial reaction

    (B) the drift theory

    (C) a double bind

    (D) reciprocal inhibition

    (E) a goal gradient

154. An epidemiologist might investigate

    (A) species-specific behavior

    (B) the etiology of neurosis

    (C) therapy outcomes

    (D) the drift theory

    (E) brain chemistry

155. With reference to any particular language, such as English or French, language tends to

    (A) have more morphemes than phonemes

    (B) become more complex as the civilization becomes *higher*

    (C) have an invariant surface structure

    (D) become more lexically marked as it develops

    (E) create greater distinction among unfamiliar objects than among familiar objects

156. Experimental animals shocked for 20 minutes are tested for pain sensitivity. Their pain sensitivity is virtually nil, an example of stress-induced analgesia. The analgesia

    (A) is mediated by the action of endorphins

    (B) is mostly psychological, as Masserman demonstrated

    (C) is mediated by the action of ACTH

    (D) is caused by overstimulated PAG sites

    (E) cannot be explained by gate control theory

157. Specific identifiable skin receptors have been found for

    (A) hot

    (B) cold

    (C) pain

    (D) kinesthesia

    (E) none of the above

158. According to Bernice Neugarten, the *social clock* is

    (A) an individual's expectations of his own social achievements at various ages

    (B) an individual's sense of society's expectations of him at various ages

    (C) an individual's actual achievements at various ages

    (D) the social roles an individual must fulfill at various ages

    (E) the pace of social change in a society

159. To answer a test question, the respondent must circle a number from 1 to 5 to signify the degree of agreement or disagreement. This test uses a

    (A) psychometric scale

    (B) Likert scale

    (C) Guttman scale

    (D) Bogardus scale

    (E) nominal scale

160. Hair cells in the inner ear

    (A) vibrate in rhythm with the cochlea

    (B) serve no apparent function in hearing

    (C) interfere with hearing because they accumulate foreign matter

    (D) start electrochemical reactions that are transmitted to the brain

    (E) attenuate audial vs. auditory acuity

161. A "behavioral contract" would be drawn up in which of the following forms of therapy?

    (A) Implosion therapy

    (B) Flooding therapy

    (C) Biofeedback therapy

    (D) Experiential therapy

    (E) Cognitive therapy

162. The post-Freudian theorist most likely to ask clients for their earliest memories is

    (A) Lazarus

    (B) Bartlett

    (C) Adler

    (D) Jung

    (E) Rogers

163. Anorexia nervosa, a disorder which tends to occur among late-adolescent females,

    (A) is now considered "psychosomatic," meaning that it is a psychological disorder which needs to be treated with psychotherapy

    (B) has been found to be associated with abnormalities of the hypothalamus

    (C) has been found to result in self-starvation in up to a quarter of the cases in some studies

    (D) is only rarely found overlapping with bulimia, which is now known to have physiological causes

    (E) is increasing significantly among college-age males who engage in extensive weight training

164. Ahmed is the best speller in his elementary school class. He takes a nationally standardized spelling test and achieves a ranking in the 15th percentile. Ahmed's score can be interpreted to mean

    (A) Ahmed's classmates are poor spellers

    (B) Ahmed's aptitude for spelling exceeds his ability

    (C) the national spelling test is unreliable

    (D) Ahmed spells better than 85% of the population

    (E) Ahmed's score has "regressed to the mean"

165. A particular teacher shows favoritism to the *teacher's pet* in most classroom activity. As the school year goes on, the teacher reports steady progress in the academic achievement of the *teacher's pet*. This is an example of

    (A) meritocracy

    (B) the self-fulfilling prophecy

    (C) ego involvement

    (D) the personal equation

    (E) Type II error

166. A controversial study by Getzels and Jackson found that

    (A) intelligence and creativity are monotonically correlated

    (B) intelligence and creativity are related, but not necessarily in a simple, straight-line manner

    (C) intelligence and creativity are orthogonal

    (D) creativity is primarily the result of convergent thinking, not divergent thinking

    (E) creativity cannot be taught by example

167. The term *educably mentally retarded*

    (A)   is reserved for conditions where there is a demonstrable biological condition

    (B)   is synonymous with *Down syndrome*

    (C)   refers to individuals in the 50 to 70 IQ range

    (D)   refers to individuals in the 75 to 90 IQ range

    (E)   refers to individuals who cannot benefit from *mainstreaming,* although they can be educated

168. When given to hyperactive children, drugs that stimulate CNS activity, such as amphetamines, can

    (A)   compensate for minimal brain dysfunction

    (B)   produce tardive dyskinesia

    (C)   reduce CNS activity

    (D)   compensate for dyslexia

    (E)   cause hyperphagia

169. In an experiment on radical environmental change, subjects lived for weeks in a cave. This procedure caused

    (A)   a change in circadian rhythms to a 28-hour day

    (B)   sleep and wakefulness cycles to vary almost at the will of the subjects, depending on the tasks the subjects desired to perform

    (C)   little change in 24-hour sleep cycles, with sleep periods varying little from day to day

    (D)   complete disruption of sleep and wakefulness cycles, accompanied by uncomfortable mental states

    (E)   diminished performance on cognitive tests with no apparent reduction of physiological measures

170. The terms *Krause bulb, Ruffini cylinder,* and *basket ending* refer to

    (A)   skin receptors

    (B)   optical illusions

    (C)   visual receptors

    (D)   psychophysics laboratory apparatus

    (E)   mental-set problems

171. If an individual stares straight ahead at an object in such a way that the retinal image continually stimulates the same visual cells, after a while

    (A)   scotopic vision ensues

    (B)   the image fades and disappears

    (C)   the image reverses color

    (D)   the image becomes autokinetic

    (E)   the image clarifies

172. The sensation of *hot* on the surface of the skin

    (A) can be attributed to specific nerve structures that are primarily distributed on the arms and legs

    (B) is not perceived unless the temperature difference between skin surface and object is 10°C

    (C) bypasses the action of *cold* receptors

    (D) involves the action of both *warm* and *cold* receptors

    (E) is a result of the paradoxical action of *cold* receptors

173. According to Weber's law, if a subject can detect a temperature difference of 3 degrees at 60°C, how much difference in temperature can that subject detect at 40°C?

    (A) 1 degree

    (B) 2 degrees

    (C) 3 degrees

    (D) 4 degrees

    (E) 5 degrees

174. Human taste sensitivity

    (A) is more acute than animal taste sensitivity

    (B) increases when the temperature of the object tasted increases

    (C) is equally sensitive to four distinct tastes—sweet, sour, salt, and bitter

    (D) is independent of other senses because of the unique nature of the neural pathways

    (E) is more sensitive to acid and bitter than to sweet and salt

175. Which of the following is a reversible figure illusion?

    (A) Color solid

    (B) Vestibular window

    (C) Ganzfeld illusion

    (D) Moon illusion

    (E) Necker cube

176. It appears that the persistence of perceptual constancies such as size and shape

    (A) can be overcome by experiences such as wearing glasses that invert images

    (B) indicates that perception is organized around retinal images

    (C) does not support the theoretical position of nativists

    (D) is primarily a function of language usage, as predicted by the Whorf hypothesis

    (E) indicates that perception is organized by conceptions of things or objects

177. If a painter wishes to paint an object in the distant background, which of the following devices best gives the illusion of distance?

    (A) Place the object at the crossing of two lines

    (B) Depict the object in schematic form rather than realistic form

    (C) Draw two versions of the object near each other to create a stereoscopic illusion

    (D) Place the object higher in the picture

    (E) Draw the object as if it were lying down *on its back* to decrease its retinal size

178. Which of the following would *not* give a viewer information about the color of an object?

    (A) wavelength of reflected light

    (B) information about illuminating light

    (C) binocular cues

    (D) information about surrounding objects

    (E) opponent coding

179. A student is studying for an important exam. The phone rings, a car crashes in the street outside, and the cat scratches the new couch. Nothing distracts the student from her studies. This is an example of

    (A) compulsive neurosis

    (B) hypomania

    (C) selective attention

    (D) retrograde amnesia

    (E) psychokinesis

180. The Durham Rule (1954) on the insanity defense says that

    (A) a defendant must be able to understand the workings of the court

    (B) a defendant is considered competent to stand for trial if he or she is assisted by competent counsel

    (C) a defendant is not permitted to stand for trial if diagnosed with a psychiatric disorder

    (D) all formerly mentally-institutionalized defendants are subject to institutionalization for observation before trial

    (E) mitigating circumstances may excuse an otherwise-criminal act

181. A person has episodes in which she engages in uncharacteristic behaviors for extended periods of time but, on later questioning, vehemently denies that she did these unusual things. This person has been in a

    (A) hypnopompic state

    (B) hypnogogic state

    (C) petit mal seizure

    (D) fugue state

    (E) multiple personality state

182. Imagine that this sample examination is being presented to you on a computer. You get the answer to the previous question wrong. Instead of allowing you to go on to the next question, the computer requires you to answer correctly two more questions on the subject matter of the previous question before you can go on. This is an example of

    (A) divergent thinking

    (B) linear programming

    (C) a flow chart

    (D) feedback

    (E) branching

183. Of the following, the method of reward that would most likely produce response competition is

    (A) extrinsic rewards

    (B) intrinsic rewards

    (C) punishment

    (D) branching

    (E) learning set

184. Rosenhan and colleagues complained of hearing voices and were hospitalized with a diagnosis of latent schizophrenia. The mental hospital doctors

    (A) produced more accurate diagnoses after being informed that they were part of an experiment

    (B) showed extra sensitivity to the needs of indigent ward patients

    (C) refined their diagnoses with standard classification batteries once the patients were in the hospital

    (D) justified their incorrect diagnoses, even though clearly inappropriate

    (E) reviewed the patients' documentation and released most of the patients before completion of the experiment

185. The word *smart* is usually used to mean *of high intelligence*. In addition, the word *smart* is often taken to mean *good*. The latter meaning, *good*, is referred to by psychologists as a(n)

    (A) semantic differential

    (B) connotative meaning

    (C) denotative meaning

    (D) morpheme

    (E) heuristic device

186. Eros and Thanatos

    (A) represent opposing aspects of super-ego functioning

    (B) control secondary process thinking

    (C) account for the human being's desire for self-actualization

    (D) are considered instinctive drives and are therefore unlikely to be completely socialized

    (E) are resolved in the Oedipal conflict

187. On the basis of a study finding that children born to schizophrenic mothers and placed in foster homes at three months of age were more likely to become schizophrenic in later life than children taken from nonschizophrenic mothers at three months of age and raised in foster homes, a researcher concludes that schizophrenia is genetically transmitted. The researcher's conclusion about genetic transmission

    (A) is flawed because even in the first three months of life some aspect of schizophrenia can be communicated

    (B) is unnecessary because it has already been shown that schizophrenia is genetically transmitted

    (C) is inconclusive because it does not use identical twin controls

    (D) supports the *medical model* of schizophrenia because of its reliability

    (E) supports Szasz's view that schizophrenia is not a *disease*

188. Studies of *executive* monkeys and subsequent follow-up studies of rats found that the incidence of ulcers can be reduced by

    (A) providing terry cloth *mothers*

    (B) isolating the most fearful animals

    (C) providing targets for outlet of aggression

    (D) narrowing the range of activities

    (E) providing immediate feedback to problem-solving attempts

189. A process schizophrenic would probably be described as having

    (A) poor premorbid state, deteriorated presenting symptoms, poor prognosis

    (B) adequate premorbid state, deteriorated presenting symptoms, good prognosis

    (C) poor premorbid state, minimal presenting symptoms, good prognosis

    (D) adequate premorbid state, minimal presenting symptoms, poor prognosis

    (E) poor premorbid state, deteriorated presenting symptoms, good prognosis

190. Although most behavior therapists are critical of psychoanalytic methodology, a behavior therapist who is engaged in counter-conditioning a phobic response might possibly ask his or her patient to *free associate* about the phobia in order to assist in developing

    (A) transference

    (B) abreactions

    (C) a response hierarchy

    (D) relaxation training

    (E) **token economies**

191. In studies of bystander intervention it was often found that subjects who did not respond to an emergency justified their behavior by *pluralistic ignorance,* that is,

    (A) the victim was not a member of the group, so intervention was inappropriate

    (B) the experimenter is responsible for any unusual activities

    (C) the experimenter or group leader is supposed to take charge

    (D) the emergency seemed too far away and unlikely

    (E) if no one else responds there must not be a real emergency

192. According to the findings of attribution theory, self-perception theory, and cognitive dissonance,

    (A) behavior cannot be made to change unless attitudes and self-esteem are changed first

    (B) forcing subjects to comply with experimental manipulations produces permanent attitude change, usually in a negative direction

    (C) self-esteem change precedes attitude change, which in turn precedes behavior change

    (D) the less the pressure to comply the greater the attitude change

    (E) the less the attitude change the less the pressure to comply

193. You are engaged in a public debate over a political issue. According to recent findings of social psychologists, which is the best method to make the audience resist the persuasive appeals of your opponent?

    (A) *Preach to the converted* by rallying your supporters behind you.

    (B) Make yourself the *underdog* by viciously attacking your opponent, then apologize graciously.

    (C) Pick at minor points in your opponent's argument, knowing that he or she will be able to correct your objections easily.

    (D) Monopolize as much time as possible until you are certain your point of view has prevailed.

    (E) Build up your own virtues at the expense of your opponent's.

194. The rate of response to a given stimulus varies greatly, from almost no response at some predictable times to high frequency of response at other predictable times. This is probably because the schedule of reinforcement is

    (A) variable interval

    (B) variable ratio

    (C) fixed interval

    (D) fixed ratio

    (E) monotonic

195. One of the problems encountered by people who work at computers for long periods of time concerns the rate at which displays on the screen blink on and off. Displays blinking at a rate close to the critical flicker frequency may induce

    (A) schizophrenia

    (B) epileptic-like seizures

    (C) depression

    (D) motor paralysis

    (E) repetitive stress injury

PRACTICE EXAMINATION 1
ANSWER KEY

1. B	29. D	57. D	85. E	113. E
2. A	30. B	58. A	86. D	114. B
3. E	31. E	59. C	87. B	115. B
4. A	32. A	60. C	88. A	116. C
5. A	33. B	61. C	89. C	117. C
6. E	34. C	62. A	90. B	118. E
7. B	35. A	63. B	91. E	119. C
8. B	36. D	64. B	92. E	120. E
9. B	37. B	65. A	93. B	121. D
10. A	38. B	66. C	94. C	122. B
11. A	39. A	67. B	95. C	123. C
12. C	40. A	68. D	96. A	124. C
13. B	41. A	69. A	97. B	125. D
14. D	42. A	70. D	98. A	126. C
15. E	43. A	71. A	99. D	127. D
16. B	44. E	72. B	100. E	128. D
17. B	45. B	73. D	101. B	129. A
18. B	46. E	74. C	102. E	130. A
19. A	47. D	75. D	103. E	131. D
20. C	48. C	76. C	104. D	132. D
21. D	49. A	77. C	105. C	133. E
22. D	50. A	78. C	106. C	134. A
23. B	51. B	79. B	107. E	135. D
24. A	52. A	80. E	108. E	136. D
25. A	53. E	81. B	109. D	137. B
26. B	54. D	82. E	110. B	138. A
27. B	55. B	83. C	111. C	139. E
28. C	56. C	84. D	112. C	140. B

141. **A**	152. **B**	163. **C**	174. **E**	185. **B**
142. **B**	153. **C**	164. **A**	175. **E**	186. **D**
143. **D**	154. **D**	165. **B**	176. **E**	187. **A**
144. **A**	155. **A**	166. **B**	177. **D**	188. **E**
145. **D**	156. **A**	167. **D**	178. **C**	189. **A**
146. **E**	157. **E**	168. **C**	179. **C**	190. **C**
147. **D**	158. **B**	169. **C**	180. **C**	191. **E**
148. **B**	159. **B**	170. **A**	181. **D**	192. **D**
149. **A**	160. **D**	171. **B**	182. **E**	193. **C**
150. **E**	161. **E**	172. **D**	183. **A**	194. **C**
151. **E**	162. **C**	173. **B**	184. **D**	195. **B**

EXPLANATORY ANSWERS

1. **(B)** Hull's theory is based on the assumption that learning takes place gradually as the goal substance reduces the level of drive; thus, he is considered a drive-reduction theorist. Tolman put greater stress on the cognitive component of learning, including the development of *cognitive maps* of the environment. Cognition about the environment, i.e., information, includes expectations based on past experiences. To know: Dollard; Doob; N. Miller; Sears.

2. **(A)** A Z-score of 3 represents those scores that fall above or below 3 standard deviations from the mean, which are the extreme scores. Another term to describe an extreme score is *outlier*. To know: standard score; T-score; (per)centile score.

3. **(E)** Stated in more formal terms, punishment is an aversive stimulus that follows an undesired response, resulting in the diminution of the rate of response. Diminution of rate of response is not synonymous with extinction. In more familiar terms, punishment reduces the number of times a response is given, but it does not eliminate the response—the undesired response "goes underground."

4. **(A)** Sociobiology, sometimes also called evolutionary psychology, assumes that the mind is an information processor that has evolved through natural selection. It assumes that biological species adapt in a Darwinian fashion: selecting out those adaptations which lead to more successful survival.

5. **(A)** In almost all graphic presentations of data, the independent variable is plotted along the abscissa, the horizontal axis of the graph. To know: ordinate.

6. **(E)** Wundt was the founder of the first psychology laboratory. Although not the same, his work can be considered the precursor of information theory.

7. **(B)** According to Freud, the thought patterns associated with the most primitive parts of the psyche, such as the id or libido, are irrational and timeless. The ego and superego strive to be rational, realistic, and time-oriented. To know: primary process; secondary process.

8. **(B)** In the preoperational period (roughly two to five years of age), the child begins to develop relatively strong, repeated, and tightly interrelated patterns, i.e., schemata, around stimuli that have symbolic meaning for the child. Although language emerges during the same period, Piaget was usually reluctant to rely on language alone as an indicator of development in other areas because of the problems of misinterpretation of the child's language. To know: assimilation; accommodation.

9. **(B)** A secondary reinforcement does not directly satisfy a need, although it has gained the capacity to be a reinforcer by previously being associated with a primary reinforcer.

10. **(A)** Although Piaget did not consider himself an educator, he occasionally commented on educational issues. He felt that children, especially those below formal operational age (approximately 11 or 12 years old), learn much more through their own actions and activities than through verbal instruction. Indeed, because adults are such authority figures and have their own adultocentric ideas, Piaget felt their verbal communications with children are often less informative than the communications of the children's peers.

11. **(A)** A genotype, as in this case, is the genetic constitution of an individual that consists of both dominant and recessive (for example, color blindness) traits.

12. **(C)** Dement concluded that we need to dream and that dream deprivation produces some kind of pressure. After a period of deprivation, there is an attempt to make up for lost dream time, a phenomenon that has come to be called "REM-rebound." The loss of dream time results in mild, non-debilitating anxiety.

13. **(B)** The implants allow some wearers to recognize familiar voices and use the phone. They are placed in the skull and are connected by wire to the cochlea.

14. **(D)** While pheromones released by females of many species serve to attract male sexual interest, among humans, pheromones seem to have a greater effect on other females than on males.

15. **(E)** Vygotsky, unlike Piaget, believed language is communicative from the beginning and that as the child develops, it becomes more adept at thinking clearly to itself. To know: zone of proximal development; apprenticeship.

16. **(B)** Panic attack sufferers tend to withdraw from society to "hide" their disorder, leading to fear of public places, agoraphobia. *Sequela* means a condition left as a result of a disease.

17. **(B)** Seligman developed the term *learned helplessness* to describe the learned attitude or belief that an individual has no control over the environment. Some have advocated that learned helplessness plays a prominent role in clinical depression.

18. **(B)** The smell would be a reminder of the more primary reinforcement, the consumption of bread.

19. **(A)** There seems to be no single motivational style that overrides all other factors in the workplace. What works in one situation at one time may not work elsewhere or later.

20. **(C)** Hue, the perceived dimension of color, depends primarily on wavelength of light, although the intensity of stimulation and contrast effects do contribute to hue perception.

21. **(D)** According to Kohlberg, only about 25% of the population achieves the fourth stage of moral development, let alone the more rarefied sixth stage, represented by alternative (D).

22. **(D)** The amount of variance accounted for by a coefficient of correlation is obtained by squaring the correlation, which in this case equals .49, or 49%.

23. **(B)** One of the most consistent findings of research on bystander intervention is that the smaller the bystander group, the greater the likelihood of intervention. Also, interestingly enough, it is consistently found that happy people are more helpful people.

24. **(A)** Fromm, Sullivan, and Horney are often described as *neoanalytic* or *neo-Freudian* theorists. Each in his or her own way adopted many of Freud's ideas, but revised them in an attempt to broaden the concept of personality to include more social factors. They felt Freud's idea of personality excluded too much of the *outside* world and that it gave the false impression that a person's personality is encapsulated within his or her own skin.

25. **(A)** When used to describe an ego defense mechanism, *displacement* refers to the discharge of hostile feelings against a substitute object when the discharge of these feelings against the actual object is perceived as too dangerous.

26. **(B)** In a normal distribution, 68.3% of the cases fall within 1 standard deviation above and below the mean, 95.4% fall within 2 standard deviations above and below the mean, and 99.7% between 3 standard deviations above and below the mean.

27. **(B)** A longitudinal study investigates an individual or process over an extended period of time or at selected points in time. To know: cross-sectional method.

28. **(C)** As a rule of thumb, tests of mental development administered before the age of five years do not strongly correlate with test scores later in life.

29. **(D)** In the early stages of moral development, Kohlberg feels a child's understanding of *right and wrong* derives from vaguely external standards that only incidentally relate to a person's needs or standards. Only later in moral development do rules become conventional and standardized. Piaget referred specifically in his research to the young child's inability to understand that in *winning,* one person gains while the other loses. A young child, according to Piaget, equates *winning* more or less to *having a good time.*

30. **(B)** Paranoid thinking tends to be very self-centered, and thus the term *ideas of reference* describes how paranoid thinkers tend to assume that the rest of the world is concerned with and focused on them.

31. **(E)** The term "g factor" is associated with Spearman, who, along with Wechsler and most earlier researchers in the field, postulated that there is a single, unitary intelligence. Gardner and most more recent theorists take the opposite position, assuming there are many kinds of intelligences.

32. **(A)** The two types of images can be shown by brain scan to involve different areas of the brain. A person can lose one type of image without necessarily losing the other.

33. **(B)** The sophisticated machinery of the 1990s, such as CAT and PET scans, has opened up new areas of research which allow scientists to map brain activities.

34. **(C)** A controversy between classical Freudian theorists and ego psychologists, such as Erikson, centers on the issue of whether or not some portion of ego functioning exists from birth. Classical Freudians tend to think not. Ego psychologists believe that since people usually can maintain contact with reality even in the face of extreme stress, this indicates that the ego can function relatively independently. To know: conflict-free zone.

35. **(A)** The superego, which contains internalized moral values learned as a child, consists of the conscience and the idealized self-image.

36. **(D)** John Locke, known as an Associationist or Empiricist, propounded the notion of *tabula rasa.* This claims that the mind at birth is a blank which becomes filled with experiences predominately from the outside world.

37. **(B)** McGuire has done extensive research on the phenomenon he calls *inoculation,* which refers to information given to experimental subjects about characteristics of the source of information, e.g., the speaker, that qualify or limit his or her power to change attitudes.

38. **(B)** Wundt, one of the early Structuralists, founded the first psychology laboratory.

39. **(A)** A zero-order correlation coefficient tests the degree of relationship between two variables.

40. **(A)** Although it is virtually impossible to do detailed research on cognitive development without using language, Piaget felt that using a child's language alone as a guide to cognitive development was inadequate. He attempted to get around this problem by placing his subjects in testing situations in which they were unlikely to have learned solutions from their previous verbal experiences.

41. **(A)** A child beginning to master concrete operations is very much bound by the appearance of immediate physical objects. Thus, a child in the early concrete operational period has not yet developed the concept: "If stick A is larger than stick B and stick B is larger than stick C, then stick A must be larger than stick C." The child is likely to test each relationship.

42. **(A)** The chi-square test, a nonparametric statistic, is the most frequently used test of differences in frequencies or proportions.

43. **(A)** Although every individual tends to be dominated by at least one of the four functions, according to Jung a severe imbalance between the four functions results in psychological difficulties.

44. **(E)** The quotation, from Neisser, expresses the cognitive psychologists' view that the cognitive interpretation of the world determines an individual's orientation.

45. **(B)** This example is based on the experiment of Lewin, Chein, and Murphy in which they found that perception can be mediated by motivational state.

46. **(E)** Face validity refers to the apparent validity of a test. There is a great danger, however, that in the absence of other tests of validity, face validity can be deceptive. A test that appears to be valid on its face may not be a true measure of the desired criterion.

47. **(D)** Sally might be diagnosed as having a character or personality disorder.

48. **(C)** A theory states the relationships between hypothetical constructs. A law states the relationships between empirically measurable variables. The popular notion that a theory is a vague set of ideas awaiting empirical testing does not accord with the way the term *theory* is used in the hypothetico-deductive method.

49. **(A)** In a projective test, the subject is presented with an ambiguous stimulus, and the responses of the subject are assumed to reflect his or her motivational or emotional state.

50. **(A)** Type I error is the error of rejecting the null hypothesis when it is true. Type II error is the error of accepting the null hypothesis when it is false. To know: inferential statistics.

51. **(B)** The peripheral nervous system connects the receptors to the central nervous system, and connects the central nervous system to the effector muscles and glands.

52. **(A)** The somatosensory area of the cortex is organized in a relatively systematic topographic fashion so that input from lower parts of the body is received higher in the cerebral hemisphere and input from higher parts of the body is received lower in the hemisphere.

53. **(E)** Delgado conducted a dramatic experiment in a bullring in which he stopped the charge of a bull by the remote electrical stimulation of the animal's limbic system.

54. **(D)** Both human males and females have 23 pairs of chromosomes. The typical male has one more Y chromosome than the typical female.

55. (**B**) Tryon (1940) selectively bred maze-bright rats with other maze-bright rats and maze-dull rats with other maze-dull rats until he developed two strains, maze-bright and maze-dull, which clearly differed in their maze-running performance. The exact nature of the genetic components that caused this difference in performance has not been determined.

56. (**C**) Although research on the effects of early environments on the development of human brain and nervous system capacity is still open to question, a growing body of evidence indicates that early enriched environments affect the brain activities of rats. For example, an extensive study done at the University of California found that environmental complexity and training resulted in differences in weight of the cerebral cortex and differences in chemical activity.

57. (**D**) Evoked potential is the electrical activity recorded from the brain or nervous system (generally by means of electrodes on the skin surface or implanted in the brain) produced by a stimulus. To know: action potential.

58. (**A**) The location of the functions in the cerebral cortex is generally a mirror image of the location of the organs controlled: the higher in the cortex the function, the lower the bodily organ.

59. (**C**) Anxiety disorders are found commonly in the general population; these include panic disorders, phobias, and obsessive-compulsive disorders.

60. (**C**) Studies of stopped (stationary) images have shown that either eye or stimulus movement is necessary for continued perception of a stimulus. The dominant direction of eye movement is to the left. To know: Ganzfeld.

61. (**C**) Penfield found that when the brain is electrically stimulated long-forgotten memories may be vividly evoked. This is sometimes taken as evidence against the trace theory of memory, which claims that over time unused memory traces fade away and eventually disappear.

62. (**A**) The galvanic skin response (GSR) measures changes in electrical conductivity of the skin. It has long been studied as an indicator of emotional activity and is frequently incorporated as part of *lie detection*. It is not, however, a reliable measure of brain activity.

63. (**B**) The forebrain includes the cerebrum, thalamus, and hypothalamus. These areas are sometimes referred to as the new brain, indicating that they are later evolutionary developments, more specialized in humans than in lower animals.

64. (**B**) Efferent nerves or fibers carry messages from the central nervous system to responding organs. Afferent nerves or fibers carry messages produced by internal and external stimuli to the central nervous system.

65. (**A**) The telencephalon is part of the forebrain and includes the basal ganglia, cerebral cortex, cerebral hemispheres, and corpus callosum.

66. (**C**) The temporal lobe, located in front of the occipital lobe and beneath the lateral fissure, plays an important role in memory storage.

67. (**B**) Conductive deafness occurs when sound waves are not properly transmitted to the cochlea; nerve deafness occurs as a consequence of damage to cochlea, auditory nerve or hair cells.

68. **(D)** Apgar scores are taken one and five minutes after birth and reflect heart rate, respiratory effort, muscle tone, reflex irritability, and color.

69. **(A)** Arousal theory claims people differ in the optimal amount of arousal they seek out. The Yerkes-Dodson law claims different tasks are performed best at different levels of arousal. Easy tasks may require more arousal than hard tasks, for instance.

70. **(D)** Zajonc's theory of emotions suggests that we first respond to a situation with an emotional reaction, and only later do we try to understand the situation or our reactions to it. This theory is the opposite of, for example, Lazarus's theory.

71. **(A)** The medulla, an enlargement of the spinal cord, is a part of the hindbrain, along with the pons and cerebellum.

72. **(B)** Studies of maturation rates find that both boys and girls who mature early tend to have positive self-images, although early maturing girls seem to run into greater social difficulties. Early maturing girls have difficulty adjusting to pubertal changes, particularly when they have no parental or peer support.

73. **(D)** The cerebellum plays a vital role in the coordination of balance and voluntary movement. Although many people naively assume alcohol is a stimulant, in fact alcohol depresses cerebellum activity. Common roadside tests, such as "walking a straight line," administered to detect drunkenness, are dramatic illustrations of the effect of alcohol on the cerebellum.

74. **(C)** Children afflicted with Down syndrome, formerly mistakenly called *mongoloids,* are generally educably retarded. The life span of children with Down syndrome has increased dramatically in recent years because of medical advances.

75. **(D)** In Parkinson's Disease, dopamine is not used properly because of the death of axons. Modern treatment for Parkinson's is L-DOPA, not the use of artificial dopamine.

76. **(C)** In Selye's GAS model, if resistance to stress is not successful, the person proceeds to the next stage, exhaustion, which can include debilitating, permanent physiological damage. Some psychologists argue that the perception of stress and the individual's capacity to resist it varies more than Selye's model can predict.

77. **(C)** The children in this famous study were reared by parents of above-average IQs, and the children's average IQ scores, 106, were above those of the general population. In addition, the younger the age of adoption, the higher the IQ scores tended to be.

78. **(C)** Pain pathways send signals through the reticular and limbic systems, influencing alertness and emotional responses. Descending pathways may suppress the conscious experience of pain. Salicylates, most commonly aspirin, have a selective depressant effect on the central nervous system.

79. **(B)** Judges agree with the decisions of juries about four times out of five.

80. **(E)** Bowlby proposed that certain responses—sucking, crying, smiling, clinging, and following—are instinctive, and the mother-child bond is a necessary evolutionary adaptation.

81. **(B)** Patient compliance with treatment instructions, which varies from 40 to 70% in various studies, is influenced by the degree of satisfaction the patient has with the physician, the physician's expressed interest in and friendliness with the patient, and the amount of knowledge and control the patient has in the treatment.

82. **(E)** The Court found that the defendant must: (1) be oriented as to time and place and have some recollection of events; (2) must have the ability to consult with an attorney with a reasonable degree of rational understanding; and (3) have an understanding of the proceedings against him or her.

83. **(C)** Shared participation in a group, especially requiring participants to give a presentation, has been found to increase the likelihood of subsequent behavior change.

84. **(D)** Decentralized communication networks have been found to produce greater worker satisfaction, although this can be influenced by the complexity of the job to be done and the work load of each participant. Rigid, hierarchical communication patterns produce the lowest worker satisfaction.

85. **(E)** Although it may intuitively appear that a poll of 1200 people, the standard for most nationwide polls in the United States, is too small to represent the entire population, it can be shown mathematically that this sample size works well. When a population is extremely large, doubling the size of a sample does not double its effectiveness.

86. **(D)** Structuralism holds that the contents of thought can be analyzed into mental elements by means of introspection. Phenomenology holds that subjective human experience is the first and most important level to analyze in order to understand an individual's point of view.

87. **(B)** Bonding in humans can take place successfully regardless of age, given proper conditions independent of sex, race, or intelligence. Bonding among many animal species seems limited to critical periods.

88. **(A)** According to Popper, science is distinguished from pseudoscience by its falsifiability. That is, science states its tenets and theories in such a way that at least in principle they can be found false if put to a test.

89. **(C)** The answer alternatives (A to E) describe, in order: the symptoms of fetal alcohol effects (FAE); rubella; fetal alcohol syndrome (FAS); effects of cocaine use by the mother; and the effects of smoking by the mother.

90. **(B)** T-score is a form of standard score, which is a method of converting raw scores into numbers more easily and intuitively interpretable.

91. **(E)** Attribution theory deals with the inner dispositional and situational factors on the basis of which we decide the causes of the behavior of others. There is a tendency to judge other people by supposed dispositional variables, minimizing the importance of situational variables.

92. **(E)** Other studies confirm Levinson's findings. Newer studies separate job satisfaction, which seems based on intrinsic rewards, from job dissatisfaction, which seems related to extrinsic rewards and frustrations.

93. **(B)** According to Hering's theory, revised by Hurvich and Jameson, blue stimulation increases sensitivity to yellow, and red stimulation increases sensitivity to green.

94. **(C)** Eysenck is also known for his controversial studies of the effectiveness of psychotherapy, which he found to be ineffective.

95. **(C)** The relationship between perceived size and perceived distance is such that as an object moves away from an observer its perceived size remains the same as long as its perceived distance changes proportionally.

96. (**A**) Traumatic brain injuries (TBIs) are one of the leading focuses of the emerging field of neuropsychology. Younger people are more at risk of death and permanent injury from TBI than from any other disorder.

97. (**B**) Primate language researchers have clearly demonstrated that their animals can employ linguistic symbols. However, Terrace, the man who trained Nim Chimpsky, feels that other researchers exaggerate their findings. He asserts that at best chimps only imitate the linguistic symbols of their handlers.

98. (**A**) Edwards, Crowne, and Marlowe studied social desirability, especially the tendency of people to *fake* responses on questionnaires to make themselves appear more popular. Those who are high on the trait of social desirability tend to wish to appear acquiescent.

99. (**D**) The sympathetic system, a subdivision of the autonomic nervous system, is involved in extreme or emergency states of the organism, such as reactions to drastic changes and extreme emotion.

100. (**E**) Type II error is not rejecting the null hypothesis when it is false. Type I error is rejecting the null hypothesis when it is true.

101. (**B**) An ogive indicates the cumulative running total of the variable being measured. It rises monotonically (without going down).

102. (**E**) In backward conditioning, the CS is presented before the UCS.

103. (**E**) In this case, the patient is *acting out* hostile feelings toward the therapist, which likely is a reflection of the manner in which hostile feelings toward past authority figures have been handled.

104. (**D**) Countertransference refers to irrational feelings the therapist has towards the patient. When the therapist *breaks the frame*, or acts out inappropriately, the therapist is probably reenacting his or her own past unresolved feelings.

105. (**C**) The perception of the color white can more easily be explained by the opponent-process theory of color vision of Hurvich and Jameson than by the color vision theory of Hering, the alternate dominant theory in the field.

106. (**C**) Vicarious punishment seems to have a weak effect. Vicarious reinforcement has the strongest effect on behavior at which the observer believes he or she can succeed, that is, where self-efficacy and self-reinforcement are high.

107. (**E**) Transient global amnesia (TGA) is one of the common symptoms of mild traumatic brain injury (TBI) and of Alzheimer's disease.

108. (**E**) Since the brain contains no receptors for pain, brain surgery can be conducted using only local anesthetic for the scalp.

109. (**D**) The MMPI-2, which is an update of the MMPI, is designed to identify people suffering from psychological disorders. Personality profiles, such as the 16-PF test, are more appropriate as tests of the general population.

110. (**B**) *Halstead-Reitan*, developed in the 1940s, and *Luria Nebraska*, developed in the 1970s, are two of the most frequently used test batteries in neuropsychological evaluation because they have now been standardized on large populations.

111. (**C**) N100 refers to the first negative peak in the measurement of evoked brain potentials, about 100 milliseconds after the stimulus. P300 refers to the positive peak, which tends to occur 300 to 500 milliseconds after the stimulus.

112. (**C**) It appears that making a large purchase, such as a car, causes some dissonance because the purchaser has to justify why a particular choice was made and why that choice seemed best under the circumstances. Therefore, people tend to look at advertisements a great deal after making such a purchase, presumably to find information to support the choice.

113. (**E**) Migraines, which are associated with dilation of cranial arteries, frequently begin with "auras," which indicate a reduced blood flow to parts of the brain.

114. (**B**) Although immediate physical contact between mother and newborn is a popular practice, emphasis on long-term, extensive postnatal infant-mother physical contact has fallen out of favor because studies have failed to show any significant effects.

115. (**B**) Studies that show increased intellectual performance of children in day-care have been used to support continued federal funding of Project Head Start. The positive gains shown after exposure to Head Start can be lost over time without continued supplemental stimulation.

116. (**C**) Studies have indicated that frequent, long-term alcohol users develop a tolerance for alcohol. Their cell membranes lose elasticity and the ability to transmit messages. In the alcohol withdrawal syndrome, symptoms such as tremulousness, hallucinations, seizures, and delirium tremens occur due to the decreased level of alcohol in the blood and the central nervous system. Messages carried across cell membranes misfire, causing over-activity of the central nervous system.

117. (**C**) In a spinal reflex, such as the flexion reflex, the message is sent from the sensory neuron (in the dorsal root) to an interneuron (generally) to a motor neuron (on the ventral root). Since the signal may or may not be sent up the spinal cord to the brain, there may be no higher-level neural intervention.

118. (**E**) The Diagnostic and Statistical Manual (DSM) of the American Psychiatric Association lists and classifies the major psychiatric categories. The Mental Measurements Yearbook (MMY), originally edited by O.K. Burros, lists and classifies the major published psychological tests.

119. (**C**) Signal detection theory seeks to explain and predict the psychological factors at play in our ability to identify stimuli.

120. (**E**) The .05 level of significance represents a 1 in 20 chance that an event may occur, a convention used in much psychological literature. This level of significance has been adopted because it seems reasonable, although there is no mathematical proof it is the only possible criterion.

121. (**D**) Steinberg also claims that most adolescents traverse their teen years with only a modest amount of turmoil or bickering, unlike those who see adolescence as a tumultuous era.

122. (**B**) Heisenberg, who studied atomic particles, concluded that due to the nature of experimental observation one could not simultaneously study, say, both the size and speed of atomic particles without altering one or the other of these factors. Therefore only one factor can be studied at a time.

123. (**C**) In his book *Experimenter Effects in Behavior Research,* Rosenthal studied the effects an experimenter and his or her expectations have on experiments.

124. **(C)** Three sets of cells on the retina are directly aligned to transmit information to the brain—rods and cones, ganglion cells, and bipolar cells.

125. **(D)** Motion parallax is a binocular depth cue. It has to do with the apparent movement of one object in the visual field in comparison with another object. As we move, objects in front of the fixation point appear to move away from us, objects at the fixation point stay stationary, and objects behind the fixation point move with us.

126. **(C)** Not only is male initiation of sexual contacts and relations the overwhelming norm in most societies, male social dominance is also the norm in the overwhelming majority of known societies at the present time.

127. **(D)** Anadamides are neurotransmitters found in the frontal lobes and hippocampus, areas of the brain involved in the formation of memories. One of the most commonly-observed effects of marijuana on behavior is the sporadic and unreliable nature of short-term memory.

128. **(D)** In this example, a change from 500 to 600 millimicrons represents a change in hue of the object, which has no effect on the size of the pupil.

129. **(A)** In order to achieve a meditative state not dominated by the "inner voice," techniques such as chanting or focus on breathing are used.

130. **(A)** Teratogens are external agents, such as viruses, chemicals, and radiation, studied by teratologists. Although teratogens can cause damage to the growing organism at any time, the first eight weeks and last months of development are considered the most critical periods.

131. **(D)** Reticular formation plays an important role in wakefulness and attention. It is not as highly developed in animals below mammals and appears less developed in most mammals than in humans.

132. **(D)** Research on the serial order effect indicates that information in the middle of a series is the most difficult to retain.

133. **(E)** Habituation to smell occurs rapidly after onset, then falls off rapidly. This indicates that plotted as a curve, olfactory sensitivity is a positively accelerated falling curve.

134. **(A)** In this example, the Z-score of 50 is 2 standard deviations higher than the mean of 40, so that multiplying the raw-score standard deviation of 36 by 2 and adding it to the mean yields a score of 284.

135. **(D)** The phobic can usually identify the object of his or her phobia (although, according to analytically oriented therapists, not necessarily its psychological meaning), whereas the obsessional tends to be so consumed by thought and ritual that the source of the original anxiety is neglected.

136. **(D)** In order to obtain the standard deviation, the variance squared is divided by the number of cases, then the square root of this number is found.

137. **(B)** "Constraint satisfaction" means the set of limits (or constraints) that satisfies the criterion, in this case the simulation of pilots' perceptions.

138. **(A)** An "accidental sample" includes members chosen without a systematic schedule of selection; that is, they happen to be nearby when the sample is chosen. Most modern surveys use the stratified random sampling technique, which insures representation of several important "strata," or subgroups, of the larger population.

139. (**E**) It has been hypothesized that Type As release more catecholamines into their bloodstream than do Type Bs. The Type As appear under constant stress, and the increasing fatty deposits in their arteries eventually lead to heart disease.

140. (**B**) Massed practice, which tends to produce more stable learning, requires more practice time than spaced learning to achieve equal results.

141. (**A**) Retroactive inhibition is the interference of other learning after subject matter has been learned. It is lessened if the learner does not engage in thought-interfering activity after learning.

142. (**B**) Some of the early reflexes listed in this question can show signs of abnormality in the first day of life, assume a more "normal" form for several months or years, then reemerge later in their abnormal form. Thus, the imperative of early testing.

143. (**D**) In the eye, for example, closing the sodium channels in receptor cells by transduction causes the release of neurotransmitter substances by the receptor cells.

144. (**A**) By administering the test to representative groups, the tester can compare average scores of different samples with some confidence.

145. (**D**) Glucose (blood sugar) is not one of the behaviorally significant neural transmitters that constitute the rest of the list of alternatives.

146. (**E**) The Strong Vocational Interest Blank was standardized on representative groups of people already in the occupations listed.

147. (**D**) Suicide is attempted more by women, but more men succeed in committing suicide. The rate of suicide has increased dramatically in the past few decades, especially among white males.

148. (**B**) Phenomenology is the study of direct human experience with a minimum of elaboration or analysis.

149. (**A**) The Minnesota Multiphasic Personality Inventory (MMPI) was designed originally as an instrument to differentiate psychiatric symptoms by means of forced-choice questions. Projective tests like the Rorschach and TAT do not use forced choice questions, and CPI and 16 PF are not designed for psychiatric evaluation.

150. (**E**) According to psychoanalysis, the use of defense mechanisms is universal, since motivational conflicts are impossible to avoid. In this view, the goal of psychotherapy is to make conscious as many of these conflicts as possible so that the individual is less subject to the undesirable effects of unconscious conflicts.

151. (**E**) Obsessive reactions are repetitive thoughts difficult to remove from one's attention. Compulsive reactions are rituals, such as hand washing or touching a *lucky* object, that are used to ward off unwanted thoughts or outcomes. Compulsions are often accompanied by obsessions, but not usually vice-versa.

152. (**B**) DSM-I (published in 1952) contained 60 diagnoses, and DSM-II (published in 1968) contained 145 diagnoses. The increasing number of diagnoses reflects, among other things, the recent advances in brain imaging and genetics, which seek to identify biological causes for psychological conditions.

153. (**C**) A double bind is a situation in which incompatible messages that cannot be reconciled by the subject are transmitted. Its excessive occurrence was once thought to be a major cause of schizophrenia.

154. (**D**) According to epidemiologists, the drift theory predicts that schizophrenic individuals tend to migrate to impoverished urban areas.

155. (**A**) Morphemes are the smallest unit of language with a definable meaning. They are made up of phoneme combinations.

156. (**A**) Endorphins are believed to act in the spinal cord and lower brain stem where pain neurons enter. They bind opioid receptors and stimulate the PAG, a site also responsive to morphine.

157. (**E**) The reception of the sensations on this list are conducted through specialized parts of sensory neurons, not separate cells.

158. (**B**) Members of a given culture tend to share age-range markers for defining events. Even Neugarten admits our culture has recently placed less emphasis on the social clock.

159. (**B**) Likert scales measure approval or disapproval of each item, usually by having the subject respond to one of five levels of agreement from *strongly approve* to *strongly disapprove*.

160. (**D**) In the cochlea, the hair cells located in the organ of Corti start a reaction that produces a generator potential, which in turn is transmitted by nerve fibers to the brain.

161. (**E**) Used in cognitive or behavioral therapy, a behavioral contract specifies the goals of the therapy for the patient and the responsibilities of others involved in the therapy (therapist, institution, family members, for example) to provide tangible rewards for meeting goals.

162. (**C**) Adler felt a person's earliest memories contain clues to the person's sense of inferiority. Striving for power or superiority is the most fundamental goal of personality, according to Adler.

163. (**C**) Anorexia nervosa can indeed lead to fatality; the rate of death in most studies is below 10%, but higher rates have been found on occasion. Less than half the identified anorexics eventually reach a state of satisfaction with their weight; about 20% remain chronically anorexic.

164. (**A**) Since Ahmed's performance falls below that of 85% of the national sample, it can be inferred that his classmates are poor spellers.

165. (**B**) The self-fulfilling prophecy states that performance can be influenced by the expectations of the judge.

166. (**B**) Getzels and Jackson found that students who measured high in intelligence were not necessarily also high in creativity, although in their study the students who measured high in creativity were at least above average in intelligence.

167. (**D**) Educable mentally retarded children are superior in performance to trainable mentally retarded children, who in turn are superior to the profoundly or severely mentally retarded.

168. (**C**) This phenomenon is known as the *paradoxical drug effect*. There is great controversy on the question of whether stimulants, especially ritalin, are being overprescribed to children.

169. (**C**) The results of the Mammoth Cave experiment concerning sleep cycles were that even radical environmental change did not alter most subjects' usual circadian patterns; most people seem to stick to their usual sleep patterns despite disruption in their environments.

170. (**A**) The italicized structures in the question are all skin receptors. Research has not yet indicated clearly unique functions for each of these structures. They all seem to do the same things.

171. (**B**) Under ordinary circumstances the eye is in constant motion, called saccadic movement, so that visual images are not constantly applied to the same receptors.

172. (**D**) Certain areas of the skin seem to be especially sensitive to warmth and cold. There appear to be separate receptors for warmth and cold, although this distinction has yet to be confirmed.

173. (**B**) Weber's law is a constant ratio that holds for moderate levels of stimulation. The amount of energy added that is perceived as different divided by the intensity of the stimulus is a constant.

174. (**E**) Human taste is more sensitive to noxious stimuli than to pleasant stimuli.

175. (**E**) In the Necker cube illusion, the perception of foreground and background are in tension.

176. (**E**) Perception appears to depend less on the physical attributes than on interpretation of the stimuli.

177. (**D**) Distance is often perceived by the observer by height in the vertical plane as well as by linear perspective and textural gradients. Higher objects tend to be perceived as more distant.

178. (**C**) For a person of normal vision, color can be perceived by either eye. Binocular cues usually refer to perception of distance and motion.

179. (**C**) Selective attention is a term used to describe focused attention which excludes extraneous stimuli.

180. (**C**) The Durham Rule, sometimes called the "irresistible impulse" defense, is now observed in few jurisdictions. The more common criterion in most jurisdictions is a variation of the M'Naghten Rule.

181. (**D**) In the latest revision of the DSM, a fugue state or dissociative fugue is also said to involve a flight from one's usual residence.

182. (**E**) A branching program, if used as part of computer-assisted instruction (CAI), diverts wrong answers onto a separate branch until the material is mastered, in which case the learner returns to the main program.

183. (**A**) Extrinsic rewards produce greater response competition.

184. (**D**) Rosenhan's now-classical study demonstrated that patient care can often be minimal and perfunctory. It also demonstrated that mental health professionals can often deviously justify their behaviors after-the-fact.

185. (**B**) Connotative meaning refers to the evaluative or emotional aspects of meaning.

186. (**D**) Freud's ideas of Eros and Thanatos, which he elaborated in part as a consequence of his interpretation of the effects of World War I, implied that certain drives, which he considered instinctive, could not be completely erased or socialized.

187. (**A**) A great deal of research, especially that of modern ego psychologists, is directed toward the influences of mothering in the very earliest stages of life. Because of this research, it cannot be assumed that even very early infant care is uniform and has no influence on later development.

188. (**E**) It appears from the studies of executive monkeys that lack of feedback exacerbates conflicts.

189. (**A**) A process schizophrenic would present a poorer clinical picture than a reactive schizophrenic.

52. The pitch of low-frequency tones below 400 Hz is detected by

    (A) the rate of hair cell responses

    (B) basalar membrane localization

    (C) action of the stirrup and anvil

    (D) wave vibrations in the auditory canal

    (E) auditory nerve firing frequency

53. Of the following statements, which is *not true* of recent understanding of autism?

    (A) Autism is a response to "cold" or emotionally rejecting mothering.

    (B) Most mothers of autistic children have toxicity or bleeding during pregnancy.

    (C) Autistic and neurologically brain-damaged children have similar neurological findings.

    (D) Autism tends to be diagnosed earlier than childhood schizophrenia.

    (E) Whereas autistic children rarely survived into adulthood in the past, many now survive well into adulthood because of medical advances.

54. When using the Rorschach test, it has generally been found that the more intelligent the subject, the

    (A) more the subject objects to using the test at all

    (B) more the subject gives quick and concise answers

    (C) more the subject's responses are filled with references to animated actions of humans and animals

    (D) more detailed and elaborate the responses

    (E) greater the total number of responses

55. Immediately after a particular neuron has been fired it is said to be in an absolute refractory period. This means that for this period of time it

    (A) cannot be excited

    (B) will react paradoxically to excitation

    (C) will react more globally to excitation

    (D) will reverse polarity

    (E) will temporarily decrease in size

56. Withdrawal from heroin addiction is painful because

    (A) while addicted, the addict's brain stopped producing serotonin

    (B) the pain is a secondary gain, not physical

    (C) heroin addiction destroys certain neuro-transmitter receptacles

    (D) endorphin production is heightened

    (E) while addicted, the addict's brain stopped producing endorphins

57. According to the Tarasoff decision

    (A) a therapist has the responsibility to warn a clearly identified intended victim when a patient threatens harm

    (B) police authorities must be warned of threats of harm made by patients in therapy

    (C) therapists accept vicarious responsibility for violent acts of non-medicated patients

    (D) a therapist has the responsibility to protect a patient from suicide

    (E) a therapist has the responsibility to hospitalize a potentially homicidal or suicidal patient

58. Of the following, which has research shown to be most reliably correlated with the development of adult homosexuality?

   (A) Stress experienced by the mother in the middle trimester of pregnancy

   (B) Family pattern of dominating mother and weak or absent father

   (C) Homosexual rape during childhood

   (D) Heterosexual rape during childhood

   (E) Childhood diet low in protein

59. According to G. Miller's work on the encoding of information, the number of units of information encoded after a single brief presentation is

   (A) influenced by the individual's nutritional state

   (B) correlated with the individual's IQ

   (C) about eight, plus or minus one or two

   (D) a constant fraction of the individual's age

   (E) not influenced by training strategies

60. "Jake is usually a happy person, but his affect is predominantly depressive." This statement

   (A) describes a dysthymic personality

   (B) is inconsistent and misleading

   (C) describes an example of the neurotic paradox

   (D) is incomplete because it omits situational variables

   (E) describes Jake's demand characteristics

61. Experimenters, especially in social psychology, sometimes subtly exert influence on their subjects to produce results to fulfill the experimenter's expectations. Of the following, the best way to reduce this experimenter influence (also called *demand characteristic*) is to

   (A) use counterbalanced designs

   (B) control organismic variables

   (C) use double-blind technique

   (D) do nomothetic research

   (E) include a placebo group

62. A group of subjects is given the Thematic Apperception Test (TAT) as part of a study of creativity. Given one test administration, which is the best way to determine the reliability of the TAT scores assigned each subject?

   (A) Reliability cannot be determined unless the test is given at least twice.

   (B) Correlate TAT scores with creativity test scores.

   (C) Compare the scores assigned by different judges.

   (D) Compare TAT scores with an outside measure, such as Rorschach scores.

   (E) Discard extremely high and low scores and use only the middle scores.

63. Social and organizational psychologists suggest that conflicts between groups are least likely to be resolved if the groups

   (A) come from differing cultures

   (B) compete for the same goals

   (C) fail to bargain over goals and the means to achieve them

   (D) appeal to differing moral values

   (E) submit to arbitration

64. Glucocorticoids are hormones released by the adrenal cortex which circulate in the blood and have an important role in stress reduction. When functioning properly, glucocorticoids suppress the formation of _____. If this function were not performed, the immune system would not operate properly.

    (A) proteins

    (B) glucose

    (C) ACTH

    (D) steroids

    (E) carbohydrates

65. "Traditional scientific thought has been based on the Newtonian model of cause and effect. Since the advent of quantum theory in physics, Newtonian logic is under siege. Studies of systems as large as ecosystems to as small as sub-atomic particles seem to elude our old ways of understanding. Change seems to happen in jumps, beyond our powers of precise prediction." This statement introduces

    (A) creationism

    (B) transactional analysis

    (C) Gestalt theory

    (D) reductionism

    (E) chaos theory

66. Jung contributed a number of important ideas to clinical psychology, including all but which of the following?

    (A) Introversion-extroversion

    (B) Archetypes

    (C) Self-realization

    (D) Overcompensation

    (E) Will to power

67. A three-year-old English-speaking child guesses that the plural of the nonsense word *glarp* is *glarps*. This demonstrates the child's

    (A) mastery of transformational grammar

    (B) eidetic imagery

    (C) use of morphological rules

    (D) Zeigarnik effect

    (E) semantic differential

68. Children about one year old like to play *hide and seek,* which Piaget would ascribe to their growing mastery of

    (A) assimilation

    (B) accommodation

    (C) object permanence

    (D) horizontal decalage

    (E) egocentrism

69. Dynamism is a concept employed by

    (A) Hebb

    (B) Weber

    (C) Lashley

    (D) Sullivan

    (E) Jung

70. An undesirable side effect of the frequent use of psychotropic drugs is

    (A) invalidism

    (B) Korsakoff's syndrome

    (C) tardive dyskinesia

    (D) violent outbursts

    (E) infertility

71. Correlation coefficients lose some of their power to detect real relationships between variables when

 I. Measurements are made in the form of standard scores

 II. Measurements are made using scores of restricted range

III. Measurements are made on variables that have no apparent relationship to each other

   (A) I and III only

   (B) II only

   (C) III only

   (D) II and III only

   (E) none of the above

72. Anthropologists divide societies into *guilt societies* and *shame societies,* the difference being whether infractions of norms are viewed as violating individual conscience or group expectations. Psychologists are likely to predict that

   (A) schizophrenia would be more prevalent in shame societies

   (B) neurosis would be more prevalent in shame societies

   (C) psychosomatic illness would be more prevalent in shame societies

   (D) schizophrenia would be more prevalent in guilt societies

   (E) depression would be more prevalent in guilt societies

73. Simon, your buddy, doesn't show up for a picnic you planned in the park. You conclude Simon is an untrustworthy person. Your assumption about Simon is an example of:

   (A) foot-in-the-door

   (B) cognitive dissonance

   (C) the illusion of correlation

   (D) fundamental attribution error

   (E) self-fulfilling prophesy

74. According to a frequently quoted study of Californians, the majority of visits by medical patients to health-care facilities

   (A) take place well into the development of chronic medical conditions

   (B) are emergency visits as a result of accidents

   (C) are the result of improper treatment by stand-alone health care providers

   (D) are the result of over-generous HMOs and insurance policies

   (E) involve no clearly diagnosable disorders

75. The patient reports that she was picked up by the police while rummaging through garbage cans in back alleys. She claims she has lived this way for months, after having been kicked out of her home by her family. The patient appeared indifferent about her present life circumstances and the prospects of hospitalization. Based on the facts given above, the attending psychologist is most likely to diagnose the patient as a

    (A) simple schizophrenic

    (B) hebephrenic schizophrenic

    (C) depressive neurotic

    (D) person suffering from a character disorder

    (E) catatonic schizophrenic

76. An experimenter divides his or her subjects into two groups. Group I is administered experimental condition A, then condition B. Group II is administered experimental condition B, then condition A. The experimenter is trying to

    (A) test for retroactive inhibition

    (B) test for proactive inhibition

    (C) use a matched-group design

    (D) counterbalance for order of presentation

    (E) randomize the sample

77. The *regression fallacy* refers to the finding that extreme scores tend to change over time. Another way of expressing this is by the term

    (A) primacy effect

    (B) recency effect

    (C) gambler's fallacy

    (D) regression to the mean

    (E) genetic fallacy

78. A student strongly dislikes a particular course, but studies very hard, gets good grades in the course, and brags about how much he knows. This might be considered an example of

    (A) identification with the aggressor

    (B) displacement

    (C) reaction formation

    (D) repression

    (E) rationalization

79. Compared to that of lower animals, the associative area of the brain in humans

    (A) is smaller

    (B) is larger

    (C) serves the same functions and is the same size

    (D) is located in a different region of the brain

    (E) develops much later prior to birth

80. An injury to approximately half of the medulla would most likely result in

    (A) death by asphyxiation or loss of heartbeat

    (B) loss of vision and/or hearing

    (C) loss of ability to engage in higher functioning, such as thinking and reasoning

    (D) motor paralysis, especially of the large muscles

    (E) loss of coordination of incoming and outgoing messages of the brain

81. A subject exhibits extreme docility, poor memory, and minimal motivation. These symptoms might lead one to suspect that the subject has suffered damage to the

    (A) corpus callosum

    (B) medulla

    (C) limbic system

    (D) reticular formation

    (E) basal ganglia

82. In all likelihood, you are highly emotionally aroused and vigilant as you take this examination. Hormonally speaking, you might credit some of this arousal to the secretion of

    (A) the posterior pituitary gland

    (B) the thyroid gland

    (C) hormones that affect the parasympathetic nervous system

    (D) the adrenal medulla

    (E) follicle-stimulating hormones

83. Learning to control alpha waves is an example of

    (A) REM sleep

    (B) programmed movement

    (C) biofeedback training

    (D) implosion therapy

    (E) behavior modification

84. The axon is surrounded by a semipermeable membrane that

    (A) keeps the axon from receiving a positive charge

    (B) contains chemicals that can be discharged into the synapse

    (C) consists primarily of sodium ions

    (D) is sensitive to oncoming stimuli from surrounding membranes

    (E) keeps sodium ions outside when the neuron is in a resting phase

85. When polarized, an axon

    (A) is essentially unable to fire or is frozen

    (B) has potassium ions concentrated on the inside of its membranes

    (C) is firing an impulse

    (D) has a positive charge on the inside of its membranes

    (E) causes the synaptic vesicle to burst

86. The reticular activating system

    (A) alerts the brain that important information is on the way

    (B) treats all incoming information as equally important, but routes information to different parts of the brain

    (C) passes information through the front side of the brainstem

    (D) plays a less important role in brain functioning the higher on the evolutionary scale the organism is

    (E) is dormant during sleep

87. A nerve impulse travels from sensory nerve to spinal cord to motor nerve. This indicates

    (A) a failure of brain functioning

    (B) a blockage of transmission in the hindbrain

    (C) the presence of a reflex

    (D) an emergency reaction

    (E) a typical autonomic nervous system reaction

88. The firing of axons of a nerve cell and the operation of binary computer circuits have been compared because both

    (A) exhibit the same flow of positive to negative ions

    (B) require the intervention of central control programs

    (C) undergo absolute refractory periods

    (D) adhere to the all-or-none principle

    (E) have similar action potentials

89. A patient is unable to verbally identify objects presented behind a screen to his left hand although he can identify them when they are presented to his right hand. What would your diagnosis be?

    (A) Destruction in Wernicke's area

    (B) Severance of the corpus callosum

    (C) Destruction in the associative area

    (D) Destruction in the somatic sensory area

    (E) Malfunctioning of the midbrain

90. The transmission of messages between neurons is facilitated in part by

    (A) the ion pump

    (B) sodium ions

    (C) ACh

    (D) norepinephrine

    (E) reserpine

91. "Once an action potential has been initiated, its characteristics are independent of the stimulus which initiated it." This quotation describes

    (A) the law of functional autonomy

    (B) the ion pump

    (C) inertia

    (D) the all-or-none law

    (E) reverberating circuits

92. The gland most frequently referred to as the *master gland* is the

    (A) testis

    (B) pineal

    (C) adrenal

    (D) thyroid

    (E) pituitary

93. A right-handed elderly adult who sustained substantial injury limited to the right hemisphere of the brain would most likely lose interest in

    (A) reading

    (B) crossword puzzles

    (C) physical exercise

    (D) art museums

    (E) checkbook balancing

94. Tracts : nerves ::

    (A) central nervous system : peripheral nervous system

    (B) axons : cell bodies

    (C) roads : cars

    (D) gyri : sulci

    (E) synapses : transmitter substances

95. At one time, physiological psychologists downplayed the role of the limbic system because they thought its function in humans was no more important than to

    (A) create dreams

    (B) transmit ESP

    (C) activate sexual hormonal secretions

    (D) adjust to extreme rapid movement

    (E) participate in the sense of smell

96. Numerous proposals have been devised to explain the occurrence of dyslexia. On the basis of a general knowledge of brain functioning, which of the following explanations appears to have the greatest intuitive appeal?

    (A) Malfunctioning of components of the limbic system

    (B) Lack of coordination between hindbrain and forebrain

    (C) Failure of one cerebral hemisphere to dominate the other

    (D) Lesions or tumors in the forebrain

    (E) Insufficiently myelinated nerve cells

97. A psychologist who isolates a single nerve cell in the cortex and wishes to demonstrate the relationship between that nerve cell and a specific memory may be attempting to disprove the theory of

    (A) Pfaffman

    (B) Wernicke

    (C) Lashley

    (D) Sperling

    (E) Sperry

98. Some people who take the GRE do so without great physical inconvenience, for example, by taking the test at their home universities. Others travel great distances at great expense to take the exam. Cognitive dissonance theory predicts that

    (A) students who have an easy time scheduling their exams tend to do better

    (B) students who have a hard time scheduling their exams dislike the exam more

    (C) students who have an easy time scheduling their exams brag more about their scores

    (D) students who have a hard time scheduling their exams study less

    (E) students who have a hard time scheduling their exams claim that the exam was harder

99. What percentage of scores in a distribution falls between the first decile and the median?

    (A) Cannot be determined from the data given

    (B) 90

    (C) 50

    (D) 40

    (E) 30

100. Evidence that even very young infants can coordinate visual perception with motor skills has been obtained from experiments on

    (A) stimulus deprivation

    (B) the Babinski reflex

    (C) the visual cliff

    (D) imprinting

    (E) sex-role development

101. In a conditioning experiment, children are shown red and blue triangles and red and blue squares. The children are rewarded each time they choose the triangles. Without warning, the pattern of rewards is changed so that the correct response now becomes the response to blue objects, whether they be squares or triangles. This is an example of

    (A) reversal shift

    (B) higher order conditioning

    (C) stimulus generalization

    (D) disinhibition

    (E) risky shift

102. The zygote

    (A) exhibits the first signs of a heartbeat

    (B) contains 23 chromosomes

    (C) must bury itself into the uterine wall before mitosis can occur

    (D) is covered with a protective wall

    (E) is impervious to teratogens

103. A sudden, loud noise occurs near a very young infant lying on its back, resulting in a reflex action that looks as if the infant is trying to embrace something with both arms. This is termed the

    (A) Babinski reflex

    (B) rooting reflex

    (C) fight-or-flight stress response

    (D) bonding reflex

    (E) Moro reflex

104. According to Erikson,

    (A) sex differences appear as early as the first months of life, when boys have more difficulty than girls in developing basic trust

    (B) males accomplish generativity more easily than females in Western culture

    (C) the construction activity of boys takes on a form different from that of girls

    (D) sexual differences can be minimized by modern psychotherapy

    (E) girls are more likely than boys to be caught up in rigid personality patterns that are not amenable to change by therapy

105. When identical twins are separated at birth and reared apart,

    (A) they nevertheless tend to have similar personalities and lifestyles

    (B) they are as similar to each other in personalities and lifestyles as other separated siblings

    (C) they are similar to each other in medical histories, but dissimilar in personality traits

    (D) they undergo strenuous efforts to discover their missing twin

    (E) they score higher on tests of extra sensory perception than do fraternal twins

106. Of the following mental disorders, which is *least* likely to be considered *just a passing phase* when exhibited by an adolescent?

    (A) Schizophrenia

    (B) Psychosomatic illness

    (C) Depression

    (D) Obsessive-compulsive disorder

    (E) Manic behavior

107. According to research on group dynamics, which of the following would most likely increase the chances of having members of a lecture audience follow through on suggestions for change made during the lecture?

    (A) Offer a large reward for the best compliance

    (B) Threaten disastrous consequences, such as increased likelihood of disease, for disobedience or neglect

    (C) Use the most physically attractive spokespersons and most elaborate surroundings

    (D) Have members of the audience participate; for instance, by having them vote

    (E) Produce endorsements from prominent social figures, such as movie stars and sports figures

108. Among the best predictors of people who will file injury reports and subsequent lawsuits are

    (A) MMPI and Rorschach results

    (B) SES and GPA

    (C) therapy usage and hypochondriac symptoms

    (D) job satisfaction, hysteria, and antisocial traits

    (E) DSM-IV and income

109. Which of the following would most likely be considered a *hypothetical construct*?

   (A) Deprivation

   (B) Performance

   (C) Fear

   (D) Aversive behavior

   (E) Deviation from the mean

110. The usual result of the prisoner's dilemma game is that

   (A) subjects become frustrated and enervated

   (B) alliances against the authority are formed

   (C) subjects tend to be more competitive than cooperative

   (D) subjects role-playing guards get so involved in their roles that the game is terminated early

   (E) subjects break into small, competing subgroups based on perceived commonality

111. Measurement of the time rent checks arrive in landlords' offices would

   (A) yield a skewed distribution

   (B) be platykurtic

   (C) be homoscedastic

   (D) require Baysian analysis

   (E) require nonparametric analysis

112. Let Z stand for the dominant gene, z for the recessive gene. If a male with ZZ genes is mated with a female with zz genes, the resulting offspring will

   (A) be half phenotype Z and half phenotype z

   (B) be one quarter phenotype Z, one quarter phenotype z, and the other half mixed

   (C) all have the same genotype

   (D) all be genotype ZZ

   (E) all be genotype zz

113. Loss of sensitivity, but not necessarily loss of movement, of parts of the body could result from destruction of

   (A) the pons

   (B) descending tracts

   (C) efferent fibers

   (D) dorsal roots of the spinal cord

   (E) descending tracts

114. The color with the longest wavelength is

   (A) violet

   (B) blue

   (C) white

   (D) orange

   (E) red

115. Balance is related to the

    (A) basilar membrane

    (B) cochlea

    (C) temporal lobe

    (D) organ of Corti

    (E) semicircular canals

116. Compared to a person with normal vision, a person wearing an eyepatch over one eye would most likely

    (A) move his or her head more frequently in order to determine depth cues

    (B) rely more on retinal disparity to determine depth cues

    (C) have more restricted spectral images

    (D) rely more on aerial perspective to determine depth cues

    (E) develop more acute exteroceptive sensitivity

117. According to the classic definition of William James, the sensation of *sourness* can be produced by the perception of

    (A) the taste buds

    (B) the sides of the tongue

    (C) sweetness

    (D) habitual stimuli

    (E) lemons

118. Stimulus substitution is said to take place when a(n)

    (A) conditioned stimulus is followed by an unconditioned stimulus

    (B) unconditioned stimulus is followed by a conditioned stimulus

    (C) reinforcer for a goal-oriented behavior is changed

    (D) previously desirable goal substance is replaced by a noxious goal substance

    (E) goal substance previously used to satisfy one drive is now used to satisfy another

119. The psychological aspects of house design fall within the field of knowledge called

    (A) ethology

    (B) environmental psychology

    (C) informatics

    (D) health psychology

    (E) psychophysiology

120. You give an aptitude test to two groups of employees. For group A, you use a split-half odd-even technique to test the reliability of the scores. For group B, you retest after three months to determine reliability. You are likely to find

    (A) higher scores in group B

    (B) more valid scores in group A

    (C) lower reliability in group A

    (D) lower reliability in group B

    (E) no major difference in reliability of scores if both groups have been chosen randomly

121. Guthrie : Hull :: movement : _____

    (A)   drive reduction

    (B)   reinforcement

    (C)   anticipatory goal response

    (D)   hypothetico-deductive reasoning

    (E)   mathematical model

122. A psychologist has a "double agent" prob-
     lem. There is a conflict between the inter-
     ests of the _____ and the interests of the
     patient.

    (A)   insurance carrier

    (B)   government

    (C)   law

    (D)   spouse

    (E)   psychologist

123. Down syndrome

    (A)   results from an extra chromosome

    (B)   results from a recessive gene

    (C)   leads to severe mental retardation

    (D)   can result from traumatic childbirth

    (E)   results from a dominant gene

124. Mental set has been measured by

    (A)   Ishihara plates

    (B)   Venn diagrams

    (C)   Luchins water jars

    (D)   Poincare's cubes

    (E)   Aristotelian syllogisms

125. The most common birth difficulty in the
     United States associated with later mental
     disorder is

    (A)   poor procedures in the maternity
          ward

    (B)   overmedication of the mother

    (C)   malnutrition

    (D)   low birth weight

    (E)   domestic abuse

126. According to Maccoby and Jacklin, children
     of three years of age tend to

    (A)   have few sex preferences in their play
          groups

    (B)   be more hostile with each other than
          cooperative

    (C)   be more cooperative with each other
          than hostile

    (D)   play in sex-segregated groups

    (E)   segregate each other in height-based
          groups

127. When people talk about "gray matter" they
     are referring to

    (A)   the natural color of the cerebellum

    (B)   the natural color of the fiber tracts

    (C)   cranial nerves

    (D)   the color of preserved brains in labs

    (E)   nuclei in the central nervous system

128. You take an exam for a difficult course. According to learning theory research, what is the best way for the professor to proceed with your exam results in order to improve your chances of learning from the exam?

    (A) Distribute exam scores in public so that social comparisons can be made

    (B) Mete out rewards and punishments based on exam scores

    (C) Give more exams in the same room and under the same conditions to reduce test anxiety

    (D) Give a second exam on the same subject matter to improve the reliability of the test scores

    (E) Report correct answers as soon as possible

129. Camille believes her upcoming job evaluation will be a disaster and a cause for being fired. Her therapist encourages her to think of her job evaluation as an opportunity to work out problems with her boss. Camille's therapist is likely a follower of

    (A) Maslow's hierarchy of needs

    (B) Horney's individual therapy

    (C) Ellis's RET

    (D) Rogers' client-centered therapy

    (E) Paglia's woman-centered therapy

130. A pigeon first learns to peck at a blue circle to open a door, then learns to go into the next cage and hop twice, then learns to pull a chain, and finally earns a reward. This sequence can be called

    (A) secondary reinforcement

    (B) discrimination learning

    (C) shaping

    (D) chaining

    (E) higher order conditioning

131. Some experiments on animals reared in isolation cages have demonstrated that they will perform work just for the opportunity to peer out of the cage for brief periods of time. These results appear to contradict which long held theory or principle of many theorists?

    (A) Adaptation

    (B) Evolution

    (C) Drive states

    (D) Arousal

    (E) Homeostasis

132. First-born children

    (A) achicve less later in life possibly because of their dependence on their parents

    (B) tend to be more immature than their siblings

    (C) tend to have lower college grade point averages than their siblings

    (D) tend to be loners

    (E) experience more difficulties early in life than their siblings

133. The term best describing overeating that results in obesity is

    (A) adipocytis

    (B) aphagia

    (C) hyperphagia

    (D) bulimia

    (E) anorexia

134. Since computers are designed to follow carefully devised instructions, some people claim that the most beneficial consequence of working with computers is that it requires the investigator to draw a diagram or flow chart of the sequence of steps of the problem being analyzed. Another term for flow chart is

    (A) algorithm

    (B) form board

    (C) program

    (D) paradigm

    (E) mathematical model

135. Phylogeny is to ontogeny as

    (A) nature is to nurture

    (B) genetics is to environment

    (C) the plant kingdom is to the animal kingdom

    (D) species is to individual

    (E) Darwinism is to Creationism

136. Most of the social psychological theories concerning attitude change are based on

    (A) Freudian ego defense mechanisms

    (B) social conformity

    (C) hedonic tone

    (D) conflict between behavior and common sense

    (E) cognitive consistence

137. Cannabis intoxication can be associated with

    (A) factitious disorder

    (B) Alzheimer's disease

    (C) gender identity disorder

    (D) tardive dyskinesia

    (E) catatonia

138. Among the elderly, the most common cause of dementia (pathological loss of intellectual functioning) is

    (A) infarction (stroke)

    (B) accidents

    (C) Alzheimer's disease

    (D) natural causes (normal aging)

    (E) Parkinson's disease

139. One of the leading precepts of Freudian psychology is: "Where the id is, there the _____ should be."

    (A) superego

    (B) defense mechanisms

    (C) gratification

    (D) ego

    (E) pleasure

140. The neurotic paradox is that

    (A) neurosis increases the more the individual is educated

    (B) if the neurosis is not cured properly, a psychosis may develop in its place

    (C) neurosis is much more common in industrial societies than in societies less advanced

    (D) neurosis is found more frequently among psychotherapists than in the general population

    (E) neurotic behavior often persists even when it leads to great personal discomfort.

141. In the latest revision of the Diagnostic and Statistical Manual of the American Psychiatric Association, the disorder once called *depressive reaction* is now called

    (A) dysthymic disorder

    (B) depressive neurosis

    (C) paraphrenia

    (D) dependent personality disorder

    (E) unipolar manic-depression

142. In one form of psychotherapy, patients are asked to construct a hierarchy of stimuli. This is done

    (A) in order to systematically review the patient's past history with each stimulus

    (B) in order to determine the point of implosion

    (C) as a way of drawing the patient's cognitive map

    (D) as a part of systematic desensitization

    (E) **as a kind of projective test**

143. Most of the presently available psychotropic drugs

    (A) produce altered states of consciousness

    (B) affect synaptic transmission

    (C) are used only to treat psychoses and manic-depressive disorders

    (D) have their primary chemical effect on brain centers located in the hindbrain

    (E) derive from folk medicines

144. Suicide is least likely to be committed by

    (A) a young married woman

    (B) a recently retired athlete

    (C) a middle-aged black man

    (D) a middle-class young male executive

    (E) a recently divorced middle-aged woman

145. Allport proposed a principle of functioning stressing that

    (A) most behaviors have complex roots

    (B) most behaviors drift away from their original purposes

    (C) particular behaviors may become goals in themselves even though their historic roots were attached to other ends

    (D) behaviors not attached to survival instincts are easily displaced

    (E) all meaningful behaviors are learned by means of reinforcement or punishment

146. A bimodal distribution would likely be found in a

   (A) follow-up reliability study

   (B) study in which the sample was not randomly drawn

   (C) sample with two frequently occurring but separated values

   (D) study of sex differences

   (E) study of two correlated variables

147. Many people, including some of Freud's philosophical descendants, object to Freud's idea of the Oedipal conflict. Which of the following accepted Freud's idea of the importance of the Oedipal conflict but reinterpreted it to diminish his stress on its sexual-aggressive component?

   (A) Rank

   (B) Fromm

   (C) Bettelheim

   (D) Breuer

   (E) Horney

148. The classic study in industrial psychology often cited to demonstrate that subjects may alter their behavior merely to satisfy the perceived demands of the experimenter was performed by

   (A) Hollingshead and Redlich

   (B) Bass

   (C) McGregor

   (D) Roethlisberger and Dickson

   (E) Flesch

149. Under what conditions of light stimulation is visual acuity best?

   (A) In dim light

   (B) In moderate light

   (C) In bright light

   (D) In light shifted to the red end of the spectrum

   (E) In light shifted to the blue end of the spectrum

150. The principle of Gestalt psychology illustrated by the Rubin vase is

   (A) similarity

   (B) proximity

   (C) closure

   (D) contour

   (E) networking

151. J.J. Gibson explains the persistence of perceptual constancies

   (A) by citing innate perceptual structures

   (B) as a ratio of the characteristics of the background in relation to those of the object

   (C) as a function of previous experience with similar perceptual structures

   (D) as a function of Gestalt principles

   (E) as a function of their relationship with the personal equation

152. Of the following, the one that is *not* one of the primary taste sensations is

    (A) sweet

    (B) sour

    (C) salty

    (D) crispy

    (E) bitter

153. A researcher collects gross sales figures from 100 retail clothing stores in a particular city, not only sales from the half dozen extremely successful department stores, but also those from the overwhelmingly large number of small *mom and pop* clothing stores. When comparing sales figures,

    (A) the mean and the mode of the sample will be approximately equal

    (B) the mean and the median of the sample will be approximately equal

    (C) the mean will be greater than the median

    (D) the median will be greater than the mean

    (E) measurement of the mean, median, and mode will be irrelevant because the distribution of sales figures will not be normal

154. A researcher plots a scatter diagram based on results of a study comparing two discrete variables. The results seem to fall along a straight line parallel to the ordinate. A Pearson product-moment correlation coefficient based on these results is

    (A) highly positive

    (B) highly negative

    (C) near 0.00

    (D) indeterminable based on the data given above

    (E) an inappropriate statistical test to use

155. When Esperanza does well in school, she attributes her performance to her work habits, but when she does poorly, she attributes her performance to environmental distractions. According to social psychologists, Esperanza is exhibiting

    (A) attribution error

    (B) cognitive dissonance

    (C) looking-glass stereotyping

    (D) self-serving bias

    (E) innocent bystander effect

156. Which of the following developmental conflicts is most associated with Margaret Mahler?

    (A) Assimilation-accommodation

    (B) Introversion-extroversion

    (C) Separation-individuation

    (D) Elektra-Oedipus

    (E) Disasthesis-stress

157. The "little brain" that controls spontaneous movement prior to the guidance of sensory feedback is the

    (A)   brain stem

    (B)   pons

    (C)   frontal lobes

    (D)   reticular formation

    (E)   cerebellum

158. When driving, many people turn up the volume of their radios, have windows of tinted glass, and close their windows. You are advising a Safety Council ready to begin a road safety campaign. Based on research on differential reaction times, you suggest warning the public that

    (A)   turning the radio volume up is the most dangerous because reaction times to sound are quicker than reaction times to other stimuli

    (B)   tinted glass is the most dangerous because reaction times to visual stimuli are quicker than reaction times to other stimuli

    (C)   closing windows is the most dangerous because air-conditioning lulls drivers into a false sense of security

    (D)   tinted glass is the most dangerous because foveal vision is less acute than peripheral vision

    (E)   senior citizens should not be allowed to drive after dark, especially if their cars have tinted glass

159. It seems almost impossible for humans to remember events in the first few years of life. This is due to

    (A)   other than sleeping, eating, and evacuation, there's not much to remember

    (B)   late maturation of the hippocampus

    (C)   late maturation of the cortex

    (D)   late development of hormones related to memory

    (E)   the traumatic nature of early experience which we tend to repress

160. The circadian clock is located in the

    (A)   pons

    (B)   hypothalamus

    (C)   medulla

    (D)   brain stem

    (E)   thalamus

161. "Munchhausen's syndrome" and "Munchhausen's syndrome by proxy," both of which involve people's glorifying the role of patient in the absence of any underlying physical problem, would be classified in the DSM-IV as examples of:

    (A)   hypochondria

    (B)   somatoform disorders

    (C)   factitious disorders

    (D)   stress disorders

    (E)   personality disorders

162. The validity of a new test as measured in comparison to a previously standardized test is found to be .50. Other things being equal, the greatest the reliability of this new test is likely to be

    (A) .50

    (B) .25

    (C) .75

    (D) indeterminate

    (E) −.50

163. *Slugger* Jones has a contract with the Beagles baseball team that provides a bonus if his batting average falls within the top 15% in his league. The mean batting average is .270, with a standard deviation of .055 (meaning that the average batter gets a hit 27.0% of the time, with a standard deviation of 5.5%). How high does Jones have to hit (what percent of the time does he have to get a hit) to win his bonus?

    (A) .850 (85.0%)

    (B) .310 (31.0%)

    (C) .330 (33.0%)

    (D) .270 (27.0%)

    (E) .275 (27.5%)

164. With respect to the relationship between binge eating and obesity, which of the following statements is the most accurate?

    (A) Binge eating and obesity are highly correlated; binge eating is frequently found among obese people.

    (B) There is no demonstrable relationship between binge eating and obesity.

    (C) Binge eating and obesity are highly negatively correlated; binge eating is found almost exclusively among extremely thin people, where it is usually followed by purging.

    (D) Binge eating is sex-related; obese men binge eat far more than obese women.

    (E) Binge eating is socio-economically related; it is not related to obesity except in the lowest socio-economic groups.

165. According to Seligman, author of the concept, "learned helplessness" is on the rise because of the

    (A) increase in television talk shows

    (B) increase in models of learned helplessness on television

    (C) increase in psychotropic medication

    (D) failure of behavior therapy

    (E) decline of the family

166. Abraham Maslow and Erik Erikson would most likely share which of the following beliefs?

    I. Whereas societies are basically unjust, individuals strive for justice.

    II. Psychological development proceeds in stages.

    III. Psychotherapy is necessary for the majority of people.

    (A) all of the above

    (B) I and II

    (C) II and III

    (D) II only

    (E) I only

167. Intelligence is "the sum-total or global capacity of the person to act with purpose, to think in a rational manner, and to deal efficiently with his or her environment, not solely facility in specific abilities." This definition could have come from

    (A) Spearman

    (B) Gardner

    (C) Bender

    (D) Wechsler

    (E) Piaget

168. Of the following, which is most likely to appear earliest in the human developmental sequence?

    (A) Smiling

    (B) Cooing

    (C) Object permanence

    (D) Fear

    (E) Distress

169. Dr. Psychometrics gives a sophisticated examination to her students. White gets a score of 50; Brown scores a 25. Dr. Psychometrics does not claim that White is twice as good as Brown because the professor knows the test is not measured on a(n) _____ scale.

    (A) ordinal

    (B) ratio

    (C) inferential

    (D) interval

    (E) nominal

170. An investigator wishing to know how members of a group will perform in a driver education course administers a test of achievement in mathematics and discovers that it is a reasonably good predictor of driving skills. Of the following, in relation to driving skills, the mathematics test can be said to have low

    (A) equivalent-form reliability

    (B) standardization

    (C) face validity

    (D) predictive validity

    (E) concurrent validity

171. An employer has to choose a small group of future employees from a large pool of applicants for a job requiring a lot of mathematical ability. Of the following, which procedure is best for the employer to follow in order to choose employees most likely to profit from further job training?

    (A) Administer an interest inventory

    (B) Administer an achievement test

    (C) Find out past grade-point average

    (D) Administer a personality test

    (E) Administer an aptitude test

172. Of the following disorders, the *least* likely to be found to be genetically-determined is

    (A) schizophrenia

    (B) depression

    (C) bulimia

    (D) anxiety disorder

    (E) obsessive-compulsive disorder

173. The clergyman's child who drinks to excess and scours through pornographic magazines can be said to be exhibiting the defense mechanism of

    (A) identification with the aggressor

    (B) reaction formation

    (C) rationalization

    (D) denial

    (E) splitting

174. A secondary gain often occurring as a result of frequent illness is

    (A) prompt medical attention

    (B) decrease in motivation

    (C) attention from others

    (D) reduction in inhibition

    (E) more focused reality contact

175. Assuming a correlation coefficient of .50, in which of the following cases would an experimenter have the greatest confidence in this statistical finding?

    (A) If the sample is small and the level of statistical significance is .01

    (B) If the sample is large and the level of significance is .05

    (C) If the sample is large and the level of significance is .01

    (D) If the sample is small and the level of significance is .05

    (E) Sample size has no bearing on conclusions based on the study or on statistical significance

176. A researcher wanting to study magazine reading patterns at a college bookstore collects sales figures for all magazines and then divides the magazines into categories such as news magazines, hobby magazines, professional journals, etc. Within each category, the researcher chooses only three titles and then computes statistical tests on the resulting data. This is an example of

    (A) discrete sampling

    (B) random sampling

    (C) stratified sampling

    (D) selective sampling

    (E) poor sampling technique

177. A depression that follows the loss of a job can be referred to as

    (A) psychosomatic

    (B) chronic

    (C) endogenous

    (D) exogenous

    (E) ego syntonic

178. In classical conditioning terminology, enuresis occurs because

    (A) the CR of urination occurs without the UCR

    (B) the CS of bladder tension precedes the UCR of bladder release

    (C) bladder tension has not become a CS

    (D) conscious control of bladder release has not become a UCR

    (E) dreams of urination have become a UCS

179. Educational psychology began in America with the publication of

    (A) Thorndike's *Elements of Psychology*

    (B) Cattell's *Journal of Educational Psychology*

    (C) Binet and Simon's *La mesure du développement. . . .*

    (D) Galton's *Inquiries Into Human Faculty. . . .*

    (E) Dewey's *Experience and Education*

180. Of the following, the child classified as *exceptional* is

    (A) an overachiever

    (B) an underachiever

    (C) a gifted child

    (D) an emotionally disturbed child

    (E) a child of parents of different races

181. Which of the following statements about the Montessori method is *not* true?

    (A) The teaching of writing is encouraged before the teaching of reading.

    (B) Piaget's findings support many of the methods used in Montessori schools.

    (C) The role of the teacher is to encourage independent discovery, not to provide direct reinforcement.

    (D) Several sensory modalities are used to teach similar lessons.

    (E) Disadvantaged learners are unlikely to benefit from Montessori methodology.

182. Electroconvulsive therapy

    (A) has been all but abandoned in modern psychiatric practice

    (B) is used in conjunction with behavior therapy in correctional institutions

    (C) has been found to be effective with delusional depressives, suicidals, acute paranoid schizophrenics, and catatonia in the adolescent

    (D) has not been found to be effective in geriatric populations

    (E) has stimulated more legal challenges than any other psychiatric procedure

183. A 65-year-old female executive complains of mild forgetfulness. Her mother, an otherwise-healthy 83-year-old, has developed full-blown Alzheimer's disease. It is most likely that

    (A) the 65-year-old woman is showing signs of early-onset Alzheimer's disease

    (B) although Alzheimer's disease may not be present, the 65-year-old woman is showing signs of depression

    (C) only genetic testing can rule out Alzheimer's disease

    (D) the mother probably does not have Alzheimer's disease, since her health is otherwise not remarkable

    (E) there is little reason to suspect Alzheimer's disease in the 65-year-old given the symptoms presented

184. During depolarization of an action potential, the neuron receives a surge of

    (A) potassium ions

    (B) sodium ions

    (C) dopamine

    (D) serotonin

    (E) ACTH

185. The "plant studies" by Langer and Rodin indicated that

    (A) routine work in large plants or factories is debilitating and leads to socially destructive behavior

    (B) subjects whose work growing plants was difficult and time-consuming were more vocal defending their efforts than subjects whose plant-growing was less effortful

    (C) people attribute more positive social values to plant lovers than to non-plant lovers

    (D) giving nursing home residents control over their decisions increases satisfaction, participation, and longevity

    (E) subjects showed more destructive behavior toward plants when placed in large, authoritarian experimental groups than when placed in small, democratic experimental groups

186. Males consistently show superiority to females in tests of

    (A) mathematical ability

    (B) hormonal balance

    (C) spatial ability

    (D) sex drive

    (E) fine motor coordination

187. Patient X continually repeats the same set of words and cannot be convinced to stop her inappropriate rambling. Her behavior can be described as

    (A) flight of ideas

    (B) asthenia

    (C) perseveration

    (D) confabulation

    (E) illusional

188. S. Papert has worked extensively with a computer language and an accompanying *discovery-learning* approach for elementary school children called

    (A) Carmen Sandiego

    (B) BASIC

    (C) LOGO

    (D) Head Start

    (E) Nintendo

189. The eight-week post-conception embryo has developed all of the following organs except:

    (A) nose

    (B) sex organs

    (C) toes and fingers

    (D) skeleton

    (E) knees and elbows

190. The voice at the other end of the phone asks you to answer a few innocent-sounding questions about your buying habits. You answer. Then the voice asks if you would be available to answer a more extensive list of questions on the phone if you are called again within the week. This survey technique is called

    (A) focus group interview

    (B) depth interview

    (C) cold calling

    (D) in-home survey

    (E) foot-in-the-door

191. Many children one or two years old latch onto a special object—a doll, a soft object, or a blanket—that they carry around with them and rely on for comfort. This object is referred to as a(n)

    (A) behavior modifier

    (B) ego ideal

    (C) model

    (D) generalized stimulus

    (E) transitional object

192. A treatment program set up by a therapist assumes that the underlying reason why shy people have difficulty is that when they are in challenging social situations their thoughts are preoccupied with fears about how others evaluate them. To counteract these preoccupations, the therapist places the *shy* person in simulated social situations and actively challenges any of the patient's fearful thoughts as they arise. This form of therapy is called

(A) implosion therapy

(B) behavioral therapy

(C) psychoanalytically oriented psycho-therapy

(D) psychodrama

(E) cognitive therapy

193. Learning of one's impending death sets off a series of reactions, including defense mechanisms, as the person attempts to come to grips with his or her vulnerability. According to Kübler-Ross, the stages of death and dying are

(A) protest, preparation, depression, resolution

(B) denial, anger, bargaining, depression, acceptance

(C) disbelief, pleading, guilt-removal, acceptance, depression

(D) help-seeking, help-denial, independent action, resolution

(E) denial, fantasy, protest, depression, resolution

194. Depth perception depends on both monocular and binocular cues. Of the following, the process that is a part of monocular depth perception is

(A) muscle strain during convergence

(B) retinal disparity

(C) changes in shape of crystalline lens due to action of the ciliary muscles

(D) expansion and contraction of the iris of the lens

(E) location of image on retina in relation to fovea

195. A person diagnosed as having a schizoid personality disorder would *not* exhibit

(A) close relationships with only one or two people

(B) emotional coldness and distance

(C) eccentricities of thought, behavior, or speech

(D) indifference to feelings of others

(E) indifference to praise or criticism of others

PRACTICE EXAMINATION 2
ANSWER KEY

1. C	29. C	57. A	85. B	113. D
2. D	30. B	58. A	86. A	114. E
3. E	31. D	59. C	87. C	115. E
4. B	32. A	60. B	88. D	116. A
5. A	33. A	61. C	89. B	117. E
6. A	34. A	62. C	90. C	118. A
7. B	35. A	63. D	91. D	119. B
8. D	36. D	64. A	92. E	120. D
9. C	37. C	65. E	93. D	121. A
10. A	38. B	66. E	94. A	122. E
11. D	39. C	67. C	95. E	123. A
12. E	40. C	68. C	96. C	124. C
13. C	41. C	69. D	97. C	125. D
14. B	42. D	70. C	98. E	126. D
15. C	43. B	71. B	99. D	127. E
16. A	44. D	72. E	100. C	128. E
17. C	45. E	73. D	101. A	129. C
18. E	46. E	74. E	102. E	130. D
19. B	47. C	75. A	103. E	131. E
20. E	48. A	76. D	104. C	132. E
21. A	49. B	77. D	105. A	133. C
22. E	50. C	78. C	106. A	134. A
23. A	51. E	79. B	107. D	135. D
24. B	52. E	80. A	108. D	136. E
25. B	53. A	81. C	109. C	137. E
26. D	54. C	82. D	110. C	138. C
27. A	55. A	83. C	111. A	139. D
28. C	56. E	84. E	112. C	140. E

141. A	152. D	163. C	174. C	185. D
142. D	153. C	164. B	175. C	186. C
143. B	154. C	165. E	176. C	187. C
144. A	155. D	166. D	177. D	188. C
145. C	156. C	167. D	178. C	189. B
146. C	157. E	168. E	179. A	190. E
147. E	158. A	169. B	180. C	191. E
148. D	159. B	170. C	181. E	192. E
149. C	160. B	171. E	182. C	193. B
150. D	161. C	172. C	183. E	194. C
151. B	162. B	173. B	184. B	195. C

EXPLANATORY ANSWERS

1. (**C**) Reading comprehension is closely related to mental age, and so the child in the example can be assumed to read at about the level of a 12-year-old. The child in answer (C) would also have the reading skills of a 12-year-old, which can be deduced from the formula: IQ = mental age/chronological age × 100. To know: WAIS; WISC; Galton; Spearman.

2. (**D**) After a period of no reinforcement, i.e., extinction, the reemergence of the conditioned response is called spontaneous recovery. If the spontaneously recovered response is not reinforced, it extinguishes.

3. (**E**) Schachter and Singer (1962) demonstrated that although physiological factors may influence the intensity of a response, cognitive factors, such as a belief about the causes of physiological reactions, also influence emotional arousal.

4. (**B**) Closure, the tendency to perceive gaps as filled in, is one of the principles of Gestalt psychology. To know: Zeigarnik effect.

5. (**A**) Excess dopamine in the system is associated with delusions, hallucinations, and paranoia. All major antipsychotic drugs reduce dopamine levels.

6. (**A**) Infants between four and six months of age seem to develop the ability to be attracted by and to be attentive to familiar objects, the human face most of all. Haaf and Bell (1967) demonstrated that the more a stimulus looks like a human face, the longer the infant will fixate upon it.

7. (**B**) Although projective tests in clinical settings are used to determine psychiatric diagnosis and level of cognitive functioning (conversely, intelligence tests are used by some skilled clinicians to determine psychiatric diagnosis), projective tests are primarily used to determine emotional and motivational functioning.

8. (**D**) An additional criterion in forming a random sample is that the selection of each population member must be made independently so that the selection of one member does not influence the selection of any other. To know: accidental sample; parameters.

9. (**C**) *Genetic* refers to growth or development; *epistemology* refers to the branch of philosophy dealing with how we know what we know.

10. (**A**) This question describes the Stroop color-word test which has been used to measure level of anxiety or reaction to conflict.

11. (**D**) This is a typical example of the kind of research work done by ethologists, who espouse a strong preference for naturalistic observation—systematic observations using a minimum of experimental controls and minimizing the use of systematic sampling.

12. (**E**) The location of gustatory receptors (including, but not limited to taste buds) on the tongue, the back of the mouth, and the throat has been carefully mapped. In general, taste sensitivity is not nearly as good as smell sensitivity, and our sensitivity for acids and bitters is greater than that for sweets and salt. To know: papillae.

13. (**C**) Wilhelm Wundt, who is considered a structuralist, founded the first psychology laboratory in Leipzig, Germany, in 1879. To know: empiricist; trained introspection.

14. (**B**) The term "paradigm" means "model" or "pattern." In science, the replacement of an old theory by a new model or theory is not *disproof* of the old theory; it is merely an indication that the new theory is more powerful, more capable of explaining more phenomena. Thus when an old paradigm is replaced, it is not destroyed, it is *shifted* out of the way, so to speak.

15. (**C**) Handedness exhibits itself almost from birth. About 90% of the population is right-handed. For unknown reasons, the left-handed are overrepresented among mental retardates, epileptics, the reading disabled, and alcoholics.

16. (**A**) Both boys and girls who mature early tend to be associated with the "in" groups at school. Early maturing girls tend to have greater difficulty dealing with their sexuality than do boys.

17. (**C**) If the acquisition time (interval between presentation of UCS and CS) is 0.5 seconds, conditioning requires the smallest number of trials. To know: delay conditioning; trace conditioning.

18. (**E**) In 1885, Ebbinghaus published his classic studies on memory based on numerous exhaustive experiments on nonsense syllables he performed using himself as the main subject. Chomsky developed a powerful approach to language behavior that attempts to deal with language from the simplest elements, such as morphemes and phonemes, to the most complex sentences. To know: savings method; recall; recognition; relearning; transformational grammar; psycholinguistics.

19. (**B**) Subjects in an experiment in which they were deprived of sleep for 200 hours bounced back virtually completely after a single night in which they had twice their usual amount of sleep. The theory that sleep restores bodily functioning is called into question by the observation that older people tend to need less sleep than younger people.

20. (**E**) Lashley's pioneer studies of induced lesions found that the amount of tissue removed or destroyed was more important than the location of the tissue in determining loss of functioning.

21. (**A**) Some have interpreted "natural childbirth" techniques as a form of self-hypnosis. One of the most controversial recent uses of hypnosis among therapists has been in restoring childhood memories among sufferers of multiple personality disorder. This use of hypnosis has been heavily litigated.

22. (**E**) Heavy-drinking pregnant women have a higher incidence of spontaneous abortions, stillbirths, and premature births. There also seems to be an association with behavior problems and attention deficit disorder in the children of alcoholic mothers.

23. (**A**) Parkinson's disease is associated with the loss of dopamine production in the nigrostratial system. Experiments with L-dopa produced favorable results—but only for a few years. Now a favored treatment is adrenal implants which take on neuron-like properties when placed in the brain.

24. (**B**) Experimental psychologists tend to prefer definitions made in the form of operations to be performed, rather than in the form of hypothetical assumptions. To know: logical positivism.

25. (**B**) Flashbulb memories—as if the scene were captured by a photo taken with a flashbulb—tend to stand out in vivid recollection. A distinct stimulus is recalled more vividly. This phenomenon has been given the name *von Restorff effect*.

26. (**D**) Gardner argues that there are perhaps seven different types of intelligence, not just the single type that traditional tests have measured. As proof, Gardner cites examples of people who score high on one type of intelligence, but low on others.

27. (**A**) In 1986, the American Psychological Association adopted a resolution labeling the evidence for the effectiveness of polygraphs "still unsatisfactory." The US Congress bars the use of polygraphs for job screening. Even the American Polygraph Association admits that the error rate hovers around 10%.

28. (**C**) The obstruction box, used as part of the obstruction method, tests the strength of motivation by examining how much or what combination of noxious stimulation the organism will tolerate.

29. (**C**) "DNR" ("do not resuscitate") written on a chart probably indicates that the patient has consented to treatment termination. There is a general tendency in modern medicine to leave the ultimate authority regarding terminal cases up to the patient.

30. (**B**) Schemata are cognitive patterns or structures that have been developed by the individual through accommodation. They relate the individual's actions to goals. To know: assimilation; accommodation.

31. (**D**) Of the choices given, the most appropriate is that the test is of questionable value. Had this test not been labelled "new," other issues might have been open to question, such as the composition of the sample given the test.

32. (**A**) Level of aspiration is that level at which a person sets goals. If it is consistently too high, the person experiences failure. Successful coaches, for example, set reachable goals for their teams, not goals beyond the team's capability.

33. (**A**) Latent learning is learning that becomes evident only when the occasion for its use becomes evident. The relationship between latent and manifest learning is usually indirect. To know: incidental learning.

34. (**A**) Watson wrote during an era in psychology when experimentation was dominated by Structuralism, which proposed notions Watson felt were too *mentalistic* and unverifiable.

35. (**A**) Normative group influence is the influence to conform to group norms. Some of the classic studies in this area were conducted by Sherif and Asch.

36. (**D**) Behavior medicine, or health psychology, studies etiology, host resistance, disease mechanisms, patient decision-making, compliance with medicine regimens, and effects of medical interventions.

37. (**C**) EBS studies, rendered less popular recently by PET, CAT, and MRI scanning, demonstrate the localization of functions in the brain. For example, a lesion at one location in a rat's brain reduces eating even to the point of starvation, while a lesion in a nearby brain area produces overeating.

38. (**B**) Written releases are imperative if a therapist is to contact an outside agency or professional, but are not necessary within the treating institution, such as within a hospital.

39. (**C**) A "lexicon" is a dictionary, so "lexical processing" refers to the retrieval of the meaning of the word from the reader's internal lexicon, or dictionary.

40. (C) In the disorders listed in this question, anxiety is defended against by an almost total removal of awareness of the source of anxiety. Denial is a more severe and primitive form of repression, which also would be the correct answer in some cases.

41. (C) A 1987 report indicates that about 30% of abused children become abusive parents, a rate six times higher than the national rate of child abuse. Other less comprehensive reports put the rate as high as 50% of abused children who turn into abusing parents.

42. (D) Szasz argues that diagnosing people stigmatizes and dehumanizes them since it implies they no longer have control over their actions—rather, the disease has control. He believes psychiatry has been used improperly to control society's unwanted.

43. (B) As a result of their spinal cord injuries, these men are no longer capable of easily acting out their feelings. It appears that as a way of coping, these men have learned to suppress strong emotional responses that they cannot act upon.

44. (D) Since latent learning or incidental learning occurs so commonly, learning often develops in the absence of direct reinforcement. This phenomenon is taken advantage of, in reverse, in deconditioning.

45. (E) "Primary prevention" attempts to foster social institutions that promote general mental health and attempts to eradicate conditions that encourage poor mental health. "Secondary prevention" includes crisis intervention, consultation, and education. "Tertiary prevention" includes the hospital community.

46. (E) An asymptote would indicate a leveling off of the response rate on the dependent variable.

47. (C) The purpose of comparing an experimental group with a control group is to determine if the experimental procedure yields differences that cannot be accounted for by chance. The results of this experiment yielded no significant differences, indicating that the experimental procedure used was ineffective.

48. (A) The modern rubric for Freud's conversion hysteria is somatoform disorder. Two ways in which "conversion" symptoms differ from actual physical disorders are (1) the common presence of belle indifference and (2) failure of conversion symptoms to conform to symptoms of known diseases.

49. (B) This investigation concerns the relationship between two sets of variables measured on the same subjects, which makes the data analyzable by the use of the Pearson product moment coefficient of correlation (r).

50. (C) Proactive interference is the term used to describe the interference or degradation of performance produced by material learned prior to learning the target material. To know: proactive inhibition; negative transference.

51. (E) Avicenna's work was published in the eighth century A.D. Chung Ching, sometimes referred to as the Hippocrates of China, published his works, including his discussion of emotional balance, around 200 A.D.

52. (E) Pitch perception seems to be based on two mechanisms: high frequencies are coded using place of excitation, while low frequencies are coded using neural rate of firing. To know: place theory; frequency theory.

53. (**A**) The "cold mothering" hypothesis, proposed by Kanner in the 1940s, has since been supplanted by more biologically oriented theories, even though to date no single cause has been found for this baffling condition.

54. (**C**) Rorschach testers feel they can estimate a person's intelligence based on the number and kinds of human and animal movement responses made by the subject. Conversely, they feel that a predominance of static, vague, and nonliving responses indicates a lower intellectual level.

55. (**A**) During the absolute refractory period, which lasts for a few milliseconds, the axon is unexcitable and cannot be fired. This is followed by a relative refractory period, during which the axon can be fired by a greater than usual excitation. After the relative refractory period, the level of excitability returns to normal.

56. (**E**) Heroin and other opiates seem to act like endorphins, occupying the brain's receptors for pain-killing. Apparently, during the course of addiction, the brain ceases to produce the normal supply of endorphins.

57. (**A**) Although originally a California state court decision, variations on the Tarasoff decision have now been adopted by most state legislatures in the US.

58. (**A**) Although the evidence for the relationship between second trimester stress and homosexuality is not overwhelming, it is the most consistently found relationship of the alternatives given.

59. (**C**) Miller felt that the human capacity for memory storage is optimal at about eight units, although the amount of information contained in each unit is variable.

60. (**B**) "Affect" is a person's immediate emotional state, which can be subjectively or objectively recognized. The quoted statement is confusing because Jake is described as having contradictory affects.

61. (**C**) In a double-blind experiment, both subject and tester are blind to which experimental condition is administered each subject. While easy to use in some areas of testing, double-blind is more difficult to perform in social psychology.

62. (**C**) Comparing scores arrived at by different judges is called inter-judge or inter-rater reliability. It is a procedure often used in nonobjective testing, such as the TAT or Rorschach.

63. (**D**) Social and organizational psychologists have generally found that the most intractable group differences are those involving deeply held moral values.

64. (**A**) Glucocorticoids stimulate the release of ACTH and beta-endorphins. Both are significant stress hormones. The release of proteins is suppressed by these hormones. ACTH, in turn, stimulates the release of follicle-stimulating hormones, lutenizing hormones, and growth hormones.

65. (**E**) According to chaos theory, scientists can plot the probability and results of interactions between things, but no "thing" can be drawn independent from others.

66. (**E**) Will to power is an idea advocated by Adler, who claimed that the fundamental human motivation is the desire to overcome inferiority by striving to achieve power or superiority.

67. (**C**) Morphology, and its associated morphological rules, refers to the study of the formation of words in a language and their usage.

68. **(C)** Object permanence refers to the idea that objects continue to exist even when they are not immediately perceived. Piaget found that until the child was approximately nine months of age it was unlikely to act as if an object disappearing from its field of vision continued to exist. Some psychologists have related this development to *stranger anxiety*.

69. **(D)** Dynamism, Sullivan's nearest approximation to what most theorists refer to as *personality*, refers to enduring patterns of behavior the individual persistently exhibits in a wide variety of circumstances.

70. **(C)** Tardive dyskinesia, which includes uncoordinated body movement, is a frequent negative side effect of the overuse of psychotropic drugs.

71. **(B)** The narrower the range of scores entered into a correlation coefficient, the less is the *power* of the test to detect real differences.

72. **(E)** Dynamic psychotherapists view depression as a function of the failure to achieve internalized goals or standards. Thus depression would be more prevalent in a guilt society, which is oriented toward internalized standards.

73. **(D)** According to attribution theory, people first assume they understand others' motivation and do not take environmental factors into consideration when evaluating others. This phenomenon is referred to as fundamental attribution error (FAE).

74. **(E)** Cummings and VandenBos coined the term "the worried well" on the basis of results of their 20-year-long study of patients at Kaiser-Permanente, a major health insurer in California.

75. **(A)** The example describes a person known in the vernacular as a *bag lady*, traditionally diagnosed as a simple schizophrenic. There are some diagnosticians, however, who would diagnose the person in the example as suffering from schizotypal personality disorder or manic-depression.

76. **(D)** Counterbalancing is a method of varying the order of presentation of stimuli or experimental conditions to subjects so that the effects of order of presentation are minimized.

77. **(D)** As a general rule, extreme scores tend to regress to the mean. Extreme scores are considered less stable than those closer to the mean.

78. **(C)** Reaction formation is the ego defense mechanism in which a person's conscious attitude and behavior are the opposite of his or her unconscious attitude.

79. **(B)** The associative area of the human cerebral cortex correlates and integrates functions of the sensory and motor areas. It is larger than the homologous area in lower animals.

80. **(A)** The medulla, which is in the hindbrain, contains centers for the control of breathing and heart rate as well as centers that relay sensory input to higher parts of the brain.

81. **(C)** The limbic system, a region of the forebrain that includes portions of the amygdala, the hypothalamus, the septal area, and the hippocampus, was once thought to control only the sense of smell, but now is thought to control both the perception and expression of emotions.

82. **(D)** The adrenal medulla, the inner part of the adrenal glands located at the top of the kidneys, secretes adrenalin and noradrenalin, which affect blood pressure, heart rate, and blood sugar level.

83. **(C)** Until the work of N. Miller it was generally thought that internal body processes such as blood pressure and brain waves were not amenable to change through conditioning. Biofeedback, the name given to the process of changing internal body processes, often uses sophisticated electronic devices and variations on conditioning (generally classical) techniques.

84. **(E)** When the neuron is resting, sodium ions are kept outside and potassium ions inside the axon by the nerve's semipermeable membrane. When the neuron is excited, the locations of the ions are reversed. To know: sodium pump.

85. **(B)** When an axon is polarized, sodium ions are on the outside and potassium ions on the inside of the axon.

86. **(A)** Also called the reticular formation, the reticular activating system passes through the medulla in the hindbrain into parts of the forebrain. Its apparent function is to control wakefulness, attention, sleep, and some simple learning processes.

87. **(C)** A reflex is a simple, specific, unlearned response to a stimulus in which the impulse travels from the sensory nerve to the spinal cord (without necessarily having to be transmitted to the brain) to the motor nerve.

88. **(D)** The all-or-none principle states that the neuron, like the circuit, fires at maximum amplitude or it does not fire at all.

89. **(B)** The corpus callosum connects the cerebral hemispheres. Studies have shown that when the corpus callosum is severed, the ability to coordinate activities in the two halves of the brain is impaired. To know: cerebral specialization; lateralization of functioning.

90. **(C)** ACh, acetylcholine, is a transmitter substance in the nervous system. AChE, acetylcholinesterase, is an enzyme that inactivates ACh.

91. **(D)** The all-or-none law or principle states that once fired a neuron is maximally activated, whatever the stimulus. The neuron itself does not mediate the amplitude of the response, although the number of neurons fired and the transmitting substances may affect the response.

92. **(E)** The pituitary gland, located beneath the hypothalamus, is often referred to as the *master gland* because it secretes hormones regulating the action of other glands. It also secretes hormones controlling body growth.

93. **(D)** Spatial construction and nonverbal ideation—functions associated with the visual arts—are associated with the right, or minor, hemisphere.

94. **(A)** The term *tracts* is generally reserved for use in describing groups of axons in the central nervous system, as in the terms *ascending tracts* and *descending tracts*. *Nerves* refer to collections of axons in the peripheral nervous system.

95. **(E)** The limbic system is located toward the upper end of the brain stem; it is now known to play a vital role in attention, emotion, memory, and motivation.

96. **(C)** The exact causes of dyslexia—as well as other disorders associated with the term *minimal brain dysfunction*—have not been established. However, a popular explanation centers on the concept of cerebral dominance.

97. **(C)** Lashley proposed the principle of equipotentiality which says that all parts of the brain have an equal potential for storing memories and that the whole of the cerebral cortex is involved in memory.

98. (**E**) The students who traveled great distances expended greater effort so, according to cognitive dissonance theory, they would tend to justify their effort, perhaps by exaggerating the difficulty of the test.

99. (**D**) The first decile represents the first 10% of the scores, the median 50% of the scores. So the difference between the two is 40%.

100. (**C**) Experiments on the *visual cliff*, a device originated by Gibson, have shown that even at very young ages an infant has some capacity for depth perception and can do a fairly good job of avoiding the danger of changes in depth of the color field by coordinating visual information with motor control.

101. (**A**) The reversal shift, a problem studied by the Kendlers, is often used as a test of verbal mediation and abstract thinking in young children.

102. (**E**) The zygote, or fertilized egg, requires approximately 10 to 14 days after fertilization to be implanted in the walls of the uterus.

103. (**E**) The Moro reflex described here tends to disappear at three to four months of age. It seems to be controlled more by the brain stem than by the cerebral cortex, so its early disappearance coincides with generally greater control of higher brain centers.

104. (**C**) Erikson found that in playing with blocks girls tend to build horizontal structures while boys tend to build vertical structures.

105. (**A**) Unless their separate environments are extremely enriched or restricted, identical twins reared apart nevertheless show remarkable similarities in personality styles and tastes, academic achievements, vocational choices—and even characters of spouses.

106. (**A**) Although no serious condition should be ignored at any stage, many of the conditions that first exhibit themselves during adolescence tend to diminish in severity with time. Various forms of schizophrenia, however, tend to exhibit themselves first during adolescence and are more intractable.

107. (**D**) One of the most stable findings of group dynamics research is that public commitment, such as a show of hands or a public statement, increases the likelihood of further action.

108. (**D**) Battie and Rigos reported these results in 1991.

109. (**C**) A hypothetical construct is an abstract concept that includes but goes beyond direct empirical reference. Increased heart rate or aversive behavior are observable components of fear, but are not synonymous with the concept *fear*.

110. (**C**) In the prisoner's dilemma game, each subject is given a choice: confess or be silent. Being silent yields a moderate penalty if both players are silent. Confessing yields a favorable result only if the other prisoner does not confess, otherwise it yields a large penalty. Most subjects confess. Competition is more common than cooperation. This result parallels some life situations, such as many business decisions and national decisions concerning armaments.

111. (**A**) Nearly all rent checks would arrive on or very close to the due date. Skewness refers to the degree to which a distribution departs from the symmetrical. A distribution having a long tail at its higher end is positively skewed. A distribution with a long tail at the lower end is negatively skewed.

112. (**C**) When an individual with only dominant genes is paired with an individual with only recessive genes, their offspring will have one gene from each parent, and thus will be of a mixed genotype.

113. (**D**) The dorsal roots of the spinal cord conduct afferent nerves, meaning that they conduct sensation from the stimulus to the central nervous system. The ventral roots contain efferent nerves.

114. (**E**) Red has the longest wavelength, violet the shortest.

115. (**E**) The vestibular (sometimes called labyrinthine) sense and kinesthesis, the sense of balance and movement, are related to the semicircular canals and the otolith organs.

116. (**A**) In this example, the person wearing the eyepatch would be taking advantage of the monocular depth cue referred to as motion parallax, meaning that objects closer to the observer seem to move faster than objects farther away.

117. (**E**) According to James, we first perceive, then we react, and finally we experience a sensation or emotion. In this case, we perceive a lemon, then experience the sensation of sourness.

118. (**A**) *Stimulus substitution* is sometimes used as a synonym for *classical conditioning.* Both refer to the substitution of a conditioned stimulus for an unconditioned one. To know: simultaneous conditioning; trace conditioning; delayed conditioning.

119. (**B**) Environmental psychology studies the transaction and interrelatedness of people and their social and psychological surroundings, both man-made and natural.

120. (**D**) Testing for reliability by re-administering a test (or an alternate version of a test) after a period of time has elapsed tends to produce scores that regress to the mean; that is, the extreme scores tend to wash out.

121. (**A**) Guthrie thought that movement is essential for learning. Hull thought drive reduction is essential for learning.

122. (**E**) In most instances in modern psychological treatment, the patient's interests are at the top of the ethical hierarchy. If there is a conflict between the interests of the psychologist and the interests of the patient, the psychologist is ethically bound to attempt to resolve the problem in favor of the interests of the patient, even if that means withdrawing from the case in an orderly fashion.

123. (**A**) Down syndrome results from extra chromosome 21 material. Trisomy 21 is directly related to maternal age, being common to older mothers. The overall incidence is 1 in 600 births.

124. (**C**) The Luchins water jar experiment was devised to test mental set. A related concept, *functional fixedness,* is a tendency to avoid using familiar objects in creative ways.

125. (**D**) Low birth weight is frequently associated wth prematurity, which is often, although not always, associated with the effect of teratogens like alcohol and drugs.

126. (**D**) Maccoby and Jacklin also found that play groups had sex-related characteristics: at three years of age, boys' play is more vigorous and girls' play is more orderly. They attribute the differences to hormonal influences.

127. (**E**) Layers or masses of brain cells are considered *gray matter* and fiber tracts are *white matter*. The cerebral lobes are covered by a layer of neurons or cortex called gray matter.

128. (**E**) One of the most consistently observed phenomena of reinforcement is that the sooner the reinforcement is given after the response, the greater the likelihood of learning.

129. (**C**) Rational-emotive therapy (RET) says anxiety, guilt, depression, and other psychological states are not caused by external events but by how the individual thinks about these events.

130. (**D**) Chaining is learning a series of responses to a series of stimuli on the way to achieving a goal. To know: shaping.

131. (**E**) The theory of homeostasis predicts that behavior is instrumental in reducing needs or drives, especially physiological needs. The example in this question can be used to describe behavior that satisfies no apparent need, yet is persistent and virtually a drive in itself.

132. (**E**) Research on birth order indicates that first-borns tend to have more difficult childhoods, although later in life first-borns seem to achieve more than later-borns, and especially more than middle children.

133. (**C**) Hyperphagia, the problem of eating abnormally large quantities of food, is associated with improper functioning of the hypothalamus.

134. (**A**) Although the use of the computer holds great promise for research in psychology, there is a controversy in the field about the benefits of computer-assisted instruction (CAI), with some psychologists now saying that it may impair human interaction.

135. (**D**) Phylogeny is a description of the evolution of a species, while ontogeny describes the evolution of an individual. The recent emphasis in psychology on evolutionary explanations of survival-oriented behaviors makes the topic of the comparison of phylogeny and ontogeny of great explanatory importance.

136. (**E**) Most social psychological theories on attitude change are based on the assumption that the most pleasing or satisfying state in which a chooser can find himself or herself is the one in which cognitions, beliefs, attitudes, and feelings are consistent.

137. (**E**) Neuroleptic malignant syndrome (NMS) can occur under drug-induced conditions, including excessive use of marijuana. It is characterized by high body temperature, autonomic instability, and muscle rigidity.

138. (**C**) Alzheimer's, which accounts for about 70% of dementia among the elderly, is characterized by an excess of fluid pressing on the brain.

139. (**D**) The expression "where the id is, there the ego should be" refers to the principle that behavior controlled by unconscious or unknown forces could become more manageable if controlled by known forces.

140. (**E**) The neurotic paradox results when the sufferer feels no choice in his or her mode of behavior, so that the neurotic behavior persists despite whatever discomfort accompanies it.

141. (**A**) Dysthymic disorder refers to a depression that is not severe enough to be considered either a major depressive episode or a psychotic reaction. Some of the symptoms include insomnia, low energy level, or chronic tiredness; reduced self-esteem; decreased productivity, interest, and pleasure; and social withdrawal.

142. (**D**) The purpose of desensitization is to make the person feel comfortable in situations that previously aroused anxiety. Wolpe is a leading exponent of a desensitization technique that he calls reciprocal inhibition.

143. (**B**) Most widely used psychotropic drugs seem to have their main effects on neuronal transmission. The MAO inhibitors, for instance, used to treat severe depression, seem to increase the levels of the neurotransmitters serotonin and norepinephrine. To know: psychopharmacology.

144. (**A**) Although more women than men attempt suicide, men succeed more often in completing the act. Suicide seems to be becoming more frequent among adolescents, but in the middle years suicide increases with age. The single, divorced, and separated commit suicide more frequently than the married.

145. (**C**) Allport called this the principle of functional autonomy.

146. (**C**) Bimodal implies that there are two modes, or two frequently occurring values.

147. (**E**) Horney posited the concept *basic anxiety*, which assumes anxiety arises from conflicting influences on the developing child. Freud's idea is that anxiety arises from conflicts within the individual, such as between id, ego, or superego.

148. (**D**) This study is known as the *Hawthorne* or *Western Electric* study because it was carried out at the Hawthorne plant of the Western Electric Company. No matter how the researchers changed the working conditions of the subjects, worker output improved.

149. (**C**) Under bright light, the cones transmit the greatest amount of information. Since the cones are most centrally located, visual acuity or sharpness is greatest for objects directly in front of the eye.

150. (**D**) The Rubin vase can be seen either as a vase or as two faces staring at close range at each other. It is an example of the principle of contour.

151. (**B**) Perceptual constancy is the apparent stability of a retinal image despite changes in size, shape, color, brightness, or location.

152. (**D**) Although chefs have discovered that Americans like the sensation of crispy food, the chemical taste receptors of the mouth are geared to detect sweet, salty, sour, and bitter.

153. (**C**) In a sample in which a few elements have larger values than the majority of others, the mean is larger than the median.

154. (**C**) Since the variable measured along the abscissa does not change as the variable along the ordinate changes, it can be said that little correlation exists between the two variables, yielding a coefficient near zero.

155. (**D**) In clinical psychological terms, it can be said that in blaming the outside world Esperanza *projects* her problems outward.

156. (**C**) Mahler studied how children learn to understand that they are separate from others, especially from their parents/caretakers, so that eventually they face the world as individuals. To know: transitional object.

157. (**E**) The cerebellum is the motor structure on the dorsal side of the pontine region that uses sensory input to determine the size and timing of movements.

158. (**A**) Reaction times to sound are quicker than reaction times to other stimuli at optimal levels of stimulation.

159. (**B**) The hippocampus is part of the limbic circuit and is a relay between the cerebral cortex and the hypothalamus. Lesions of the hippocampus are known to produce memory problems.

160. **(B)** The hypothalamus also regulates several other important functions, such as maintaining homeostasis, regulating temperature, and regulating survival drives, such as eating, drinking, sex, fighting, and nurturing offspring.

161. **(C)** DSM-IV no longer specifies variations of Munchhausen syndrome as separate entities; it is considered a factitious disorder. In Munchhausen, the person goes to excessive lengths to be a patient and receive the attention given a patient. In Munchhausen by proxy, the person presents another person, such as a child, for medical attention in hopes of gaining maximal attention for the patient role.

162. **(B)** The validity of a test cannot be greater than the square root of its reliability.

163. **(C)** Since 85% of all cases fall below the mean plus one standard deviation, Slugger has to hit one standard deviation or more higher than the mean in order to hit in the top 15% of his league. Thus, he would have to hit at least .270 (27.0%) + .055 (5.5%), or .325 (32.5%).

164. **(B)** Normal-weight people binge eat in the same proportion as obese people.

165. **(E)** Seligman attributes much of the increase in the incidence of depression in modern American society to the decline of the family and religion and to the growth of pop-psych nostrums which imply personal responsibility for failure to achieve happiness.

166. **(D)** Maslow's theory postulates five basic needs that have to be fulfilled if one is to achieve the highest level of functioning; Erikson posited eight stages in development.

167. **(D)** Wechsler, like Binet and Thorndike before him, felt intelligence is an aggregate or an amalgam rather than a collection of different types of abilities. Most recent theorists stress the role of components or subcategories of intelligence; the current assumption is that there are different types of intelligence.

168. **(E)** Studies on the development of differentiation of human emotions find that the earliest and most consistent emotional reaction is distress.

169. **(B)** A ratio scale can determine not only the relative performance of each subject, but also the relationship of one score to another. Since most psychological tests fail to achieve the status of ratio scales, inference about differences in scores is limited.

170. **(C)** Since mathematical skill does not appear on its face to be related to driving skill, in this example it can be said that the test of mathematics has low face validity.

171. **(E)** Since achievement tests can reflect differences in past training, aptitude tests can be used in this situation to attempt to predict future performance after further, more equalized training.

172. **(C)** Bulimia and anorexia nervosa seem to be culture-bound. Both conditions are found overwhelmingly in advanced industrial societies and are almost absent in other societies.

173. **(B)** Reaction formation is the defense mechanism of expressing in overt behavior the opposite feelings and reactions to those of the unconscious.

174. **(C)** In this example, the primary gain is to avoid the difficulties that would have to be faced if one were not ill, while the secondary gain is the attention one receives from others.

175. **(C)** In addition to level of significance, the size of the sample is a consideration in determining the value of a correlation coefficient. The larger the sample, the greater is the power of the statistical test.

176. **(C)** In the stratified sample, the elements are divided into strata, usually defined by their common characteristics, and samples are then taken from each stratum.

177. **(D)** Exogenous refers to the influence of external factors, endogenous to that of internal factors.

178. **(C)** Bladder tension does not become a conditioned stimulus for liquid retention (a CR), and so the liquid is released.

179. **(A)** Thorndike proposed classical principles of learning that later influenced both research psychologists and educators.

180. **(C)** In educational psychology parlance, *exceptional* can mean a person at either end of the intelligence spectrum, either exceptionally bright or dull.

181. **(E)** Maria Montessori began her work by structuring learning environments for children in Italian slums. Her success with these children caused her philosophy to spread.

182. **(C)** Although its mechanism is still a mystery, ECT (electroconvulsive therapy) is used in modern psychiatric practice in response to a number of diagnoses. The method of administration of ECT and the accompanying medication and treatment are subject to constant revision as research results become known.

183. **(E)** Mild forgetfulness is common in middle-aged people and not necessarily indicative of Alzheimer's disease.

184. **(B)** Upon stimulation, the closed sodium gates in the cell membrane open, sodium rushes into the axon, the next gate opens, and so on down the line. The spread of depolarization and entry of sodium is called an action potential. When this occurs, the cell is said to fire.

185. **(D)** Langer and Rodin found that personal power and control over one's life-decisions is an important element in a happy, productive, and long life.

186. **(C)** While males tend to score higher on mathematics tests, the sex differences in math scores disappear when geometry scores are left out. It has been suggested that hormonal differences in prenatal development account for the generally superior spatial ability of males over females.

187. **(C)** Perseveration is inappropriate repetition of behavior, speech, or thought. It is sometimes a feature of frontal lobe lesion.

188. **(C)** LOGO is a simple programming language developed by Papert and his associates. With the aid of devices called *turtles,* it teaches children the basics of computer language design.

189. **(B)** Sex organs develop last among the organs listed. Prior to the eighth week, the embryo does not show distinct sexual organs. They generally develop after the eighth week, when the child is in the fetal period of development.

190. **(E)** The *foot-in-the-door* technique is a method of reducing nonresponse among survey respondents. First the respondent is asked to complete a small questionnaire, then asked for a commitment for a later time to complete a larger questionnaire.

191. **(E)** Modern Freudian psychoanalysts such as Mahler and Jacobson claim that *transitional objects* represent an attempt to maintain contact with the warmth and familiarity of the parental figures while the child is making a transition to the social world.

192. (**E**) Cognitive therapists claim psychological difficulties are the result of conflicting thought patterns (thus the term *cognitive*) that can be corrected by variations on conditioning techniques.

193. (**B**) Many researchers working with dying individuals confirm that this is a common sequence of defense mechanisms, although these stages of coping are not invariant.

194. (**C**) The ciliary muscles control accommodation of the eye to visual stimuli by thickening the lens when they contract and flattening the lens when they relax.

195. (**C**) Although persons diagnosed as having a schizoid personality disorder are aloof, cold, and distant, the presence of thought disorders is unusual.